Ralph Johnson Bunche

Ralph Johnson Bunche

Public Intellectual and
Nobel Peace Laureate

Edited by
BEVERLY LINDSAY

Foreword by
JOHN HOPE FRANKLIN

University of Illinois Press
URBANA AND CHICAGO

© 2007 by the Board of Trustees
of the University of Illinois
All rights reserved
Manufactured in the United States of America
1 2 3 4 5 C P 5 4 3 2 1
∞ This book is printed on acid-free paper.

Library of Congress Cataloging-in-Publication Data
Ralph Johnson Bunche : public intellectual and Nobel
peace laureate / edited by Beverly Lindsay.
p.   cm.
Includes bibliographical references and index.
ISBN-13: 978-0-252-03225-7 (cloth : alk. paper)
ISBN-10: 0-252-03225-X (cloth : alk. paper)
1. Bunche, Ralph J. (Ralph Johnson), 1904–1971.
2. Bunche, Ralph J. (Ralph Johnson), 1904–1971—
Political and social views. 3. Bunche, Ralph J. (Ralph
Johnson), 1904–1971—Influence. 4. Statesmen—
United States—Biography. 5. Intellectuals—United
States—Biography. 6. Nobel Prizes—Biography.
7. United Nations—Biography. 8. African
Americans—Biography. 9. International relations—
History—20th century. 10. United States—
Intellectual life—20th century.
I. Lindsay, Beverly.
E748.B885R355   2007
973'.0496073092—dc22 [B]   2007020858

Contents

Foreword

Ralph Bunche: A Personal Memoir

JOHN HOPE FRANKLIN

Ralph Johnson Bunche was, above everything, a sensitive, disciplined, and warm-hearted human being. To be sure, he was a carefully trained, highly disciplined, and widely respected political scientist. In his later years, he was celebrated for his talents in mediating international disputes and helping to keep the lid on a series of highly volatile crises in the Middle East. He never regarded his successes as out of the ordinary or even deserving special praise. His self-effacing modesty argued, silently, that his training and temperament led him to perform his duties at a level that, to ordinary mortals, was extraordinary in every sense.

I first met Ralph Bunche on one of his visits to Harvard where I was a graduate student in the late 1930s. He, like Robert Weaver and others who recently had completed their own studies there, enjoyed returning to the old haunts in the very few rooming houses available to African American graduate students in Cambridge. He was warm, cordial, and encouraging, traits that a novitiate in his mid-twenties would greatly appreciate. When I was teaching at St. Augustine's College in 1943, the president of the college asked me to assist him in persuading Ralph to visit and speak at the seventy-fifth anniversary of the college, a celebration that had been postponed because of the onset of the war. Ralph came, delivered a timely address and spent much of a day with Aurelia, my wife, and me in our modest apartment reading the galleys of my first book, *The Free Negro in North Carolina, 1790–1860,* which would be published later that year. I was greatly flattered by the time he devoted to my work, so characteristic of him, and the flattering comments he made about it.

From that point on, I counted Ralph Bunche as a friend, and we saw each other whenever we could. One year, 1945, when I was teaching at North Carolina for Negroes, now North Carolina Central University, I was spending some time in Washington doing research at the Library of Congress. I took time off to attend the spring commencement at Howard University. To my great surprise, I encountered Ralph Bunche, who had been away from Howard during the war, Sterling Brown, and Rayford Logan, all in their academic regalia and in a festive mood. For several years they had boycotted the commencement exercises to protest the "autocratic" rule of President Mordecai Johnson. They had just won some great concession from him and were celebrating by "rejoining" the university. In this experience I saw another side of Ralph. He was unyielding in his fight for the principles in which he believed.

Ralph Bunche could be gracious and honorable in his interpersonal relations. In 1950 I witnessed one example of this. That year I was teaching in the summer session at Harvard. Ralph and his wife, Ruth, visited that summer to arrange for yet another postponement of the professorship at Harvard that he had accepted. He had recently completed the mediation of yet another Middle East crisis for which he would receive the Nobel Peace Prize later that year. When he, Ruth, Aurelia, and I went to a Cambridge restaurant for lunch, the line was long, and the four of us waited patiently while chatting and exchanging experiences. During the wait, several couples came up to him offering their table or their place in line. He graciously declined each offer, indicating that he was quite content to wait his turn. These acts of grace were also acts of humility that were so characteristic of him.

Toward the end of his public activities, after he lost his sight, he attended a meeting about international problems. I was moved by his good cheer and obvious optimism in the face of declining health. The thing that struck me most was his reaction to some remarks I had made. From across the room, he said that he did not know I was present until he heard my voice, and he greeted me as if I were a long-lost brother. I do not believe that I had ever been so impressed as I was by this recognition of me by a sightless friend.

In his own time and in his own way, Ralph Bunche saw and participated in a great many historic events. Most of all he saw a world flounder and stumble, and although he gave everything he had to set the world on a safe and steady course, he, as well as statesmen before and after him, would be unable to achieve the peace he sought in a world of greed and selfishness.

As they read the volume by Professor Lindsay and her colleagues, students, scholars, and diplomats will be on the road that Ralph Bunche traveled for decades. The authors' examinations and portraits of Bunche, from the young public intellectual to the seasoned statesman, provide comprehensive analyses that are vitally needed in the contemporary era when one often wonders how much has changed since the early 1970s when Bunche's career and life ended. The exceptional writings of such authors are vital to posing solutions to domestic and international challenges that remain.

Preface

BEVERLY LINDSAY

The real objective must always be the good life for all of the people.
International machinery will mean something to the common man
in the Orient, as indeed to the common man throughout the world,
only when it is translated into terms that he can understand: peace,
bread, housing, clothing, education, good health, and, above all,
the right to walk with dignity on the world's great boulevards.

—Brian Urquhart, *Ralph Bunche: An American Life* (1993), p. 106

As a graduate student and at the beginning of my career, I often wondered how professionals could postulate the ways a luminary might examine a phenomena or initiate public and international policies thereof. Currently, my coauthors and I are the professionals who present analyses and conjectures regarding one of the twentieth century's foremost diplomats. This scholar earned his Ph.D. at Harvard University, began his academic career at Howard University (where shortly thereafter he was requested to create the political science department and become its first chair), and later assumed a position in the United States Department of State. For American and international audiences, his most famous honor was being awarded the Nobel Peace Prize in 1950 for his negotiations leading to an armistice between Israel and four of its Arab neighbors—Egypt, Lebanon, Syria, and Transjordan—while he was an executive diplomat at the United Nations. His name was Ralph Johnson Bunche.

Bunche tried to refuse the Peace Prize because he believed that he was simply doing his job. He only agreed to accept the award after the UN's secretary-general Trygve Lie ordered the acceptance. Numerous schools, buildings (including the international building at the University of California at Los Angeles), and streets were subsequently named in his honor. At one time he held more honorary doctorates than any American.

Nearly sixty years later, Bunche is now known primarily in select scholarly and diplomatic arenas. To rectify this absent legacy and to commemorate the 100th anniversary of Bunche's birth, a national Centenary Committee undertook a careful portrayal and disseminated information about the diplomatic, international relations, public policy, and educational contributions of Ralph Bunche. Committee members included Presidents Jimmy Carter and George H. W. Bush, UN secretary-general Kofi Annan, a diplomat who had held six ambassadorial posts, a knighted UN executive, and a university director emeritus of the Ralph Bunche Institute for International Studies (Ralph Bunche Centenary, 2003–2004).

In the years following what would have been his 100th birthday and the centennial activities, we carefully examine in the chapters that follow the phenomenal contributions of a statesman and intellectual—Ralph Johnson Bunche—to glean further insight on the monumental roles that he played on the world stage and within the academy in order to posit models for ameliorating contemporary diplomatic, sociopolitical, and educational problems.

We review and build upon previous analyses by Brian Urquhart in *Ralph Bunche: An American Life* (1993), Benjamin Rivlin in *Ralph Bunche: The Man and His Times* (1990), and Charles P. Henry in *Ralph Bunche: Model Negro or American Other?* (1999). For example, we examine Bunche's framework about race and try to ascertain how it fared through time. We move into relatively uncharted areas as we explicate his writings on higher education that were primarily published in the *Journal of Negro Education,* where he was a member of the editorial board. Limited attention has been devoted to his perspectives on education, which we hope to illuminate, while he was a board member of the Rockefeller Foundation.

The authors of this volume include some of the nation's foremost scholars who have written on Ralph Bunche, diplomats who have relied upon Bunche's diplomatic contributions, and government officials who have initiated public policies. During recent academic years, we made concerted efforts to organize symposiums and present papers on Ralph Johnson Bunche at national conferences such as those of the Fulbright Association, the African Studies Association, American Educational Research Association, American Council on Education, American Political Science Association, and by endowed university lectureships. These forums provided valuable critiques that we hope strengthen our analyses as we relate the historical Bunche to the contemporary era.

The initiation and production of this volume is a comprehensive task. During the past five years, numerous scholars, diplomats, and policymakers have devoted their talents and time to help bring the book to fruition. Special appreciation is expressed to the contributing authors who are eminent professionals in their fields, as they devoted considerable effort amid extremely busy schedules by offering critiques, presenting at national and international conferences and symposiums, and striving to meet writing deadlines.

Sincere appreciation is expressed to the valiant professionals who contributed "behind the scenes" by facilitating networks, providing copies of original material, encouraging the development of the volume, and being interviewed as professionals who worked directly with Dr. Bunche. These include Horace Dawson, William Greaves, Robert Hill, Benjamin Rivlin, Rc Saravanabhavan, Ronald Palmer, and the current and/or past presidents and chancellors of the University of Michigan (Mary Sue Coleman), University of Massachusetts at Amherst (Marcellette Williams), University of Maryland in Baltimore County (Freeman Hrabowski), American University in Paris (Lee Huebner), St. Mary's University in Texas (Charles Cotrell), Middlebury College and Salzburg Seminar (Olin Robison), Harvard University's Dumbarton Oaks campus, and their staffs. Pennsylvania State University doctoral assistants Lorenzo Baber and Suzanne Hickey and staff assistant Sally Kelley provided valuable assistance with research and logistics. Gratitude is expressed to Kerry Callahan, Joan Catapano, Angela Burton, Copenhaver Cumpston, and other professionals at the University of Illinois Press for their cogent editorial and design skills. We appreciate the critiques from the Press's reviewers that helped us to hone our points.

I was fortunate to have an interview with Presidential Medal of Freedom awardee and president emeritus of the University of Notre Dame Theodore Hesburgh, who served on the Rockefeller Foundation Board with Ralph Bunche. Father Hesburgh's in-depth comments were very helpful in placing the life and career of Bunche within both the historical and contemporary times. Father Ted's involvement with domestic and international endeavors such as the U.S. Commission on Civil Rights, International Atomic Energy Agency, the United Nations, various higher education boards, and numerous national boards involved with civic and public engagement of universities enabled him to interact continually with Bunche for over twenty years and thus hold innumerable informal discussions with him.

Particular gratitude is voiced to eminent James B. Duke professor emeritus John Hope Franklin, who penned the forward. Professor and Presidential Medal recipient Franklin was a colleague of Bunche. Dr. Franklin inspired countless scholars and policymakers, and we greatly appreciate his lifelong contributions. Special acknowledgment is expressed to John McDonald, who spent hours with me as an executive fellow at the Institute for Multi-Track Diplomacy. Ambassador McDonald encouraged my two senior Fulbright grants in South Korea and Zimbabwe and supported the executive fellowship where my initial work on the Bunche project commenced, helped me to understand the frameworks and nuances of shifting diplomatic modes in light of matters being addressed, and reinforced a sense of optimism in moving toward diplomatic and intellectual solutions to improve human conditions.

My lifelong very special appreciation is expressed to my parents. My late father, Joseph Bass Benson Lindsay, always imbued a sense of stamina and psychological fortitude, especially when the odds were against me. Simultaneously, he always wanted me prepared academically and professionally for opportunities when they arose. Ruth Roberts Lindsay, my mother, inspired continuous curiosity about educational matters and research, beginning with her teaching me to read as a tiny preschooler. My reading small portions of newspaper articles including those about Bunche was encouraged by my mother. Both built the foundation that decades later helped me to produce this volume about an African American intellectual and statesman of my father's generation.

We ardently hope that our book will shed insight on and articulate solutions to contemporary international affairs and pressing domestic sociopolitical and education challenges of the twenty-first century. As we succeed, the contributions of one of the twentieth century's foremost statesman in the public intellectual and diplomatic arenas will carry on.

Ralph Johnson Bunche

1. Framing the Conceptual Landscape

BEVERLY LINDSAY

When we reflect about Nobel Peace Prize laureates, often the names of eminent diplomats, civil or human rights leaders, statesmen, and peace activists come to mind. During the sixty years from 1945 (when the United Nations was established) to 2005, five peace laureates (who were or became household names at the time) also devoted a considerable part of their careers to life in the academy. Ralph Johnson Bunche, the 1950 Nobel Prize recipient, was the first of these modern-day laureates who had an established career in the university and as an international diplomat. Professors such as Linus Pauling, Henry Kissinger, Elie Wiesel, and Desmond Tutu would follow him. Given that the goal of the Nobel committee is to award the peace prize to individuals who "shall have conferred the greatest benefit on mankind . . . and who shall have done the most or best work for fraternity among nations, for the abolition or reduction of standing armies and for the holding and promotion of peace congresses" (Nobel Prize, 2006), we may ask what are the conditions that enabled Ralph Bunche to engage in a successful academic career and to undertake a stellar diplomatic career that led to his becoming a peace laureate. What domestic and international lessons might be learned via an in-depth analysis of his dual careers that may shed light on contemporary sociopolitical and educational challenges?

Before and after being awarded a Nobel prize, Bunche was involved with civic and philanthropic organizations that examined domestic and international problems. Might there be some generic nexus between civic and philanthropic endeavors and those leading to the Nobel prize? Quite notable were his fifteen-plus years as a board member of the Rockefeller Foundation. His board membership, which has not been explored in depth, may shed light on ways that he used his intellectual and diplomatic skills to initiate projects to ameliorate social conditions. As a board member, he interacted with corporate chief executive officers and presidents of major universities such as Princeton and Notre Dame, and his blend of intellectual and diplomatic talents would be observed as the board wrestled with various ideas for programs (Hesburgh, 2006).

An initial analysis of Bunche's work indicates his profound concern with fairness, justice, and equality—what today we call *social justice* (Hesburgh, 2006)—for humanity in domestic and international arenas. Social justice concerns were affected by Bunche's childhood, youthful experiences, graduate study at Harvard, Howard University tenure, and United Nations career. This volume seeks to move beyond areas covered in earlier works. For example, while Urquhart (1993) and Henry (1999) examined Bunche's graduate study at Harvard University, this volume situates the place of graduate study in the United States during the 1920s and 1930s. How Bunche and peers developed intellectual freedom in light of Harvard University's disparate treatment of students from various demographic backgrounds is explicated. How the pursuit of intellectual freedom was related to justice and fairness by emerging intellectuals is significant.

Or for instance, while Bunche's role at the creation of the United Nations has been documented (Henry, 1999; Urquhart, 1993; Rivlin, 1990), we explicate how standard diplomatic practices were changing, and Bunche's roles therein, in light of tectonic changes after World War II. New modes of negotiations were mandatory. During the various eras of Bunche's life, he was called upon to separate and simultaneously mesh seemingly incongruent realities (living in segregated housing while pushing for equality at the United Nations for emerging poor nations) in order to establish and/or preserve social justice.

We begin by illuminating highlights of Bunche's life and career—to familiarize the reader—that are then examined in subsequent chapters from historical, political, educational, international, and legal perspectives. We move from Bunche's birth through the 1920s to the 1970s (when he died) as we elucidate phenomena that are still relevant for university students, scholars, and domestic and international policymakers in the twenty-first century.

Emerging Intellectualism and Career Highlights

On August 7, 1903, Ralph Johnson Bunche was born in Detroit, Michigan, the son of a barber and a homemaker, where he spent his childhood in a multiethic, yet segregated, working-class and poor neighborhood (Palmer, 2003; Henry, 1999). His family moved to Albuquerque, New Mexico, in 1914 to improve his parents' poor health. After the deaths of his mother and his favorite uncle and the disappearance of his father, Bunche's grandmother moved the family from Albuquerque to Los Angeles where he graduated from Thomas Jefferson High School as his class's valedictorian. Despite his academic accomplishments, he was excluded from the Ephebian Society, a citywide honor society, because of his race. After entering the University of California, Southern Branch in Los Angeles (now known as UCLA) on an athletic and academic scholarship, he switched from football to basketball after suffering an injury. During his undergraduate career, he excelled academically and made memorable speeches that portrayed a nascent interest in internationalization, founded upon a spiritual and idealistic basis. As an example, consider this excerpt from "That Man May Dwell in Peace," one of his speeches: "May there not be evolved a universal political society, in which each nation would retain its individuality, its nationality, if you please; extensive freedom of action and autonomy within its own domain; yet maintaining, withal, an abiding consciousness of membership in the more significant international society? Essentially, the welfare of the world body must take precedence over nationalistic interest in periods of crisis" (Bunche, 1969c, p. 19). These were amazing remarks for an undergraduate reflecting upon the 1920s when the economy was strong and Americans were in what appeared to be a postwar boom.

In the early 1940s, Bunche began his career in the Office of Strategic Services (which in the late 1940s became the Central Intelligence Agency) gathering and analyzing information that would be translated into guides for the military in parts of Africa and the Middle East. As the war commenced, considerable discussion emerged regarding the creation of an international body to address global conflicts. After accepting a position in the United States Department of State, Bunche was a member of the American delegation at several domestic and international venues where the charter was drafted for a new organization, the United Nations. Bunche's presence at these discussions was significant: he drafted material regarding the status and treatment of the colonial trusteeships of defeated powers and the newly emerging nations such as Israel (Rivlin, 1990). Influencing public and international policies were fundamental components of Bunche's contributions.

Shortly after the United Nations was formed, war ensued between Israel and its Arab neighbors. The UN Security Council appointed a Swedish Red Cross official and World War II hero, Count Folke Bernadotte, as its mediator in Palestine. Ralph Bunche was his chief assistant. Due to a series of mishaps, Bunche was late to a meeting with Bernadotte in Jerusalem from which Bernadotte left on a trip to the Government House. Upon returning, Bernadotte and his military aide were assassinated by Israeli terrorists. Bunche had also been a target. Bunche took Bernadotte's place to chair a series of intensive meetings between Egypt and Israel on the Isle of Rhodes that led to four armistices and the cessation of fighting in 1949. The next year he was awarded the Nobel prize over competitors Prime Minister Winston Churchill, President Harry Truman, U.S. secretary of defense George Marshall, and Indian prime minister Jawaharlal Nehru. Bunche stated that he was a professional optimist and that "nothing can be more sacred to free peoples than the preservation of the rights and dignity of the individual. This is the essence of democracy in our thinking. . . . In the broad field of human rights one of the most striking and difficult problems is that of minority groups within national societies. There must be no compromise on the issue of human rights; that a right compromised is not right at all" (Bunche, 1969c, p. 165). In other words, diplomatic solutions to solve human rights must be foremost.

Harvard University offered Bunche a professorship, which he accepted but never undertook. The professorship was offered by the chair of the government department, William Yendell Elliott, who as a young man reportedly objected to Negroes living on the Harvard campus in desirable housing. While Elliott capitulated, as a Harvard student he reportedly said, "Don't expect me to sit next to him," after a Black student began residing at Lowell House (Keller & Keller, 2001, p. 63). The offer occurred after World War II when Harvard president James Bryant Conant, who had interacted with Bunche during the Dumbarton Oaks talks leading to the establishment of the United Nations, espoused a more democratic environment at Harvard. Instead of assuming a Harvard professorship, Bunche remained at the United Nations working closely with several UN secretaries until his resignation in 1971 due to declining health. He died later that year. Throughout his diplomatic career, Bunche was at the forefront in helping craft solutions to the most pressing international problems. These ranged from the transition of colonies to independent nations; civil wars in African, Middle Eastern, and Asian nations; and conflict resolutions involving UN peacekeeping forces (Nzongola-Ntalaja, 2003).

While a senior diplomat at the United Nations, Bunche voiced his views about civil rights on the American home front. Despite being criticized severely by young civil rights activists and Black Power advocates, he was a featured speaker at the monumental 1963 march on Washington and protested with Martin Luther King at the historic 1965 Selma march.

Although awarded scholarships and fellowships, Bunche and other African Americans who attended Harvard University in the 1920s and 1930s faced continuous covert and overt discriminations. Some of the disparities occurred due to the administrative policies of Harvard University president A. Lawrence Lowell. Ironically, Lowell was a senior professor of government, the field that concerns itself with democracy and rights of individuals. While Lowell, an Anglophile social scientist, was concerned with eliminating some social or class distinctions among white male students—he sought to desegregate eating and social clubs based upon economic status and ethnicity—his inclusiveness did not extend to Catholic, Jewish, Negro, and Chinese students (Karabel, 2005; Lipset & Riseman, 1975). During the Lowell presidency, informal measures were established to limit the number of Jewish students at Harvard after his formal measures failed. For example, white male applicants from the Midwest and mid-Atlantic states, where fewer Jewish students resided compared to the Northeast, were encouraged. Lowell's attempts to limit Jewish inclusion were further witnessed as he publicly engaged in efforts to thwart the confirmation of Justice Louis Brandeis to the Supreme Court.

As he restricted the admission and co-curricular activities of non-white, Catholic, and Jewish students, Lowell favored restrictions on general curriculum options of Harvard undergraduates and advocated mainstream curricular content for graduate students (Keller, 1982; Lipset & Riesman, 1975). Freedom of intellectual choice was limited to particular realms. Under this backdrop, Bunche and other African American, Jewish, and Chinese students sought co-curricular and informal means—via discussions and study groups in their living quarters and in the Negro community—to strengthen their intellectual development. For the marginalized groups, serving their race or ethnic groups and addressing concrete social disparities were paramount challenges that would continue throughout Bunche's academic and diplomatic career.

After becoming the first African American to earn a Ph.D. in political science from Harvard University, he continued his academic career at Howard University while continuing to engage in research in Africa and Asia. At both Harvard and Howard Universities, he was awarded prestigious fellowships to undertake research in the United States, Paris, Geneva, London, and various parts of Africa. During his Howard career, Bunche was a primary researcher with Swedish sociologist Gunnar Myrdal (who later won a Nobel Prize in economics) as they produced the seminal work *An American Dilemma* (1944), which examined conditions affecting Negroes in America and concluded there was a fundamental dilemma between American principles of democracy and the nation's treatment of Blacks. Interestingly, a later Harvard

University president, James B. Conant, sought to revise the general education curriculum and to provide students with more course options, and he cited *An American Dilemma,* with methodology grounded in the social sciences, as a critical example of topics to be covered when studying historical and contemporary issues of American democracy (Harvard Committee, 1945).

During his Harvard graduate school days and while at Howard, Bunche and other scholars were known as young Turks. They espoused very progressive— some would contend radical—views on economic and sociopolitical inequities within the United States and in international settings. Of particular intellectual interest to the young Turks were nations with huge socioeconomic class distinctions among the racial and/or ethnic groups and colonial powers and their treatment of the indigenous populace (Lewis, 2000; Henry, 1999).

Bunche and his students demonstrated against lynchings, picketed segregated establishments in the nation's capital, and organized colloquiums and conferences critical of American presidential administrations. As a carryover from his Harvard days, Bunche initially advocated socialist government policies to ameliorate race and class problems. While at Howard, he was known as an excellent professor who challenged his students and wrote various publications, including nine articles in the *Journal of Negro Education* (where he served as an editorial advisor). The topics that Bunche addressed, such as a "Critical Analysis of the Tactics and Programs of Minority Groups" (1935a) and "Critiques of the New Deal Social Planning as It Affects Negroes" (1936a), were not readily accepted by traditional white American academic journals.

Principles and Organization of Volume

Despite his contributions, Bunche's legacy is often unknown today outside select academic and diplomatic circles. To rectify his absent legacy in the wake of the 100th anniversary of Bunche's birth, this volume provides an exploration of two dominant conceptual motifs—*public intellectualism* and *diplomacy*—that contributed to Bunche's quest for social justice. Our working definition of *public intellectualism* encompasses the interactive relationship between the "life of the mind" and critical analysis to address and/or provide solutions to domestic and international problems via "public" and scholarly modes. *Diplomacy,* at this stage, entails traditional and innovative methods of discussions, mediations, and negotiations to maintain or establish just and peaceful conditions. This book offers an in-depth analysis of Bunche's contributions to public intellectualism and diplomacy in their multiple conceptual, programmatic, and policy manifestations. His original publications and speeches; diplomatic constructs, policy initiatives, and practices; and educational and public policy initiatives are analyzed.

The various authors include some of the nation's foremost scholars who have written on Ralph Bunche, American ambassadors and diplomats who have relied upon Bunche's diplomatic contributions, and government officials who have initiated public policies. We examine their major written works concerning Bunche and those of other writers such as Urquhart (1993), Rivlin (1990), Edgar (1992), and Henry (1999) that analyze his United Nations and Howard careers. Our volume focuses on the nexuses between Bunche's multiple roles in public intellectualism and diplomacy. Some essays have appeared in a special issue of the *Journal of Negro Education* (Spring 2004).

This chapter frames the conceptual landscape and depicts conceptual patterns and explicates thematic linkages that are explored. To that end, we build upon the historical, sociological, and political science literature by and about Bunche (Bunche, 1941a; Henry, 1999; Urquhart, 1993; Keppel, 1995) and literature examining the nexuses between diplomacy and education (Clark, 1990; Lindsay 2003; Stromquist, 2002; Amin, 1997). From tenets of these works, we pose several salient questions in the chapters that follow:

1. What early family and educational phenomena influenced Bunche the man and Bunche the intellectual and diplomat?
2. What were Bunche's contributions as a public intellectual during his academic career that influenced the study (of) and public policies for African Americans?
3. What conceptual paradigms were posited and written by Bunche regarding worldviews of race that still have significant relevance for bridging theoretical and policy frameworks expressed by academicians and policymakers?
4. What intellectual and disciplinary paradigms in political science and international relations did Bunche significantly alter?
5. What administrative and executive positions were articulated by Bunche that contributed to political and educational initiatives in professional organizations, on Capitol Hill, in the United Nations, and for other international bodies?
6. What components of Bunche's scholarly and diplomatic skills may be used to facilitate contemporary college and university engagements as they address pressing diplomatic and public policies after September 11 or ongoing crises in the Middle East and other hot spots?
7. What features of Bunche's writings on social engagement pertain to today's students as they undertake practicums in various communities?
8. What is the importance of changing diplomatic modes via legal and educational considerations as new international disputes are addressed?
9. What position might Bunche articulate regarding the current role of the

United Nations in contemporary challenges on the African continent and
in the Middle East?

10. How has Bunche influenced diplomatic practices of the United Nations,
ambassadors, and other senior diplomats?

11. What overarching synthesis from the various facets of Bunche's life and
career might provide programmatic and policy directions for contemporary
challenges?

As we respond to such queries, similar data are analyzed with varying interpretations by the several authors based upon multiple disciplinary paradigms.

The chapters in part 1, "Origins and Manifestations of Public Intellectualism," reveal how the early life of Bunche influenced his intellectualism. His
publications during his Howard University career show links between public
intellectualism and activism; his world perspectives on race can be related to
contemporary aspects of globalization. His public intellectualism translated
into changing some tenets of political science as a discipline and initiating
fellowship programs designed to link the field with policies and programs
for action.

"Rethinking the Early Life" (chapter 2) by Ben Keppel, an associate professor and Bunche scholar at the University of Oklahoma, explores Bunche's
development from his birth in 1903 through his graduation from UCLA
in 1927. This contrasts to biographical and historical studies, which focus
on his mature years as a teacher, scholar, and diplomat. Drawing upon
Bunche's personal papers (located in the Special Collections Department of
the Charles Young Research Library at UCLA) and a definitive biographical
study (Urquhart, 1993), Keppel first gives attention to Bunche's difficult early
life in Detroit and Albuquerque. In 1917, Bunche's mother died and his father
disappeared, leaving Bunche in the care of his maternal grandmother, Lucy
Taylor Johnson, whom Bunche called "Nana." Nana became Bunche's chief
guardian and mentor. These family tragedies inspired the family to move to
Los Angeles. Keppel concentrates on the significance of Bunche's background
as an African American who, though not born on the west coast, nonetheless
grew up as a son of the American west. Second, Bunche's life in Los Angeles
will receive special attention, especially his public address "The Fourth Dimension of Personality," which he made as UCLA class valedictorian where
he was a city "goodwill ambassador" (Bunche, 1927a; Keppel, 1995; Henry,
1999). Finally, these formative public words are considered in their full historical context as expressions of desires by African Americans and others for
a world order based on the concepts of equality and human rights (Lewis,
2000). Bunche believed in what has come to be called "internationalism," or
the conviction that the place of the United States in the world must be defined

by the quality of its relations with the rest of it. Keppel's discussion makes the case not only for Bunche as a Wilsonian internationalist, but also locates him within a well-developed discourse in the African American community on the need for a world order based on fundamental concepts of human rights and justice.

Yale University professor Jonathan Scott Holloway's chapter 3, "Responsibilities of the Public Intellectual," explores Bunche's early scholarly and political contributions to American life in general and Black life more specifically during his tenure at Howard University. Bunche used his professorial position at Howard as a bully pulpit for a range of ideas that represented a commitment to political change in the service of social justice. Bunche was part of a cohort of radical Black scholar-activists at Howard who sought to change the terms of the political debate in America away from its focus on race and toward a new focus on class (Holloway, 2002). Bunche's politics during the Great Depression and New Deal were far more openly progressive than those he would espouse later in his career as he became a major international figure at the United Nations (Rivlin, 1990).

Drawing from authoritative sources on Bunche's early years in the academy (Holloway, 2002; Henry, 1999; Urquhart, 1993), his personal papers (Ralph Bunche Papers, Special Collections, UCLA), and his publications from the 1930s (predominantly in the *Journal of Negro Education*, 1930s), Holloway discusses the various dimensions of Bunche's political philosophies and the way that these philosophies were informed by the social realities of the world in which he and other Black scholars lived. Holloway urges readers to look beyond his important international work in the second half of his career to his earlier years when he repeatedly challenged public and private orthodoxies in service of a larger ideal of a broad and universal humanity, from his work organizing picket lines attacking race discrimination to his participation in the National Negro Congress and again to his scholarly contributions in the 1930s. He was a public intellectual before the term was fashionable.

Charles Henry, a renowned Bunche biographer and professor at the University of California at Berkeley, writes in chapter 4, "Revisiting a World View of Race," that "globalization" is a new term to explain old phenomena. As early as 1936, Bunche contended that the "inequality of peoples" was becoming an organizing theme for political and economic life across the globe. Bunche introduced the concept of "social race" to explain the consciousness of environmental and social conditions when manifested in a group of people. Economic and political systems, not biology, play a crucial role in making a "social race." Henry argues that Bunche's pioneering discussion of the concept of social race rests on three basic elements. First, his approach is comparative, including the United States and West Africa, and expanded to include Chinese, Japanese, and Mexicans as well as Blacks and Whites. Second, the source of slavery is located in economic competition rather than racial hierarchy. Thus, Bunche foreshadows the work of Eric Williams (1944), Walter Rodney (1972), and William Julius Wilson (1978) that discuss the centrality of economics. Third, Bunche attacks the view of Black lynching as irrational sexual politics. Comparable to Ida B. Wells (1969) and Arthur Rapier (as cited in Henry, 1999), he explains them as economic domination. Recent scholars (Thomas, 2001; Gilroy, 2000) have used the term "global apartheid" to describe a world system that combines political, economic, and racial antagonism. By revisiting Bunche's written works of nearly seventy years ago (at the beginning of his career) and select speeches of thirty years ago (near the end of his life), we have a conceptual framework from which to analyze the continuities and discontinuities in the world system over generations.

In chapter 5, "Political Science Educational Contributions: Integrating Theory and Practice," Hanes Walton Jr. (political science professor at the University of Michigan) explicates how Bunche's academic training and career and subsequent career in international organizations placed him in a position to shape the discipline of political science. The integration of his roles emerged from his Harvard Ph.D. in political science, his Nobel prize, and becoming the first of his race voted president of the American Political Science Association.

Using Bunche's 1954 presidential address to the American Political Science Association as well as his other scholarly writings about political science education, Walton maps out the specifics of Bunche's educational and intellectual contributions to political science. While it is true that the discipline started in 1895, created a national association in 1903, and established a journal in 1906, Bunche was able to enhance the discipline during the year that he served as president of the national association (Bunche, 1954a). For example, he started the association's fellowship program on Capitol Hill. Walton draws from Bunche's original publications to show Bunche's creation of new categories of political science analysis: African American politics, African politics, world politics and international organizations, political parties, and Southern politics.

In part 2, "Educational Venues and Public Intellectualism and Diplomacy," we explore the linkages between Bunche's public intellectual viewpoints— primarily expressed in the *Journal of Negro Education* where one-third of his academic articles and chapters were published—and current policies and programs in colleges and universities. The perspectives of liberal arts college and public research university presidents and their presidential implementation of educational policies and programs are highlighted via case studies. How students and young scholars may use public intellectualism, as posited by Bunche, for concrete service learning challenges is also a focus of this section.

In chapter 6, "Educational and Diplomatic Influences at Public Research Universities," Beverly Lindsay (a former executive fellow of multitrack diplomacy and current professor and senior scientist of higher education and international policy studies at Pennsylvania State University) builds upon the conceptual and global policy perspectives of Bunche pertaining to roles of universities. Her interview with Father Theodore Hesburgh, president emeritus of the University of Notre Dame and a fellow board member of the Rockefeller Foundation with Bunche, provides firsthand knowledge by a contemporary. In "The Roles of the University in the Political Orientation of Negro Youth," written at the eve of World War II, Bunche (1940a) maintained that universities decorate students in tinsel and glitter and turn them loose as B.A.s—babes in arms—because the students are not prepared to face the real challenges of the world. Moreover, Bunche declared that universities often have an "unceasing quest after that elusive concept 'truth' and too often our search for Truth becomes an escape device—whereby we can divorce ourselves from the tough and dangerous controversies of the world" (Bunche, 1940a, p. 222). Bunche thought that universities, in particular, have special roles to exert in preparing students for their careers and the mantles of leadership and simultaneously fostering conditions wherein faculty and administrators can develop students and themselves in solid interdisciplinary scholarship (Bunche, 1940a; Bunche, 1940b; Lindsay, 2003; Banks, 2004)

Interviews and/or participant observation with the chief executives of two major public research universities provide the salient methodological components of case studies to ascertain how these institutions responded to September 11, 2001, and to Muslim and/or Middle East conflicts, particularly the 2003 war in Iraq. In addition, Lindsay's interviews with Hesburgh, her examination of Rockefeller Foundation Web sites, and her data analysis indicate that some solutions that Bunche initiated from the 1930s through the early 1970s still provide the frameworks for addressing current-day problems, such as in-depth interactions with peers in other countries and participatory processes by all relevant stakeholders. Lessons can be learned—from Bunche's work and intentions as they play out in these contemporary postsecondary institutions—to foster equity and fairness.

In chapter 7, "Intellectual and Diplomatic Imprints at Liberal Arts Colleges," Lindsay continues her analysis based upon the responses of presidents and observations at liberal arts colleges in the United States and France. Several college presidents reflect upon Bunche's direct and indirect contributions to liberal arts education through his writings, career achievements at the United Nations, and his membership on the Rockefeller Foundation Board. In-depth consideration is devoted to public intellectualism at liberal arts institutions and its relationship to the missions and goals of such colleges, which, given their small- to medium-sized student body, offer extensive opportunities for interactions between students and faculty.

In chapter 8, Lorenzo DuBois Baber (doctoral candidate at Pennsylvania State University) and Beverly Lindsay present "An Early Vision of Education: Applying Knowledge to Social Engagement," as they scrutinize Bunche's valedictorian speech at UCLA in 1927 wherein the young scholar implored his fellow graduates to use the knowledge they gained during their four years for more than just individual pursuits. Instead, Bunche said, they should connect with the innate, but often ignored, human desire to help others for the betterment of society (Rivlin, 1990). As a student and professor of higher education, Baber and Lindsay note the current trend of educators calling for social engagement by students that Bunche articulated almost eighty years ago. There is a desire to connect classroom learning to the living world, the theoretical to the practical (Salzburg Seminar, 2005).

Baber has been part of a program that represents the visionary ideas of Bunche. The University of Maryland, Baltimore County's Shriver Living-Learning Center was named in honor of former Peace Corps director Sargent Shriver and Eunice Kennedy Shriver. The center collaborates with curricular and co-curricular departments to provide service learning opportunities for students in Baltimore, Maryland. Undergraduate students volunteer by tutoring, mentoring, and engaging in community development programs. Simultaneously, they enroll in a sociology course that covers issues involving the changing American society and the ways in which social institutions influence the sites where students participate. Chapter 8 links Bunche's early vision to current calls for similar student engagement in this Maryland case study.

In part 3, "Diplomats Articulating Diplomacy," a senior ambassador and professor skilled in diplomacy explicate various components of diplomacy as envisioned by Bunche and subsequently used for multifaceted public diplomacy. That is, diplomacy moves beyond national interest, concentrates on international and domestic civil wars, and incorporates country-specific phenomena. Shifting roles and definitions of diplomacy and international law with the advent of the United Nations are new considerations, especially as nations and international bodies encounter horrific problems not witnessed previously.

Edwin Smith, the Leon Benwell professor of law at the University of South-ern California, explicates "Diplomat in Pursuit of the International Inter-est" in chapter 9. He points out that Bunche, as one of the first members of the Secretariat of the United Nations, was an international civil servant engaged in tasks selected by the secretary-general rather than a national government—a new mode of diplomacy. Bunche participated in the forma-tion of new styles of international conflict resolution that dealt with new con-straints and opportunities arising from the relative freedom from parochial national interests. Smith discusses the manner in which Bunche contributed to new approaches to international diplomacy adopted by the United Na-tions and further posits how contemporary conditions, in the Middle East, for example, illustrate the salience of the rule of law and its fair application (Crocker, Hampson, & Aall, 1999; Crocker & Hampson, 1996). Bunche's seminal experience in international mediation provides a template from which scholars and educators can explore the prospects for the more effec-tive use of mediation as a tool for prevention of violent conflicts (Greenberg, Barton, & McGuinness, 2000).

In chapter 10, "An International Legacy: The Middle East, Congo, and United Nations Peacekeeping," Princeton N. Lyman (adjunct senior fellow and formerly Ralph Bunche Senior Fellow at the Council on Foreign Relations and former American ambassador to Nigeria and South Africa) discusses how Bunche is celebrated for his efforts to bring about peace and stability in the volatile Middle East, for his efforts to contain the crisis of Congo's independence, and for establishing the principles of UN peacekeeping that continue today. Lyman maintains that Bunche's legacy is clouded in today's world by the ultimate failure of the UN's early nation-building process in the Congo, by the decline in the UN's ability to play a significant role in the Middle East, and by conflicting views over UN peacekeeping. These clouds are not of Bunche's making, but they allow us to reflect on the period of his diplomatic efforts with the wisdom of hindsight and the perspective of more recent history.

In the Middle East, the courageous efforts of Count Folke Bernadotte and Bunche to bring an end to the first Arab-Israeli war, and Bunche's later work in the wake of the Suez crisis, ironically marked the high point of UN influ-ence in the region, according to Lyman. Thereafter, the UN gradually lost its reputation for evenhandedness and has often been shut out of the processes of peace and war. In Africa, the UN and UN peacekeeping suffered a loss of respect in the wake of the Rwanda genocide, the effects of which have spilled over to the Congo (Nzongola-Ntalaja, 2003). The UN's and Bunche's legacy in the Congo is even being called into question. Lyman concludes that Bunche's legacy may well depend on what is learned from the past. As the UN struggles with nation-building responsibilities and with new peace-keeping responsibility—challengingly, once again in the Congo—its ability to establish itself as an instrument of democracy, fairness, and effectiveness will be the test of whether the legacy Bunche intended will be realized.

Part 4, "Contemporary and Future Critical International Inquiries and Models," synthesizes aspects of public intellectualism and diplomacy. In chapter 11, "Complexities Abound: Paradigms for Future Public Intellectuals and Diplomats," Lindsay contends that the *public intellectualism* and *international diplomacy* artfully articulated and practiced by Ralph Bunche is still applicable. However, they now need adept alterations as complexities increase from a world with fifty-one members of the United Nations in 1945, to 131 in 1971 when Bunche retired, to 191 in 2003, the centenary year of Bunche's birth, and to 192 today. Innovative forms of technology that allow peace or violence in nations thousands of miles apart, new methods of violence, and instantaneous communications throughout the world were not remotely evident in 1971. Helping ascertain discrete, yet interrelated, linkages expressed herein will contribute to changing public intellectualism and diplomatic policies for the academic community, diplomats, and public policymakers. Hence institutions and nations can ardently strive toward peace, equity, and fairness using tenets articulated and practiced by Ralph Johnson Bunche.

PART I

Origins and Manifestations of Public Intellectualism

2. Rethinking the Early Life

BEN KEPPEL

Challenges of Addressing the Past

Scholarly analysis and common sense agree that an individual's formative experiences and circumstances decisively influence the direction and velocity of the rest of the journey. Exactly how circumstances and decisions become achievements, however, is a complicated process. One inherent challenge in tracing the origins of a "great life" is to see inevitable triumph in every fragment of evidence. And indeed, journalistic admirers of Ralph Bunche, writing in the late 1940s and 1950s, constructed such a picture, with some assistance from Bunche himself. Bunche's rags-to-riches life story and his gifts as a mediator were much admired in a society struggling to come to terms with many profound social changes and ideological contradictions (Keppel, 1995, pp. 61–95). Today, this symbolic work continues with Bunche's skill as a peacemaker being used to inspire at-risk African American youths to choose mediation over confrontation and peace over violence (Elster, 2003).

I approach Bunche's formative years as an historical challenge and I must, in the process, acknowledge some limitations of our knowledge. In addition, even though this inquiry strives to be scholarly and objective, this does not relieve me from the obligation of thinking about how this narrative might help us to better understand the formation of character and leadership in a society very much in need of both. As I look back on Bunche's life, I am, like my predecessors and contemporaries, *rethinking a life:* that is, trying to find in Bunche's life answers to *our own* questions about *our* world. For instance, today, when "mentoring" has become a buzzword for addressing the many problems faced by young people, it seems entirely legitimate to ask how studying Bunche's early years can help us to understand how individuals achieve in the face of great adversity and hardship. At a time when many see the American family as being "in crisis," Bunche's own illustration should cause us to rethink stereotypes about what constitutes a "stable" or "functional" family.

Interpreting Circumstances

Students of Ralph Johnson Bunche's life owe a great debt to his two most scrupulous and scholarly biographers, Brian Urquhart (1993) and Charles P. Henry (1999). Their meticulous research has given us the best account of Bunche's early years and family life. The family into which Bunche was born in Detroit, Michigan, on August 7, 1903, seems to have been a large and loving one that was also under considerable stress. Bunche's mother, Olive Johnson Bunche, came from a family under economic and other pressures with a deep commitment to education. We know virtually nothing about the family of Fred Bunche, Bunche's father, except that he seems to have been a gregarious man who never quite found his economic or personal footing in life. By 1916, Fred Bunche had vanished. The tuberculosis that afflicted both Olive Bunche and her brother, Charles Johnson, propelled the family to the drier climate of Albuquerque, New Mexico, in 1914. Within three years, both Ralph's mother and beloved Uncle Charley would be dead—Olive from tuberculosis and Charley from a self-inflicted gunshot wound. This tragic turn of events inspired the family's next move, to Los Angeles, with Bunche's beloved grandmother, Lucy Taylor Johnson, firmly at the helm (Urquhart, 1993, pp. 30–31; Henry, 1999, p. 10).

If there is one theme that emerges most strongly from Bunche's adult recollections about his youth, it is about the bedrock importance of his grandmother in his life. As Bunche wrote in 1954, "I was reared in a deeply religious family. It was a matriarchal clan ruled over by my maternal Grandmother, 'Nana.'" Bunche recalled in words that he would publicly repeat many times, "Foremost, she believed in God. In worldly matters, she believed that every person has a virtually sacred right to dignity and respect; that all men are brothers and are entitled to be treated as equals and to enjoy equality of opportunity." This egalitarian creed "came to be a very part of [my] very being" because Nana "became both mother and father to me when, in my early youth, I lost both my parents" (Bunche, 1954b). Like many members of what we have come to call "the greatest generation," Bunche emphasized the simple happiness of his childhood, rarely expressing his feelings about the tragedies and inequalities that were surely part of those years. As he wrote to some fourth-grade admirers in 1964, Bunche preferred to recall his childhood as consisting of "happy but meagre days. I was not snowed under with gifts and cash to spend and I had to learn to get much enjoyment out of very little. Because of this, I did at times have to do without, but beyond that, I did not have to make any serious sacrifices when I was young and I never felt deprived" (Bunche, 1964). Such admirable stoicism and practicality is deeply mixed into the long-standing narrative of individualism that has always been at the center of our culture. Because Bunche's words cling deeply to this rhetorical formula, they do not tell us very much.

Charles P. Henry notes that Bunche's account of his childhood omits certain important details. For instance, Bunche remembers the Detroit community as a model of practical pluralism. Bunche often wrote about his early years in a "white, working class neighborhood populated largely by German-speaking Austrio-Hungarian neighbors. We were one of the very few Negro families in the area, but we never experienced any unfriendliness from our white neighbors" (Bunche, 1969a, p. 46). Henry's research, in contrast, found Bunche's Detroit neighborhood to be an area of "high black concentration." Bunche also recalled the local YMCA as exemplary of this inclusive ethos, while according to Henry, the Detroit YMCA was "openly segregationist." What are we to make of these contradictions? Henry concludes that Bunche's "tendency to stress the integrated nature of his childhood reflects the old Black elite's optimism about race relations" (Henry, 1999, p. 11).

In addition to being sensitive to the fallibility of memory as an historical resource, we must, as I argued earlier, also be aware of how cultural conventions influence how we express our sense of the past. Our generation lives in a far less emotionally reserved culture than Bunche did, and we record our adversities in a very different language. So, the twenty-first-century interpreter of Bunche's early life must combine faithfulness to his written words with some careful intuition. As Bunche told *Reader's Digest*, "We had our problems from time to time . . . grumbling was not encouraged. Nana would say, 'We all have our troubles, but its best to keep them to ourselves and not make others unhappy about them'" (Bunche, 1969a, p. 46). These words were certainly not meant to suggest moral quietism or silence in the face of discrimination and injustice. In the same essay, Bunche recalls his grandmother's pride in her African American heritage and recounts her emphatic advice to "always protect your self-respect and your dignity" (Bunche, 1969a, p. 47). And yet, men and women of Bunche's generation kept the memory of many hardships at a distance—at least in public—by projecting on to them a warm light generated by the confident knowledge that they had triumphed against great odds. It seems reasonable to argue, then, that Bunche's early life was much more difficult than he and others sometimes portrayed. We have an obligation to question some of his nostalgia about his poor but happy beginnings.

Nana's role in young Ralph's life confirms the importance of a current theme in our public life: the importance of having a mentor. As we debate the present state of the American family, we might look to Nana Johnson as a reminder that a strong family originates often in the example provided by its strongest member. The successful family is defined less by a particular configuration of persons or by the achievement of a certain degree of material wealth and comfort than it is by the presence of people who consistently transmit love, care, and hope in actions as well as in words.

Discovering Prejudice

For at least two generations—as Americans have struggled to come to terms with ethnocentrism and racism in our society—the leading cultural figures have been drawn to ask when the concepts of race and prejudice enter the human experience. This issue became especially important after the Supreme Court's decision in *Brown v. Board of Education* (1954) placed the public school at the center of efforts to desegregate American society.

Bunche's response when he discovered prejudice is remarkable and courageous. As I discussed previously, Ralph Bunche contends that he and his family were not targets of racial prejudice during his early youth in Detroit. These, however, are not Bunche's only thoughts on the subject. He also tells us that he discovered prejudice in Detroit as an emotion *within himself*:

> During the early years of my life I was unaware of the existence of a "Negro problem," but I soon learned about prejudice—against Italians. . . . I didn't often hear the word "nigger," but I heard the words "wop" and "dago." The Italian boys had to pass through our section on the way from parochial school, and in the winter time we would bombard them with snowballs whose centers were pieces of coal. Instinctively, I knew this was wrong and kept it hidden from Nana and my parents. For, in our family circle, no unfriendly word against Italians was heard. Nana set the family line by pointing out, "Negroes have no business running down anybody. Anyhow, people who sing and like music as much as those folks do can't be too bad." (Bunche, 1969a, p. 46)

Bunche's education as to the patterns of American prejudice continued as he moved west from Detroit. In New Mexico, where Bunche and his family lived from 1914 to 1917, Bunche learned that Mexicans and Indians were among the designated outcasts; in California, the Japanese were added to this list of the excluded (Bunche, 1969a, p. 46). According to Bunche's own account, he discovered the specifically "Negro problem" in 1917 with his family's arrival in Los Angeles. When Bunche's family finally found a home at Thirty-seventh Street and Central Avenue, the family encountered a very different welcome than, according to Bunche, they had received in Detroit. As Bunche's Aunt Ethel recalled:

> We were the first Negro family to move into the block. There was resentment at once. Before a week had passed, Mother [Nana] and I were in the backyard preparing to make a vegetable garden. The neighbors . . . were carrying on a conversation across our yard. Says one, "I'm going to move"; the other says, "looks like we have to since niggers have moved in." I was boiling inside and Mother knew I was ready to explode. "Sweetheart," she said in a subdued voice with her hand on mine, "we deposited seven hundred and fifty dollars on this small Garden of Eden and we are owners. They are renters." (F. Johnson, undated, p. 6)

This incident is an appropriate preface to Ralph Bunche's own encounters with racism in Southern California. Once, while working as a newsboy, Ralph and his white peers were invited to spend a day at the beach. Because of his race, Ralph was forbidden to join his colleagues in the use of a bathhouse. Ralph was forced to wait outside while his colleagues enjoyed use of the facility (Henry, 1999, p. 17).

Another example of institutional racism occurred when, as a middle school student, Bunche was tracked into a vocational curriculum rather than one designed to prepare him for college. This action was reversed only after Nana's direct intervention with the principal of the Thirtieth Street Intermediate School. A few years later, when Bunche graduated from Jefferson High School at the head of his class in the winter of 1922, he was "blackballed" from the city's honor society because he was an African American, an event that filled Ralph with anger and almost caused him to give up academic pursuits. Bunche records that only Nana's insistence that he continue his education, as Johnson forebears had done, allowed him to "break out of the iron ring of the ghetto" (Bunche, 1969a, p. 48).

Bunche's public comments on his early exposure to prejudice are especially interesting when placed beside his scholarly work as a political scientist during the 1930s. Not surprisingly, Bunche witnessed prejudice wherever he lived. However, if the behavioral and emotional expressions of that attitude were broadly similar, Bunche also noticed that the objects of derision and exclusion differed somewhat depending upon the cultural and demographic landscape. These formative experiences no doubt influenced the scholarly agenda that

Bunche would set as a "Young Turk" faculty member at Howard University during the 1930s and early 1940s: studying how the particular details and nuances of human experience interacted with the surrounding cultural and economic system. These concepts are further explored in chapter 3.

Historicizing Personal Experiences

It is especially tempting when writing about the life of an accomplished and principled historical actor to lay great stress on *individual* action—whether by our heroic subject or by his equally admirable mentors. While not devaluing their importance, it is also important not to lose sight of the surrounding historical context. With regard to Bunche's formative years and young adult-hood, it is especially important to remember he had one important quality in common with other Angelinos, especially African Americans—he was from somewhere else. The Johnson family's movements over three generations correlate closely with the general patterns of African American migration between the early nineteenth and twentieth centuries.

As important as migration is to understanding larger developments in African American history, the written historical record is often not explicit about the reasons for moving from one locale to another. We know from Brian Urquhart's biography that Bunche's great-grandfather, James H. John-son, was a Baptist minister and freedman from Virginia who migrated to Missouri in the 1830s and married Bunche's maternal great-grandmother, Eleanor Madden. In 1842, James Johnson bought a two-hundred-acre farm near Alton, Illinois. Thomas Johnson, Bunche's grandfather, was born on that farm. Thomas Johnson met his future wife, Lucy A. Taylor (Bunche's beloved Nana), while both were students at Shurtleff College in Alton. Shortly after their marriage on September 8, 1875, the couple migrated to Fort Scott, Kan-sas, where Thomas would teach for the next ten years. In 1885, the Johnson family moved south to Waco, Texas, where Thomas became principal of an unnamed school for African American children (Urquhart, 1993, pp. 23–24). Nelle Johnson, the family historian, writes that the Johnsons were "happy and prosperous in the Lone Star State" (N. Johnson, 1953).

These facts suggest that the Johnsons were members of the small class of African Americans who were both property owners and recipients of considerable formal education. Thomas Johnson's job as a principal would have placed him firmly in the small black professional class of that era. Nelle Johnson reports that "disaster overtook the family" in 1890 when Thomas Johnson died in a malaria epidemic at the age of forty (N. Johnson, 1953, p. 1). Thomas Johnson's death placed Nana at the helm of her family, and it was she who aimed them toward Michigan and California, ultimately making the Johnson family part of the great migration of African Americans from the South to the North and West over the next three-quarters of a century. It is also clear that, if the death of Thomas Johnson in no way diminished the family's commitment to upward mobility and service through education, it—along with the untimely deaths of Olive and Charles in the next generation—toughened the material and emotional circumstances of the clan into which Ralph Johnson Bunche was born thirteen years later.

As we turn to the ideas of the young Ralph Bunche, we must consider that his family's migration west had a lasting significance beyond the pursuit of material opportunity. As Charles P. Henry has suggested, "The move north and west by African Americans represented more than a demographic change. It was also a psychological break with the past," and it was filled with intellectual and ideological significance. The city brought economic, social, and cultural opportunities. There were also continuing obstacles to personal advancement, but these were often fought through organized public protest and political action (Henry, 1999, pp. 20–21). As we shall see, Ralph Bunche's experience as a young man reflected this mix of forces.

When Bunche and the Johnson family arrived in Los Angeles in 1917, we should keep one scholar's conclusion firmly in mind: "race relations and racial practices [in Los Angeles] were quite similar to patterns which existed throughout the United States. African Americans were being restricted by segregated housing, segregated educational institutions and by limited job opportunities" (Cox, 1996, p. 23). As we have seen, this finding is certainly manifested in Bunche's individual experience. What is also important is that the community organized itself to fight these reversals. Only a few months before Ralph Bunche was born in Detroit, leading African Americans in Los Angeles founded the Los Angeles Forum to encourage "racial uplift" (Cox, 1996, p. 10). Among its early accomplishments was to raise money for African American education and force the local school district to hire African American teachers. A little more than ten years later this organization joined with the local NAACP, founded in 1913, to protest local screenings of D.W. Griffith's *Birth of a Nation*, a racist portrait of African American life during the reconstruction of the South after the Civil War (deGraaf, 1962, p. 28; Cox, 1996, p. 23).

By 1918, African Americans in South Central were large enough in number and organized well enough politically to send the first African American to the California State Assembly (deGraaf, 1962, p. 28). By the early 1920s, as Ralph Bunche prepared to cross the threshold of the University of California, Southern Branch (known today as UCLA), the local chapter of Marcus Garvey's Universal Negro Improvement Association claimed more than one thousand members (deGraaf, 1962, p. 34). While I have found no evidence

that Bunche or any members of his clan participated in these various mo-
bilizations to fight segregation, I find these facts relevant to this life story
because they suggest that Bunche, in addition to the support of his family,
had the advantage of living in a bustling and politically catalytic environment, the kind of social and political surroundings that would encourage the
young not only to dream of wider horizons but to plan, to act, and to speak
on those dreams.

Bunche took up this challenge in an address to a local service club during
his college years. In perhaps his only public reference during the 1920s to
encroaching racial segregation in Los Angeles, Bunche warned his listeners
against patronizing a newly opened "colored only" swimming pool. "If we accept this," warned Bunche, " . . . we will have separate, inferior schools, parks
and perhaps even Jim Crow street cars forced upon us" (Henry, 1995, p. 24).

These words confirm Brian Urquhart's conclusion that, although Bunche
had experienced "hints of prejudice" earlier in his youth, "it was only in Los
Angeles that Ralph first developed real racial consciousness" (Urquhart, 1993,
p. 34). Projecting Bunche's individual experience against this backdrop of
community activism compels us to remember that "racial consciousness"—
when it is as nuanced and sophisticated as it becomes in Bunche—is the
product of interaction not only with prejudice itself but with a constructive
understanding of what it is and how it must be met. It requires no dilution
of Nana's important role in Bunche's personal development to argue that her
advice and advocacy did not take place in a vacuum—there were many such
figures in Los Angeles fighting the same battle.

Becoming a Public Diplomat

Ralph Bunche entered the University of California, Southern Branch, in 1923
after a year spent laboring at various part-time jobs. He graduated summa
cum laude four years later. It was during these years that Bunche's public
life formally began. The most important evidence for understanding these
years are three speeches Bunche gave as an undergraduate student. We have
already considered one of these—"Across the Generation Gap"—in which
Bunche attacks the opening of a new segregated swimming pool—and will
consider the other two shortly.

The pages of the *California Grizzley* give us a small yet tantalizing glimpse
of someone at the beginning of an exciting journey. A front-page story in
the April 15, 1926, issue, which announced the victory of Carl V. Swisher of
Pomona College (for reflections on "Propaganda for War") in a regional intercollegiate speech contest, also makes note of Bunche's "unusually creditable
. . . showing" and reports that "Ralph Bunche has taken part in a number of

speaking contests and even last year won the intercollegiate oratorical contest between debate organizations" (Pomona speaker places first, 1926, p. 1). There is no hint in this article of what any of the participants had to say at this important conclave. One event in Bunche's early public career did not make the campus paper: he helped to establish the Southern Branch Debating Society when he was excluded because of his race from the official debating organization of the university (Henry, 1999, p. 23). Nor does this source tell us anything about the other half of Bunche's life as a college student—juggling part-time work to pay for his education. Bunche, like many students, held several part-time jobs in addition to his many on-campus involvements. John B. Jackson, a contemporary of Bunche's at UCLA, remembers that Bunche, while he played on the basketball team and served as sports editor of the yearbook, also worked on campus as a janitor and as a salesman at Campbell's Bookstore across from school (Gist, 1990, pp. 64–65, 81–82).

The address to which the *California Grizzley* alluded was an uncompromising defense of "internationalism" in an era when American public opinion generally ran counter to its precepts. Bunche strongly supported the League of Nations because the violence of the Great War had made it "manifest that no longer can the nations of the world be permitted the exercise of unabridged liberty—each forming its own laws of conduct or none at all." Bunche, in an oblique reference to the opposition to the League among the leaders of the United States, suggested that the United States, "as a nation which, in the scant one hundred and fifty years of its national existence, has fought five wars with foreign powers and the bloodiest civil strife in history, should lead rather than retard such approbation" (Henry, 1995, p. 18). Despite this unenviable record, the United States also possessed some important intellectual assets to contribute to the creation of a more peaceful and well-ordered world: "Our thirteen colonies were rent by social and economic rivalries, dislikes, distrusts, and sectional jealousies, comparable . . . to those prevalent among the nations of the world today. Nevertheless, common bonds of human interest drew them into a single political union in which their interests were dissolved and from them emerged our present great commonwealth" (Henry, 1995, p. 19). Bunche hoped for the evolution of a "universal political society in which each nation would retain its individuality, its nationality . . . yet maintaining . . . an abiding consciousness of membership in the more significant international society" (Henry, 1995, p. 19). Undergirding this world consciousness would be a more highly evolved degree of human understanding in which "all peoples and nations think of themselves as component parts of a larger whole" (Henry, 1995, p. 19). Bunche assigned to his nation a very special role: "Let us here in America assume the leadership and begin to sow propaganda for world peace just as intensely as we sowed the destructive hatred instilling propaganda during the World War. Let us call a halt to all ethnocentric chauvinism . . . Let us begin immediately the development of a universal, rational-minded citizenry converted to world peace, conscious of membership in a world fraternity of all nations and peoples, and willing to make both individual and national sacrifices to the end that world tranquility may be eternally preserved!" (Henry, 1995, p. 20).

Taken together, Bunche's collegiate writings confirm that he, like many other leaders of his generation, possessed what Brenda Gayle Plummer has called a "modern black American outlook," which was the product of "growing participation in politics, educational opportunities and more diverse social and cultural contacts." The signature of this worldview would also become the signature of Bunche's academic writing: "an emancipatory view of race in the global setting" (Plummer, 1996, p. 36).

Bunche and others among his intellectual cohort within the "talented tenth" were on the leading edge of a broader trend: the sustained emergence after World War II of a robust internationalist ideology that, if it was always somewhat less in fashion than its advocates would have liked, gained influential adherents in the postwar years. This ideology advocated a more cooperative and multilateral approach to foreign policy, using, where practical, the United Nations and affiliated institutions to prevent the emergence of a world system governed only by narrow calculations of "power politics." This approach would become the bedrock of liberal foreign policy in the next generation, uniting a diverse group of American leaders such as Eleanor Roosevelt, the leading light of American liberalism; President Dwight D. Eisenhower, the tribune of "dynamic Republicanism" at home and abroad; Governor Adlai E. Stevenson, Eisenhower's Democratic rival in 1952 and 1956; and Senator J. William Fulbright, the father of the Fulbright international fellowship program who uncomfortably combined a generous and expansive internationalism in foreign affairs with a support for racial segregation in his own country.

In passages quoted previously, Bunche advocated a standard of human understanding that has made some remarkable advances but also suffered some equally significant setbacks over the last eighty years. Despite the injunctions of postmodern academic theory against seeing too much of the future in the archival remains of the past, there is a connection that is so strong, full, and direct that it must be clearly noted.

Building a functioning international world system based on self-determination balanced by federalist institutions was such an important theme to Bunche that he devoted his most important public moment to that point in his life, his valedictory address in 1927, entirely to it. Nurturing and developing a "fully grown personality" fitted to a world becoming drawn together by multiple human interconnections was to be the continuing task of his generation "if the mission of this [higher] education be filled" (Rivlin, 1990, p. 222). There was one very important difference between Bunche's 1926 defense of the League of Nations and his celebration of the "Fourth Dimension of Personality" on commencement day a year later. The League of Nations, its World Court, and Bunche's explicit references to the seemingly escalating human impulse to war are all absent, perhaps a pragmatic concession to the requirement to unify rather than polarize on such a hallowed and "nonpolitical" occasion. Bunche removed potentially controversial examples but kept the overriding spirit of the earlier speech intact. For instance, Bunche remained true to his fundamental point when, in his very first sentence, he proffered that "humanity's problem today is how to be saved from itself," launching into an only slightly moderated general indictment: "Throughout history man has indulged in self adulation and preached the gospel of human progress. Great advancement has been made, but in spite of success, there can be no doubt that human relationships are still far from complete adjustment. There are, in short, vital conditions in human associations which bode only ill for man's future" (Rivlin, 1990, p. 220).

The valedictory version of Bunche's 1926 address, "May Mankind Dwell in Peace" focused on what individuals could do within their personal relationships with others: the fulfillment of a true "higher education"—practiced in life rather than merely theorized in a college classroom—required humans to "become more altruistic and less selfish . . . we shall love more and hate less. We shall have become more internationally-minded—less insular minded" (Rivlin, 1990, p. 222). Bunche enjoined his audience "to recognize the truth, both psychologically and sociologically, that only in proportion as our world grows does our self grow" (Rivlin, 1990, p. 223).

Ralph Bunche's final college speech was a template for the hundreds of commencement addresses he would give in later years. Bunche, like many public figures, was able to temper his public language as he matured not because he had "sold out" but because he came to understand that the most important history is made not in public but behind the scenes, building the capacity for enlightened cooperation one practical step at a time. Ralph Bunche left the University of California, Southern Branch, a consummate practitioner of public diplomacy.

Synthesizing the Early Years

Near the end of his life, Ralph Bunche volunteered in an interview to "speak a word or two against brotherhood" (Hall, 1969, p. 50). After more than forty years as a public intellectual and more than a quarter century speaking on behalf of brotherhood as either a representative of the United States government or, far more often, the United Nations, Bunche confessed to his interlocutor that "I used to make a lot of speeches about brotherhood, but I don't mention it any more. . . . Mankind will be a lot better off when there is less reliance on lip service to brotherhood . . . and much more practice of the sounder and more realistic principle of mutual respect governing relations among all people" (Hall, 1969, p. 50). It is very difficult, after reading Bunche's "Fourth Dimension of Personality"—arguably Bunche's first "brotherhood" speech—not to detect a sense of disappointment in Bunche's words of 1969.

When Bunche began his life journey, he and the rest of his generation were far more optimistic than we are today about the ability of human beings to apply intelligence and enlightened self-interest to the world's most intractable problems. Although our current pessimism has been earned, it should not overwhelm some helpfully complicating facts. While it is true that the United Nations often became a pawn in superpower politics, Bunche's innovative work in peacekeeping helped prepare it for a new era. It has become fashionable to debunk the hopes that were once held out for a postcolonial world. It is true that the transition to nationhood for many former European colonies in the "developing world" has been more difficult than many anticolonialists envisioned fifty years ago. At the same time, the ethnic bloodshed and political chaos that sometimes accompany nationalist struggles are not unique to the "dark continent" of Africa; they have also occurred in the former Yugoslavia and Northern Ireland among other places. In domestic affairs, the picture is not much different. A broadly based civil rights movement did overcome the most visible and onerous institutions of racial segregation; and yet, the underlying economic inequalities that also drew Bunche's sharply analytical mind remain stubbornly resilient.

As I look back on Bunche's formative years, I am left inspired yet unsettled: there are many worthwhile lessons in Ralph Bunche's biography. But there are also questions and mysteries (which are different from secrets) that are left unanswered, no matter how much research we do. It is ultimately impossible for us to fully understand and appreciate the human toll taken by the demands of being Ralph Bunche—a major African American icon of brotherhood in the exceptionally turbulent middle years of the twentieth century. What is beyond question a generation after Ralph Bunche's death is that there remains much work to be done if we are to fully achieve the world he fought so hard to bring into existence.

3. Responsibilities of the Public Intellectual

JONATHAN SCOTT HOLLOWAY

Ralph Bunche is remembered as one who frowned on confrontation. Internationally famous for his activities as a peace broker for the Middle East, Bunche has gone down in history as a natural mediator—one who held his opinions closely and was skilled at political neutrality. Indeed, over the last thirty years of his life, as the modern civil rights movement emerged and then matured, an increasing number of activists thought Bunche was too adept at avoiding political turmoil. In 1941, Arthur P. Davis, his colleague at Howard University, had only disparaging words for Bunche. Making reference to the hair coverings that distinguished the field slaves from those in the plantation house, Davis observed, "There [are] bandana-handkerchief-headed Negroes, and silk-handkerchief-headed Negroes, but Ralph is a cellophane-handkerchief-headed Negro—you have to get off at a certain angle to see him" (Logan diary quoted in Janken, 1993, p. 207). W. E. B. Du Bois chimed in as well, confiding to Howard historian Rayford Logan that "Ralph Bunche is getting to be a white folks' 'nigger'" (quoted in Janken, 1993, p. 206). During the late 1960s, Bunche's do-good image frustrated young black radicals such as Stokely Carmichael, who, when Bunche's success was offered as an example of civil rights progress, responded, "You can't have Bunche for lunch!" Other progressive black leaders held similar views; Adam Clayton Powell and Malcolm X dismissed Bunche as an "international Uncle Tom" (Rivlin, 1990, p. 23).

Portions of this essay were previously published in *Confronting the Veil: Abram Harris Jr., E. Franklin Frazier, and Ralph Bunche, 1919–1941* by Jonathan Scott Holloway. Copyright © 2002 by the University of North Carolina Press. Used by permission of the publisher.

Standing in stark contrast to the image of Ralph Bunche as the embodiment of the political establishment and a polished conciliator is the reality of a young intellectual who deplored capitalism on moral grounds and who openly questioned the status quo while urging others to do the same. Consider the fact that eight years before Du Bois's "white folks' 'nigger'" comment, he believed that Bunche was part of the vanguard of young, progressive black American intellectuals.

Du Bois's belief in Bunche's vanguardism grew from the fact that for the better part of the 1930s, Bunche urged everyone—from interracial betterment organizations to graduate students at Princeton to the federal government—to address the needs of the working class before all else. He organized pickets of the Department of Justice, defended Howard student protests at the U.S. Capitol, led a boycott against the segregation policy of Washington's National Theater, and helped organize the National Negro Congress (NNC) (Holloway, 2002). During these years he remained fiercely antiracialist, always trying to change the debate over the race problem in the United States into one that revolved around class. Bunche never hesitated to criticize intellectuals and other "respectable types" who refused their moral obligations and tried to remain above the fray.

By looking back over his 1930s work, we can discern several issues about which Bunche never wavered. He did not relent in his desire to eliminate what he termed "racialism" and "racialist thought"; he remained a devout believer in the important role unfettered intellectuals and universities had to play in the modern world; and he maintained an abiding faith in the promise of American democracy. If one can find any change in his opinions on these matters, it would be the increased intensity of his feelings. Bunche articulated an agenda for the black radical intellectual in the 1930s. A reading of his essays, key speeches, and correspondence makes evident Bunche believed that the progressive black intellectual of the 1930s had to be politically engaged and that the "labor question" had to matter as much if not more than the "Negro question."

Bunche emerges from this history as an independent intellectual who took advantage of opportunities for new types of scholarly inquiry and service. This intellectual biography of Bunche during his early years reveals how his generation of black intellectuals played critical transitional roles in the political, social, and racial landscapes in between the first and second world wars. These scholars came of age during a time of dramatic societal upheaval and the work they did, aimed as it was at ameliorating social discord, marked pathways for future scholarship and intellectual activism. This generation's work led to the legitimization of social science expertise on race relations via Gunnar Myrdal's *An American Dilemma* (1944) project, it broadened the scope of "accepted" intellectual discourse by blacks, and it helped enlarge the terrain of professional possibilities for black scholars.

Emerging Scholars for New Directions

Bunche received his bachelor's degree from the University of California, Los Angeles, in 1927 and then moved east to pursue a Ph.D. in political science at Harvard. In 1929, having just earned his master's degree, Bunche began teaching at Howard University. He organized Howard's first political science department and then served as its chair. Over the next several years, Bunche worked at Howard as a professor and assistant to university president Mordecai Johnson and spent summers at Harvard pursuing his doctorate.

In 1934, after having already been promoted to associate professor at Howard, Bunche completed his dissertation, "French Administration in Togoland and Dahomey," and received his doctorate in political science. He was the first black to earn a doctorate in this field in the entire country (Greene, 1946). In addition to being a "racial first," Bunche's work showed great promise in the eyes of his mentors: he won Harvard's annual Toppan Prize for the best dissertation in political science. But despite his committee's urging, Bunche never managed to publish his research as a monograph. He did, however, produce short essays on the topic in the 1930s, and he returned to Africa at the close of the decade with the intent to update his old research, gather new findings, and write the long-delayed book (Urquhart, 1993; Henry, 1999; Holloway, 2002).

During the 1930s his early research in Africa was put to good use when Bunche took the domestic orientation of race relations in the United States and placed it in an international context. Bunche drew comparisons between Africans' degraded political and economic state and that of blacks in the United States. The daily contours of life in colonial Africa and the United States were undoubtedly different, but Bunche saw close connections between the systems through which both peoples found themselves at the bottom of their social hierarchies. In Africa, the vehicle for oppression was imperialism. In the United States, the vehicle was race. In both places, the driver was capitalism.

Bunche's most complete articulation of these ideas began in early 1935 when Alain Locke, his senior colleague at Howard, invited Bunche to "join in a series of booklets for adult education groups" (Locke, 1935). Locke prompted Bunche to write on his area of expertise when he asked Bunche to generate an essay examining "World Aspects of the Race Problem including the

Imperialistic System." Bunche accepted Locke's offer and produced a ninety-eight-page pamphlet titled *A World View of Race.*

Although merely a "pamphlet" whose target audience was a population other than his professional peers, *A World View of Race* must be considered the most important publication of Bunche's early years. It is the longest piece Bunche ever published and represents the clearest nexus of his international and domestic scholarly and political interests. In this essay, Bunche examined how race was used in the modern world and offered ideas as to how the current conception of race could be changed.

Bunche argued that "race" was used toward political and economic ends. Bunche noted the promise of the Western world's political principles and determined that in the light of contemporary events, these principles—"human equality and the doctrine of natural rights"—had "fallen upon hard times" (Bunche, 1936b, p. 1). Bunche held that the "inequality of peoples" was becoming an organizing theme for political and economic life across the globe, and he argued that this inequality frequently manifested itself as race-based bias. Bunche remarked, "One of the rocks on which the noble philosophy of human equality has run afoul takes shape as the frightful bogey, *race.* No other subject can so well illustrate the insincerity of our doctrines of human equality and the great disparity between our political theory and social practice as that of race" (Bunche, 1936b, p. 2). In short, Bunche saw "race" as a concept used to explain and justify a reality of economic, political, and social oppression.

Spurred by his ideas of economic and political causation, Bunche argued that the only solution to race problems lay in a complete restructuring of society. Toward that end, Bunche urged blacks to develop a class consciousness and to establish alliances with white workers in a united front to attain economic and political justice. For Bunche, the only solution to the race problem was the creation of a new society "in which it is unnecessary for men to knife one another for jobs, and in which economic exploitation of human beings for private gain is eliminated" (Bunche, 1936b, pp. 89–90).

In his call for a biracial movement, Bunche intended that his text would initiate such social change. He was, if nothing else, a firm believer in the central role intellectuals would have to play in forging a successful biracial workers' movement. *A World View of Race,* then, needs to be read as a treatise arguing for a nuanced and sociological understanding of racial formation and as a guidebook for a progressive political and intellectual intervention into undoing group inequity.

Bunche's progressive and at least theoretically race-blind ideas about social reform were either dismissed or criticized by politically moderate black scholars and the mainstream leadership of betterment organizations like the National Association for the Advancement of Colored People (NAACP). Fisk social scientist Charles Johnson, for example, felt that Bunche's pamphlet was "dogmatic," and that the students for whom *A World View of Race* was intended "did not need it" (C. Johnson, 1938, pp. 61–62). Roy Wilkins, the relatively new editor of the NAACP's magazine *Crisis*, declared as early as 1933 that Bunche and like-minded academics were so caught up in the reveries of progressive, allegedly race-neutral politics of the day that they paid insufficient attention to the practical application of their ideas. Wilkins understood the abstract appeal of an economic solution to racial problems but also had a sense of what kind of political program would inspire most blacks. There was little doubt that race was tightly linked to economics, but in his opinion the problem was one of race *and* class rather than race *or* class. Wilkins believed there was little in the radicals' agenda that would appeal to most blacks. "This may not be as it should be," he confessed, "but . . . I am afraid that if we go off too heavily on a theoretic . . . and economic program, we will find that we shall have cut ourselves loose from the support of the bulk of our followers" (Wilkins, 1934).

This general critique—that Bunche and his radical cohort were too distanced from the masses and too enamored of economic, sociological, and political theory—was, and continues to be, articulated often. But Bunche and his colleagues did not respond to these criticisms defensively and justify further their arguments. Scholars today, therefore, do not have extended treatises rationalizing their ideas and delineating how their theories could be enacted in real terms. We do not know precisely how they intended to create the biracial workers alliance they sought because they offered no strategy beyond "workers' education" to solve the abiding problem of white worker racism. When it came to such nettlesome problems, Bunche and his peers were astonishingly silent. Given the deep entrenchment and omnipresence of racism, this was a critical failure in their analysis. They were not, however, silent when it came to attacking another problem: older black leaders who refused to pass their reins to the next generation of leaders. These younger leaders were eager to steer black social consciousness in a radically different, economically deterministic direction.

Challenging Establishment Leadership

Bunche's activist exhortations and opinions on race and racial leadership did not remain confined to the printed page. He was a much-sought-after orator who frequently spoke in the Washington, D.C., area and, as he rose in prominence, across the country. During the mid-1930s, Bunche typically used these occasions to skewer self-serving leaders in the black community. One such example can be drawn from a speech Bunche gave before the Detroit Civic Rights Committee in 1936. Bunche's critics in the 1960s would have been stunned to hear his radical attack on opportunistic black leadership and its political quiescence.

In his speech, "Politico-Economic Analysis of the Politics of Race in the U.S.," Bunche addressed issues that applied to blacks' social, political, and economic position in Detroit, and more specifically in that city's government. Despite the local flavor of much of the speech, it was clear that Bunche believed leadership styles in Detroit could be extracted and applied in different locations and on larger scales. In short, his local critique of black leadership could move and still hold true. To emphasize this point, Bunche compared his assessment of Detroit's black leadership to what could be found in Washington, D.C. Perhaps because the District leadership was what was "local" to Bunche or perhaps because what happened locally in Washington had national implications, Bunche's discussion of black leadership styles was far more caustic and aggressive than the critique he had leveled in *A World View of Race.*

In a striking departure from the social scientific tone he typically evinced in his writing, Bunche offered his feelings about the black leadership in Washington:

> I come from the nation's capitol and I awake every morning with the sickening stench of pussy-footing, sophisticated Uncle Tom, pseudo Negro leadership in my nostrils. There the race has some highly paid, so-called Negro leaders many of whom hold their positions by carrying tales about other Negroes to the "white folks"—an old plantation custom. There, Negroes . . . attempt to ingratiate themselves with their white superiors by labeling every Negro who demands justice for his group "red." There, I hear Negro governmental officials constantly attempt to whitewash every discrimination, every injustice to Negroes in order to secure their useless, boondoggling jobs. (Bunche, 1936c)

True to the tone of the speech, Bunche wanted to do more than offer theories or merely describe leadership "types." He named names. Bunche singled out one of the first blacks to become involved in Franklin Roosevelt's administration, Lt. Lawrence Oxley, head of the Division of Negro Labor for the Department of Labor, as the "champion pussyfooter of all pussyfooters." While Bunche used Oxley as an example of a groveling black leader who was only interested in "buttering his own bread," his negative appraisal of Oxley had deeper roots.

Bunche was speaking to his Detroit audience just after the conclusion of a federal investigation into alleged communist activities at Howard University after a 1935 conference on blacks and the New Deal that led to the formation of the National Negro Congress, a Popular Front–styled organization. These charges, springing from retired Howard dean Kelly Miller's sense that secularism and radicalism had combined in such way that God and American democracy were under attack, found support among a few senators and representatives but were dismissed by the black and white New Deal officials who attended the conference. Except for Oxley, that is. Because he claimed that the entire 1935 conference was communist, Oxley, in Bunche's opinion, distinguished himself during the investigation as the "head S.O.B. of all S.O.B.s" (Bunche, 1936c). These types of black leaders, Bunche told his Detroit audience, had to be discredited.

But who, precisely, were these leaders? Except in those fairly rare moments when he eviscerated a particular individual like Oxley, Bunche never offered an exact definition of who literally belonged to the establishment he decried. Specificity, however, was beside the point. Bunche's rhetorical vagueness allowed him to cast a wide net in his attack against well-known black leaders. Bunche's logic seemed to suggest that since blacks lived in such a politically and economically degraded state, "their leaders," particularly those who appointed themselves leaders by virtue of their middle-class standing, were not doing the job.

If blacks were to enjoy the fruits of American democracy, they had to be vigilant against self-serving leaders. With this sentiment, Bunche reflected the thinking expressed by his peers who believed that *they* represented the best hopes for the race. He and the other "young leaders of the race" were deeply suspicious of and impatient with established black leaders who, in their collective opinion, ignored the plight of working-class blacks. Bunche urged his listeners to join him and "turn the pitiless spotlight of publicity on [self-serving black leaders'] hypocrisy, dishonesty, and treachery. Shout their false names from the housetops and drive them from their soft seats. It is high time that the Negro group should win respect and dignity for its cause by its honesty, fortitude, and courage. The group never profits by what is gotten through the back-door. It is time we waved good-bye to the 'hat-in-hand' age" (Bunche, 1936c). Later in this same speech, Bunche made it clear that in addition to finding a new leadership, the answer to the "Negro problem" was to adopt a new tactic that focused upon building solidarity among black and white workers. Blacks, he warned, must never again be misled by the "snobbish, middle-class leadership that disdained the Negro masses" (Bunche, 1936c).

The intensity of Bunche's challenge to black America's establishment leadership is at least partly explained by the frustrating social realities of racism that limited the potential breadth of leadership "types" in the black community. For example, whereas Bunche was deeply invested in the potential for a leadership elite of intellectuals to rise up and present a class-oriented thesis of society, he had to concede that race still ruled his existence. Despite his vigorous attempts to demonstrate that solving the "race problem" would not answer this country's problems regarding blacks and whites, Bunche and virtually all of his colleagues at Howard and other black institutions were trapped in a racial discourse. Academic segregation routed Bunche and his other colleagues—all of whom received their doctorates from the best, historically white, research universities—to Howard, Atlanta, or Fisk Universities. Also, Bunche's audiences were typically all black unless he found himself talking to members of that era's radical left—an act that he would find out in the 1950s carried its own peculiar consequences when he had to defend himself against charges of affiliating with communists two decades earlier. In addition to having to lead a professional life circumscribed by race, Bunche had to live much of his private life within the same boundaries. Even when some racial barriers began to lift after the second world war, Bunche, then at the United Nations, declined Harry Truman's offer to serve as an assistant secretary of state because he did not want to return to Washington and be forced to raise his children in its Jim Crow environment (Rivlin, 1990; Edgar, 1992).

Other ironies appear when we consider that, as much as Bunche and his young progressive colleagues decried the older black establishment and its faulty leadership, the younger scholars were unable to reach the same audience or numbers as the black establishment. The NAACP had *Crisis* and the National Urban League had *Opportunity* available as ready and capable tools to disseminate their ideas on a large scale. Additionally, the ministers and their churches, the leaders and institutions for whom Bunche felt the most disdain, had the greatest access to the black community.

Responsibilities of the Public Intellectual

A substantial portion of Bunche's attention during the 1930s was devoted to analyzing the role of race in the world order. But the interwar era was also a period marked by grave social concerns: global depression, the persistence of terrorist lynchings at home, and the specter of a rising fascism, to name just a few. Bunche was certainly attuned to these issues, but he was particularly concerned about the security of aggrieved communities in a world teetering on the brink of conflagration. Bunche spoke frequently in support of policies that broadened the availability of democratic participation to poor Americans, he called for economic justice for all Americans, and he called attention to the ominous political developments in Europe. Although Bunche did walk picket lines on a number of occasions in the 1930s, his activism was largely an intellectual activism that argued for social reform. This was not "armchair radicalism" to Bunche. Instead, Bunche believed that intellectuals and universities had an extremely important role to play in shaping the public's morality and politics.

Speaking before Carter G. Woodson's Association for the Study of Negro Life and History (ASNLH) in 1935, Bunche informed the audience that in his view it was a "critical period for Negroes—for all minority and oppressed groups. Our entire future is at stake in this period" (Bunche, 1935a). Bunche began his talk with specific references to the plight of blacks in the United States:

> Now [it is] more compelling on us than ever to fight—to fight to hold every inch of ground that we have won; to demand more insistently than ever before that justice be done, that equality be given, that every man have his place in the sun.
>
> In such a period the right of freedom of thought and expression assumes double importance for the Negro race.
>
> It is a precious right of the minority and oppressed groups to be allowed to think independently, to criticize vigorously and unceasingly not only the errors of its [sic] own leadership and philosophy but also the policies of the dominant groups and the governments which they control and which result in injustice to us. (Bunche, 1935a)

Bunche's strong reference to protecting "freedom of thought and expression" is understandable for a number of important reasons. His talk to the ASNLH came on the heels of the congressional investigation into communist activities at Howard and if, as an intellectual, he were denied the freedom to share his ideas, he had no role to play in society. This is not to suggest that Bunche advanced these arguments merely to save his literal job, but rather his figurative job. Bunche took the role and responsibilities of the scholar very seriously and spoke often on the positions of the intellectual in modern society.

Just one month after Locke had enlisted his services on *A World View of Race,* Bunche spoke at the Charter Day Dinner for the Howard Club of Philadelphia. After the obligatory opening remarks honoring the school and its alumni, Bunche dove into the heart of the speech: the social mission of universities. He began by stating that the "university, like all other human institutions—like the government, the church, the foundations—is incorporated in the general social fabric of any given period." For Bunche, the university captured the spirit of its age, it reflected the "mores of contemporary society," and it played influential roles in the present and future. But in times of great social and political change, the "progressive university" had a doubly important moral role to play: "[it] must not merely be controlled by orthodoxy and existing attitudes, but should act as a dynamic factor for social purposes. It ought often to project itself ahead of the accepted ideology and grope for new principles which will make for a better world for all mankind. When and if it does so . . . it must be prepared to meet the bitter criticisms and attacks of those who are hostile to change, who vigorously, selfishly, or blindly defend the status quo" (Bunche, 1935b). According to Bunche, the university, and by extension the professoriate, could and should take an activist role in changing society. The university, in Bunche's estimation, was a social laboratory whose role was to introduce "new ideas . . . [that] may hold a promise for a world vaguely conscious of certain deep-seated defects in things the way they are" (Bunche, 1935b).

In two other speeches concerning the place of higher education in the social order, Bunche reasserted that the primary role of the university was to activate the intellects of its young students so that they could be well-prepared to deal with the world outside of the academy. In the first speech, given in November 1935 to an audience at Miner Teachers College (a school for training black educators), Bunche argued that universities must pay special attention to aggrieved and minority groups like black Americans. These students, he maintained, had the greatest need to develop the "intelligently *critical* faculty to its keenest edge" in order to deal with the many social disadvantages awaiting them upon their graduation (Bunche, 1935c).

Bunche felt it "socially criminal" that students matriculated in schools, lived off a diet of textbooks and examinations, and then collided with the real world upon graduation. In his mind, professors had to prepare their charges for what their future might hold. True to the strong economic theme that guided much of his work during the era, Bunche suggested that students first had to learn something about black workers in order to gain a "real" education. "[How] valuable to the group can the so-called 'educated' young Negro be," Bunche wondered, "if he doesn't understand the problems of the Negro workers—if he is ignorant of the conditions of Negro workers in the tobacco fields, of longshoremen, of Negro miners, steam laundry and lumber workers? Does he know about 'Jim-Crow unionism' and the significance of the relation between Negro workers and labor unions?" (Bunche, 1935c).

Teachers carried a great responsibility on their shoulders, and Bunche

wanted to make sure that those who sought to become educators understood the gravity of their social responsibility. "Teaching," he concluded,
"is no substitute for fulfilling the obligations incumbent upon the socially
valuable, informed citizen. . . . We need honest and courageous leadership;
leadership that is socially aware of all that is happening, leadership that
cannot be purchased—that has no price tag because it is too *socially minded*
to stoop to *intellectual prostitution*" (Bunche, 1935c). Six months after this
speech, Bunche would revisit a number of these themes when he launched
into his assault of self-serving black political leadership before the Detroit
Civic Rights Committee.

But before turning his attention in Detroit to political leaders, Bunche
would speak several more times about the moral responsibilities of intellectuals and the need to protect academic freedom. Even though Howard
president Mordecai Johnson vowed to protect the freedom of his faculty,
the 1935 congressional investigation made it clear that this freedom would
be challenged. Just how limited his academic freedom could be was illuminated for Bunche when he was scheduled to appear before the Capitol City
Forum—a liberal Washington, D.C.–based speaker's group—in November
1935. Just before the meeting was to be called to order, the police arrived and
stopped the proceedings. The police claimed that the forum lacked a permit
to use the building where Bunche was to speak and that the building itself
was in violation of fire codes. Bunche felt otherwise, asserting that "the police
action was another phase of the anti-communist campaign" (*Washington
Tribune*, 1935a, 1935b). Two weeks later, Bunche finally got his opportunity to
speak before the Capitol City Forum. He made his opinion plain: "[Academic
freedom is] the very *foundation* of the educational process. It involves the
right of free inquiry and discussion on the part of both students and teachers,
and protects both from discipline for nonconformity" (Bunche, 1935d).

Bunche had a deep concern that raging nationalism and an ever-expanding
federal government made it "unpatriotic to think," and that both were fueled
by this country's economic structure. Bunche argued that American universities and their endowments were captive to corporate interests, and he feared
that education supported by corporate giving was tainted by conservative,
capitalist ideology. This corporate worldview trickled down through the
university hierarchy. Bunche knew all too well that despite promises of academic freedom, professors still took risks when they applauded trade-union
movements or supported picketers and other strike activities. Universities,
he pointed out, preferred to engage in less threatening struggles: fraternity
parties, football games, and alumni fund-raising. Discussing controversial
subjects like "capitalism, race relations, the trade-union movement, the pro-

tection of civil liberties, the status of minorities, and the conflict of classes" was taboo and even prohibited (Bunche, 1935d).

Bunche knew of which he spoke, for Howard University was especially vulnerable to the whims and vagaries of corporate and federal goodwill (Holloway, 2002). In a July 1936 article for the *Journal of Negro Education,* Bunche went on at length about the dangers of a close relationship between black institutions like Howard and the capitalist system (Bunche, 1936d). The article, "Education in Black and White," presented an overview of the state of higher education in the United States especially as it related to blacks.

Bunche resumed the drumbeat he had begun seven months earlier at the Capitol City Forum. He spoke of the gloomy consequences that awaited lovers of democracy if academic freedom were curtailed, warning the reader about the "'nightriders' in the educational world" who wanted the scholar to be "an intellectual virgin, innocent of all knowledge of and contact with the world of practical affairs and its problems." Bunche also examined the extent to which universities reflected the "status quo . . . consistently harmoniz[ing] with the dominant capitalistic pattern" (Bunche, 1936d, p. 351).

Black schools' fiscal health was tenuous when compared with that of white institutions. On this issue Bunche's evidence was more than compelling. He pointed out how easy it was to trace the development of black schools in the South to the well-being of Sears and Roebuck stock (the Rosenwald Fund, which funded a massive construction effort for primary and secondary schools for southern blacks, was a philanthropic arm of Sears) (Anderson, 1988). Black colleges and universities were even worse off, Bunche added, referring to them as "inevitable puppets of white philanthropy." The concern Bunche felt over the looming loss of academic freedom was even more immediate when considering black education. Because white philanthropies were the "controlling interests" at these schools, there was little hope that "'Negro Education' could ever direct itself to really effective solutions for the problems of the masses of working-class Negroes" (Bunche, 1936d, p. 356).

Three months after "Education in Black and White" was published, Bunche traveled to Princeton's School of Public Affairs to participate in the Conference on Higher Education for the Negro. The talk he gave, "Some Implications of the Economic Status of the American Negro for Negro Education," echoed many of the same themes he had addressed in "Education in Black and White" and at the Capitol City Forum. He spoke to the fact that schools were captive to capitalist interests and urged that education not take place in vacuum, divorced from any interaction with the real world. What makes this presentation noteworthy is the setting in which it occurred and the tone with which Bunche concluded his presentation. While some black student radicals of the 1960s would come to believe that Bunche was an "Uncle Tom," it is evident that he was not one in 1936, as he had the following to say to the young Princeton scholars:

> In your reading & thinking on this prob[lem,] be honest with yourself. Think straight. Be candid—brutally so, if necessary. *Hate* the N[egro] if you will, but hate him on *honest, sound* grounds. . . . Dislike or hate the N[egro] because of the econ[omic] threat that he offers, or because he is a worker, or a strike-breaker. But not for specious reasons—not because some race maniac implements his phobia with pseudo-scientific theories of racial inferiority, or because of his body-odor, or his steatopogy. . . . And for Pete's sake don't *love* the Negro—at least never admit it publicly. The N[egro] race has too many *professional* lovers—it has too many "affairs" of this kind—& most of them do him more harm than good. Don't fall for sentimental, romantic, or prayerful approaches to the problem. (Bunche, 1936e)

After the Princeton appearance, Bunche turned his attention away from academic freedom, the role of intellectuals in the public sphere, and black education in general. Except for *A World View of Race* and several book reviews, Bunche largely disappeared from the public sphere from 1937 through the middle of 1939 as he left the country on extended research trips, became a lead researcher for Myrdal's *An American Dilemma*, and even consulted for a Republican Party–sponsored investigation on black voting behavior (Holloway, 2002).

A Final Progressive Push

After Bunche completed his work for the Myrdal project and the Republican Program Committee (the latter of which was never published as Bunche and the RPC fundamentally disagreed on numerous findings in Bunche's report), he began to accept public speaking engagements again. Bunche's return to the wide-open, occasionally ad hominem, verbal assaults of the 1930s, however, was short-lived. As Hitler's armies rolled into the Soviet Union and Japanese aggression remained unchecked, the United States' preparations for war went into overdrive. An important aspect of this effort involved developing a reliable understanding of Africa—one of the war's major theaters—and its historic connections to Europe. To this end, the newly created Office of the Coordinator of Information (COI—from which the Office of Strategic Services and then the Central Intelligence Agency emerged) sought Africanists to provide public information, generate propaganda, and wage psychological warfare. Upon the recommendation of Bunche's former mentors at Harvard

University, representatives from the COI contacted him about a position. In September 1941, Bunche accepted an appointment as a senior social science analyst for the Office of Strategic Services (Urquhart, 1993). The conversion to expert consultant was now complete.

Whereas Bunche had already considered himself part of the public sphere, now the level of his involvement—and in his view, responsibility—intensified. This was the moment that Bunche decided to step back from the fiery rhetoric that characterized his speaking and writing of the previous decade (Urquhart, 1993; Logan, 1943). It may be that Bunche's personal views never changed, and that he would share his opinions on race and economics with his close friends. But now, and for the rest of his life, Bunche was determined to prevent these private opinions from damaging or compromising the effectiveness of any organization to which he was attached. Whatever may be the true source of this new reticence, we are left with a final irony: as Bunche became more of a public figure, he also became more of a private one.

In the summer preceding his federal appointment, however, Bunche had not yet metamorphosed into this public sphinx. In the middle of July, Bunche participated in the "Conference on the Needs of Negro Youth," a gathering sponsored by the Howard University Summer School. His talk on the opening day of the meeting, "The Role of the University in the Political Orientation of Negro Youth," revisited some of the themes he had addressed prior to his international travel and extensive research projects.

In Bunche's 1936 article, "Education in Black and White," he had railed against those who wanted academics to remain "intellectual virgins." In his 1940 conference speech, Bunche continued with this theme but in a more direct and aggressive manner. He chided his audience, and laid some blame on himself as well, for being "pure scholars, intellectual vestal virgins, [who] are of the world but not in it. Rumor reaches us that the worldly world is sordid, vulgar, barbarous, lying, intriguing, and ruthlessly lacking in moral fabric" (Bunche, 1940a). Bunche chastised those who were faint of heart and afraid to venture outside the "severely insulated cloisters of the University." Bunche felt that scholars prided themselves on their unending pursuit of the truth. But this pursuit, Bunche warned, allowed professors to lose touch with real-world problems and also left the professors' students dangerously unprepared for the complications and contradictions of the modern world (Bunche, 1940a).

Bunche was not advocating a complete departure from the objective social science ideal to which he and his Howard colleagues had pledged allegiance earlier in their careers. Bunche still wanted professors to "cultivate scholars," but now he also believed academics had a moral responsibility to train a few "crusaders for democracy" as well. Bunche did not try to hide his purpose:

"Is it not clear that it is only through democracy that we can hope to continue to produce scholars? It is no secret to anyone now that the democratic principle is sorely besieged throughout the world, and is threatened with total annihilation" (Bunche, 1940a). The blood threatening to wash up on shores around the world intensified in Bunche this need to develop "social crusader-scholars."

Bunche signaled that pragmatic political concerns were overwhelming the hope he and his progressive colleagues of the early 1930s carried for a different socioeconomic and a truly democratic future. "The Negro of today," Bunche declared, "is not permitted the luxury of choosing between ideal systems. He is socially blind even if he permits himself to build his hopes in such a dream world." Although his audience probably was unaware, Bunche was making inferences to his own experiences with what had been Bunche's dream world: the National Negro Congress. Just months before he gave the speech to the Howard Summer School students, Bunche had broken with the NNC. Frustrated from the start that the NNC relied too heavily on race as an organizational tool and then did not limit its organizational scope exclusively to labor, Bunche left the NNC after its April conference in 1940 (Henry, 1999). Bunche wanted his students to understand that the NNC had become, in his view, a puppet of the Communist Party. And since he thought that Stalin's communism was "sophistry of the cheapest variety," he urged his audience to dispel any notions that they may have had to support the CP efforts or those of the NNC (Hutchinson, 1994; Henry, 1999). Communism, he made clear, failed as an ideal system for improving the quality of black life.

Fascism, based as it was on the politics of white supremacy, was clearly not an option. Conceding that there were many things wrong with democracy in America, Bunche still urged those in attendance to accept that whatever progress the race had made since slavery was due to the democratic ideal. "Democracy, even imperfect democracy," he offered, "has been the ideological foundation upon which our lives have been based. It has been our spiritual life blood" (Bunche, 1940a).

Bunche still believed that class and economics should supplant race as analytic or scientific tools for social analysis (Bunche, 1941b). He felt that black colleges had to trumpet the virtues of democracy more than ever before. Black schools, Bunche argued, had to do everything possible to develop in their students and in society at large an "ardent faith in the principles of democracy" and to make a "fetish of the worship of democracy." This was a holy mission in which all elements of the university must be engaged: "the classroom, the seminar table, the lecture platform, the university press, the chapel" (Bunche, 1940a).

Bunche concluded his lecture with a nod toward an age that had passed. In his closing thoughts, one can discern a hint of sadness at the opportunity that had been lost, but one can also note a close-the-ranks mentality that privileged national unity at a time of international crisis and declared that without sacrifice, all gains would be for naught. Bunche asserted that universities could afford to act as disinterested or objective institutions dedicated to scientific truth in times of peace and prosperity. In such times, he continued, it might be enough for schools to cultivate the next generation of truth-seekers. But that day had passed. Universities now had a moral obligation to defend national standards and to save democratic ideals. If they shirked that responsibility, their own existence was threatened (Bunche, 1940a).

Bunche remained on the faculty at Howard until he resigned in 1950, but he was essentially on leave throughout the 1940s as he moved from posts in the federal government to the United Nations. In terms of public profile and the effect his views and decisions would have on the world, Bunche would undoubtedly become the most prominent black scholar of his generation. It is ironic, then, that Bunche, the great believer in the roles the intellectual and the university had to play in modern society, rose to the heights he did only when he removed himself from those spheres. It is also noteworthy that despite his success, Bunche remained exposed to racial discrimination and never broke the shackles of a racial logic built by a racist society. These facts make it all the more surprising that Bunche was able to sustain his anti-racialist belief system for as long as he did.

We are left, then, with an enigma: a one-time radical who is written off as an Uncle Tom; an active supporter of progressive politics who at one point contracted his work to the increasingly conservative Republican Party; an objective social scientist whose most important intellectual contribution is captured in ad hominem speeches and pamphlets. In short, Bunche's legacies are difficult to discern. Because he kept accepting projects that pulled his attention away from manuscripts in progress, his scholarly publishing record is thin. Furthermore, because he was only active on the Howard faculty for little more than a decade, his legacy as an academic intellectual is limited. What is clear, however, is that in just over ten years of sustained activity, Bunche served as a model of intellectual engagement beyond the life of the mind. Scholars, Bunche felt, had a moral responsibility to speak to social injustice and then to act on their beliefs to secure a better future. According to Bunche's 1930s worldview, this was a future that ought to be defined by economic justice rather than racialized systems of degradation.

4. A World View of Race Revisited

CHARLES P. HENRY

An observer of race relations once wrote, "Why not have a ten year moratorium on all discussions and writings on the race problem? . . . This would give the present younger generation a chance to grow up without having their minds too warped" (J. Young, 1973, p. 34). After all, as sociologist William Julius Wilson declared in 1978, race was declining in significance (W. Wilson, 1978). Since then, however, we have seen the rise of diaspora studies, new attention to immigration and its racial implications, the spread of "hip-hop" culture across the globe, the development of "whiteness studies," the replacing of an East-West ideological divide with a North-South cultural divide, the formation of an American multiracial or mixed race movement, the creation of an "underclass" thesis, the intersection of race, class, and gender, the rebirth of the modern reparations movement, the clash of civilizations, and the replacement of affirmative action with diversity or multiculturalism. In short, the "globalization of race"[1] is now a worldview expressed in mass culture as well as social science. An observer might have good reason to call a time-out to sort through the maze of concepts, programs, and images related to race.

However, the observer quoted above is not University of California regent Ward Connolly or Supreme Court justice Clarence Thomas writing about current racial politics; it is Arthur P. Davis, a newspaper columnist and literary critic commenting on the 1930s. Much as it is today, in the 1930s the issue of race was in dispute and racial discourse was in transition. For the first time, a new generation of young Black intellectuals was making themselves heard both in academic and public circles. These young Black scholars, trained at some of the best universities in the country, began to challenge the dominant biological race paradigm of such White scholars as Herbert Spencer, William Sumner, E. L. Thorndike, Carl Brigham, Robert Yerkes, Lewis Terman, William MacDougall, Madison Grant, Lothrop Stoddard, and others who were trained and taught at these same universities (Gossett, 1997, chapter 15). Moreover, they also challenged the views of an older generation of "race men" who had sought in the terms of the Negritude writers of the thirties to develop an "anti-racism racism." That is, this older generation of scholars, including Carter Woodson, Kelly Miller, and the young W. E. B. Du Bois, had challenged the notion of racial hierarchy but accepted the concept of biological difference.

Both academic thinking and popular opinion were in flux after World War I. The war had cracked the notion of the superiority of Western or White civilization. Black soldiers from the United States as well as the West Indies and Africa had fought and died to "make the world safe for democracy" and were unwilling to return to the prewar status quo. The war had generated massive internal and external migrations leading to the creation of new, cosmopolitan urban centers such as Harlem and Chicago's South Side. A young Jamaican like Marcus Garvey, for example, could immigrate to Harlem and develop the Universal Negro Improvement Association (UNIA). Ella Baker, a young woman from North Carolina, moved to Harlem and pursued educational and organizational work unheard of in her hometown that would eventually lead to her key organizing roles is the NAACP and the Student Nonviolent Coordinating Committee (SNCC). In short, the conditions were present to create a formidable Black civil society or counter-public.

One organization, above all others, would become the leader of Black civil society: the National Association for the Advancement of Colored People (NAACP). Formed in 1909, the NAACP, like the Urban League (1910), UNIA (1914), and other activist groups, received a boost in membership and resources as a result of World War I and its impact. By the early 1930s, however, it was clear that the NAACP had no economic strategy for dealing with the Great Depression. At the NAACP's Amenia conference in 1933, a group of the new generation of Black intellectuals launched an attack on the NAACP and its leaders, who included Du Bois and James Weldon Johnson. Leading the charge were economist Abram Harris, sociologist E. Franklin Frazier, and political scientist Ralph Bunche. Charging that the racial provincialism and middle-class bias of the older leaders led them to neglect the economic needs of the masses of Negroes, these young academics were appointed to a follow-up committee that made specific recommendations to the NAACP (J. Young, 1973; Holloway, 2002; Henry, 1995). The report of this special committee was ultimately rejected, but the three scholars would go on to have a profound influence in shaping our racial worldview.

Three years after Amenia, Ralph Bunche had become the first African American to receive a doctorate in political science. His 1934 Harvard dissertation entitled "French Administration in Togoland and Dahomey" won the Toppan prize as the best dissertation in government that year. Bunche published a number of articles in 1935 and while teaching at Howard organized with John P. Davis a major conference on the "Position of the Negro in the Present Economic Crisis." The conference was unusual in its inclusion of workers, farmers, and labor activists along with academics, government officials, and Communists. Growing out of the conference was a new organization, the National Negro Congress, that would attempt to fill the gap created by the NAACP's lack of response to economic issues.

From 1936 to 1942, the Associates in Negro Folk Education, funded by the Carnegie Corporation and later by the Rosenwald Fund, issued nine works called the Bronze Booklet series. The overall editor was Alain Locke, who also wrote three of the booklets on art and music. Two were by Sterling Brown on fiction, poetry, and drama, one each by Eric Williams on the Caribbean, Ira De A. Reid on education, and T. Arnold Hill of the National Urban League on economics, replacing one by Du Bois that had not been accepted (Aptheker, 1985, p. 103). Bunche produced the booklet on politics, *A World View of Race,* in only a week, although he later apologized for the haste in which it had been written and seemed embarrassed by its polemical tone. Nonetheless, it represents his views at the time and is their most extensive exposition.

One senses a tension in *World View* between Bunche the pragmatic social scientist and Bunche the committed and leftist activist. The tone and language are much different from his dissertation two years earlier. In the title alone, Bunche suggests he is not dealing simply with an academic paradigm but an entire way of seeing the world.[2] The introduction of the pamphlet presents a subject that would consume Bunche for the next several years, the great disparity between our political theory of human equality and our social practice of race. Two aspects of Bunche's analysis have particular relevance for today—his formulation of race as a social construct and his comparative, historical examination of race.

Although Bunche's booklet is meant for adult education students, the first chapter reads like a graduate review of the latest scholarly literature on race. After noting the relatively recent origins of the term, he adds that definitions of race linked to broad geographic regions were too vague to permit the concept to be used as an effective instrument of national policy. Herbert Spencer, says Bunche, introduced the explanation of an evolutionary "step-ladder" of races with distinct levels of advancement tied to nature. In this scheme of superior and inferior races, color was the simplest means of identifying races. All conceptions of race, states Bunche, are in general agreement that there must be certain physical characteristics determined by heredity and passed down from one generation to the next (Bunche, 1936b, p. 5).

It is in the attempt to establish rigid racial classifications that scientists falter. According to Bunche, "*The plain fact is that the selection of any specific physical trait or set of traits as a basis for identifying racial groups is a purely arbitrary process*" (Bunche, 1936b, p. 7; emphasis in the original). Citing the commonly accepted postulate of three main racial types—the Negroid or black, the Mongoloid or yellow-brown, and the Caucasian or white—Bunche suggests that physical variations within each type are so great as to render the concept useless. Later in the essay, he challenges the notion that race can be linked to a language (for example, Aryan) or a nation (for example, French or British). Human migration, Bunche concludes, means all existing human groups are of mixed origin (Bunche, 1936b, p. 14). Based on current anthropological knowledge, Bunche believes "existing racial divisions are *arbitrary, subjective and devoid of scientific meaning*" (Bunche, 1936b, p. 7–9; emphasis in the original).

The study of heredity is central to the concept of race. Bunche argues that genetics has made rapid strides, and he reviews the role of genes and chromosomes in determining physical traits. However, it is the interaction of the hereditary constitution with environmental conditions that is of prime importance to the problem of "race" in man. With our present knowledge, says Bunche, it is impossible to determine the degree to which heredity or environment contributes to the resultant character of the human type. But it is clear that environmental and social conditions are of "tremendous importance" for the individual or the group (Bunche, 1936b, p. 13).

It is at this point in his analysis that the Howard political scientist introduces the concept of *social race* into his analysis. If we concede the significance of environmental and social conditions for the individual or the group, then it becomes clear that the inherent ability of any individual or group is dependent for its realization and expression upon the presence of proper conditions for its cultivation. At this point, contends Bunche, the social, economic, and political systems, by determining the financial, educational, and other opportunities in the society, will directly affect the physical and psychological character that the individual or group will develop (Bunche 1936b, p. 13). He cites Army intelligence tests from World War I and subsequent tests, which found that Negro recruits born and reared in the North scored higher than southern Whites, as evidence that superior environment is a determining factor in intellectual capacity. (More recently, the work of social psychologist Claude Steele on race and "test anxiety" demonstrate just how subtle environmental influences can be in affecting test performance [Steele, 1997].) Having argued that race has no scientific basis in biology, and having further argued that individual and group differences are not inherent but rather directly linked to environment, Bunche concludes, "*Group antago-nisms are social, political and economic conflicts, not racial, though they are frequently given a racial label and seek a racial justification*" (Bunche, 1936b, p. 23; emphasis in the original).

For the sake of comparison, we might group modern racial conceptions in four broad categories. At one end of a continuum, we would place those scholars who argue that race does not exist and that it is counterproductive to maintain racial labels even if we use them for "liberatory" or "compensatory" ends. Paul Gilroy, for example, has written "renouncing 'race' for analytical purposes seems to represent the only *ethical* response to the conspicuous wrongs that raciologies continue to solicit and sanction" (Gilroy, 2000, p. 41). Echoing Bunche, he adds, "Racialized conflicts . . . are now understood by many commentators as a problem of the incompatible identities that mark out deeper conflicts between cultures and civilizations" (Gilroy, 2000, p. 98). Another well-known opponent of racial discourse is philosopher Anthony Appiah. He argues that even more modern and implicit cultural concep-tions of race rely at base on biological claims, and further, that biological distinction has inevitably led to claims of racial inferiority and superiority (Goldberg, 1993).

At the opposite end of the continuum are those writers who maintain a biological conception of racial difference. Most prominent among modern-day advocates of this position are those writing on intelligence testing such as Richard Jensen, William Shockley, and Charles Murray. While these au-thors link race directly to intelligence (as measured in standardized testing), sociobiologists simply state that human organisms are frameworks for the natural selection of reproductively successful genes and that genes favoring intrakin relations have a selective advantage (Goldberg, 1993, p. 7). Both perspectives ignore the influence of social institutions and practices.

Another group of scholars labeled "melanists" also support a biological definition of race. These writers, often psychologists or psychiatrists, promote a view that sees Caucasian behavior as abnormal or deviant. Francis Cress Welsing, for example, contends that "whiteness" is a genetic deficiency that has inflicted Caucasians with an inferiority complex. This sense of inadequacy or inferiority leads them to act with hostility and aggression toward people of color (Ani, 1994, p. 451). From a different perspective, a number of schol-ars have focused on "racialized biopolitics" in popular culture. Operating almost exclusively through the visual representation of racialized bodies, often engaged in sexual or sporting activities, it represents a new form of identity politics (Gilroy, 2000, p. 185, 263).

Within these extremes reside a plethora of racial conceptions. One notable school of thought often labeled as "essentialist" argues that Africans and those of African descent are bound together over time and place by specific characteristics and values. Afrocentrists are generally seen as the main proponents of this viewpoint; however, their thinking is not uniform. Chiekh Anta Diop developed a "two cradle" theory of civilization—European and African—in which environment, not biology, determines cultural difference (Diop, 1979). Molefi Asante, on the other hand, says, "Race refers to the progeny of a fairly stable common gene pool which produces people with similar physical characteristics." But then Asante suddenly shifts from physical to geographic characteristics, stating, "The African race means the gene pool defined by the whole African continent including people in every geographical area of the land from Egypt to South Africa" (Asante, 1990, p. 17).

The final major modern conception of race is as a contingent and variable social construction that is nonetheless real. Many of these scholars writing from this position argue that the concept may be used for positive as well as negative purposes. One of the most popular works of this school is Michael Omi and Howard Winant's *Racial Formation in the United States.* They present a theory of racial formation that treats race in the United States as a fundamental *organizing principle* of social relationships. At the micro level, race is a matter of individuality and identity while at the macro level it is a matter of collectivity, of the formation of social structures. The relationship between these levels, Omi and Winant assert, takes place through "*political contestation over racial meanings*" (Omi & Winant, 1986, pp. 66–69). David Goldberg's work substitutes racial creation/constitution for racial formation because it signifies a greater subjective dimension. Goldberg adds that race is central to both science and modernity. Science, says Goldberg, rests on classification, which is central to scientific methodology. Classification, the ordering of representations, always presupposes value (Goldberg, 1993, p. 49). Classifications are central to the drive to exclude, which is not antithetical to modernity but constitutive of it, that is, it forms the measure by which racialized groups are modern and deserving of incorporation, or premodern and to be excluded from the body politic (Goldberg, 1993, pp. 108–109). Charles Mills goes even further in believing that White supremacy may become independent of feeling racism, that is, the system of accumulated, entrenched privilege can reproduce itself through motivation that is simply self- and group-interested (Mills, 1998, p. 146).

Bunche's framework and social definition of race foreshadows this last category of racial thinking. While his views have been called neo-Marxian (as have those of Diop and Du Bois), Bunche never develops a rigid or mechanistic view of race relations. He would likely agree with Mills that "Whiteness is not really a color at all, but a set of power relations" (Mills, 1997, p. 127). This perspective on race as power rather than biology helps both Mills and Bunche keep the historic economic exploitation of Blacks at the heart of their explanations of the polity and its structuring of the "racial contract." As Bunche states it, "All of the present-day relations between the disadvantaged Negro group and the majority white group are influenced by this master-slave heritage and the traditional competition between poor white and Negro masses" (Bunche, 1936b, p. 76).

Yet a contemporary Bunche would also find something of value in Gilroy's work. Both Gilroy and Bunche see the concept of "nation" as practically and theoretically limiting. Gilroy suggests that the concept of "diaspora" disrupts the fundamental power of territory to determine identity by breaking the simple sequence of explanatory links between place, location, and consciousness. "Diaspora," says Gilroy, "is an outer-national term that contributes to the analysis of intercultural and transcultural processes and forms" (Gilroy, 2000, p. 123). As a political scientist who trained himself in the latest anthropological methodologies and fieldwork techniques in the two years following *World View*, Bunche might see diaspora as a useful idea.

From 1936 to 1938, Bunche trained in the field methods cultural anthropologists were using to study culture contact. Political science (the only social science discipline originating in the United States) had not provided a method by which he could examine colonialism from the perspective of the African. Consequently he proposed, and the Social Science Research Council funded, a two-year study on the impact of colonial rule and Western culture on Africans. Prior to his fieldwork, he studied with Melville Herskovits at Northwestern University, Bronislaw Malinowski at the London School of Economics, and Isaac Schapera at the University of Cape Town in South Africa. Bunche became the only African American funded by a private foundation to make a research trip to Africa until the 1950s.

While Bunche became more sophisticated in his social analyses as a result of this experience,[3] the foundation for his research was laid in *World View*. If the ancient word diaspora acquires a modern accent as a result of the nationalisms and imperialisms of the late nineteenth century, as Gilroy maintains, then there is no better starting place than Bunche's work. He asks the question "By what devices is the African governed?" (Bunche, 1936b, p. 46). He replies that European contact has resulted in two extremes of policy: "The one, based entirely on greed, regarded him as essentially inferior, subhuman, without a soul, and fit only for slavery. The other, based entirely on sentiment, regarded him as a man and brother, extended to him the egalitarian principles of the French Revolution and attempted to 'Europeanize' him overnight" (Bunche, 1936b, p. 46). While both policies aimed at maximum exploitation, were unscientific, and devoted little attention to the African, the differences in their implementation would have profound consequences for the African diaspora.

According to Bunche, French native policy represents one extreme, the policy of assimilation, in which nothing in native civilization is good and French culture must replace it. More recently, said Bunche, the French abandoned wholesale assimilation of native populations in favor of a less ambitious policy of "association." Key to making this new policy of collaboration in colonial planning work is the creation of a privileged or elite class of natives. The elite native becomes a Black Frenchman with many civil and political privileges all designed to ensure loyalty to France. Bunche cites Martinique and Guadeloupe as prototypes for this new African policy that is a class device for the control of the country (Bunche, 1936b, pp. 50–51).

For the native elite, the French accept the native as a brother with no thought of race or color. Bunche relates several vignettes of Black French colonial officials treated as social equals both abroad and in Africa. In conversation, Bunche notes, the African colonial administrator "draws careful distinctions between 'the blacks,' 'the natives' and 'Frenchmen,' like himself" (Bunche, 1936b, p. 54). It is even possible, says Bunche, to see a White French subordinate administrator taking orders from his dark-skinned boss. Such a relationship would be impossible to find in the United States. The African elite is keenly sensitive to any suggestion of inferiority: "His education, whether French or English, has 'Europeanized' him and he has adopted European standards of conduct, culture and achievement as his own. It is slight wonder that he is captivated by a French culture which receives him with open arms. But unfortunately, only a few natives are ever able to attain this privileged status. The French policy of association has an entirely different meaning for the native African masses" (Bunche, 1936b, p. 56). By the co-opting of the most ambitious and talented natives, the native masses are left without effective leadership and appeals to race consciousness are minimized.

Like the French, the British are confident of their colonizing genius as a "superior" race, however, the British believe their culture is so superior no supposedly primitive people could ever become sufficiently elevated to absorb it. This traditional Anglo-Saxon attitude toward darker races has policy implications for colonial administration. Given that British colonial administrators can never be more than a handful, Bunche says, it is much simpler to permit native chiefs to maintain native law through tribal institutions and social organization. Although this hereditary native elite may become trained and educated, it is frozen out of English society. This can and does lead to them becoming professional agitators and troublemakers. Comparing this English racial attitude to one advanced in the United States by Lord Lugard and repeated by an American president at Birmingham, Alabama, Bunche writes, "Here, then, is the true conception of the interrelation of colour: complete uniformity in ideals, absolute equality in the paths of knowledge and culture, equal admiration for those who achieve; in matters social and racial a separate path, each pursuing his own inherited traditions, preserving his own race-purity and race-pride; equality in things spiritual, agreed divergence in the physical and material" (Bunche, 1936b, p. 60). This, says Bunche, is the essence of Booker T. Washington's well-known "separate as the fingers of the hand" analogy, and of the familiar American legal fiction of "separate but equal rights." As a result, both the Blacks in America and British Africa are extremely race conscious.

Yet Bunche recognizes a further distinction between Africans under French and British domination and African Americans. "The American Negro," writes Bunche, "is an exceptional case in that he has been torn away from his origins and dumped into an entirely new milieu in which he finds himself a minority group" (Bunche, 1936b, p. 49). This characterization of the American Negro as economically, politically, and culturally powerless foreshadows the rise of the internal colony approach to race conditions in the 1960s and 1970s (Blauner, 1972; Barrera, 1979; Carmichael & Hamilton, 1967).

Another innovative aspect of *A World View of Race* is Bunche's comparative examination of minority groups in the United States. Bunche argued that biological, cultural, and social differences only become meaningful when such groups pose an economic threat to the "settled" population. "Racial feelings," states Bunche, "are thus extremely fickle" (Bunche, 1936b, p. 70).

A prime example of the arbitrary nature of race prejudice is the case of Chinese immigrants. As long as they were not thrown into competition with White labor, they were unmolested. However, when they did begin to compete with Whites, new stereotypes began to take shape and new prejudices were invented. Quite suddenly, says Bunche, they became undesirable and had to go: "They did not make good Americans; they did not readily assimilate; they retained their Chinese customs and laws; they sent their money back to China; they lowered American standards of living; they were criminal, degenerate, dishonest, racially inferior, unclean, and unreliable workers" (Bunche, 1936b, p. 71). The hatred, mob violence, lynching, and discriminatory legislation they faced were similar to that experienced by the Negro in the South.

Similarly, Bunche analyzed the changing perceptions of Japanese and Mexican immigrants. He adds that Jews, Poles, Italians, Germans, Greeks, Irish, and Scandinavians all suffered from some form of racial persecution in different sections of the country when they first arrived in significant numbers. He notes the bitter resentment against Irish immigration by the "Know Nothing" party. Yet all these European ethnics, "with the possible exception of the Jews," have been able to throw off their minority status within one or two generations. Of course, the last two decades have witnessed the rise of "whiteness" studies, which focus on the contingent nature of European ethnic identity in the United States. Central to the overcoming of minority status on the part of European ethnic immigrants is the creation of "blackness" as the other to unite against (Jacobson, 1998; Roediger, 1991; Lipsitz, 1998; Malcolmson, 2000).

While the basic cause of the racial persecution of all these groups is the same—economic competition—the inferior status of the Negro has become fixed. Bunche believed, however, that the factors of race and the tradition of slavery do not fully explain the perpetuation of the American "race problem." After all, Brazil, Cuba, Puerto Rico, and other South American and Caribbean countries do not possess a "one drop of Negro blood" rule with its rigid and extreme racial classifications.

Contrasting the relatively free and open intermingling between the White Spanish and French settlers, the native Indians, and the Negroes in these other countries, Bunche concluded they tend to be rooted in class and caste rather than racial distinctions. He attributed this difference to the White population in the South, which both before and after emancipation was a predominantly poor population: "The determination of the ruling class of plantation owners and bankers in the South to perpetuate in law and custom the pernicious doctrine of the racial inferiority of the Negro was made possible only because the numerically preponderant poor-white population feared the economic competition and the social and political power of the large Black population. The cultural, political and economic degradation of the Negro also gave the poor whites their sole chance for 'status' in the society" (Bunche, 1936b, p. 78). It follows then that the ultimate solution to racial discrimination is a society of plenty with a fair distribution for all.

White society's tendency to view Blacks as a group has led them to overlook differences within the Negro community. "No one," says Bunche, "can describe how it feels to be a 'Negro' in this country because what the Negro is here defies description—the sum total of the social, political and economic forces have created a purely sociological being called the Negro" (Bunche, 1936b, p. 85). Racial hatreds are group hatreds that reflect a social legacy handed down from generation to generation.

What does Bunche's global analysis of race nearly seventy years ago tell us about contemporary racial discourse? Bunche considered himself a progressive social scientist, a social engineer if you will, committed to the applied use of knowledge for the betterment of humankind. Social scientists like Bunche, who saw Africans as in a transitional stage between primitivism and civilization, were working toward a world where achieved status replaced ascribed traits. It was assumed that increased contact and communication would lead toward cultural homogenization.

Yet the postmodern world provides everyday examples that science has not triumphed nor religion died in even the most technologically advanced countries. Electronic media have helped create an ethnic politics in which primordial have become globalized (Appadurai, 1996, p. 6, 41). The quantity of information available threatens to overwhelm our capacity to interpret it, and the rapid dissemination and pace of change leads to anxiety and fear. Thus, "the more explicitly universal modernity's commitments, the more open it is to and the more determined it is by the likes of racial specificity and racist exclusivity" (Goldberg, 1993, p. 4).

The role of race in this brave new world is as much in flux today as in Bunche's era. Manuel Castells, for example, states, "While race matters, probably more than ever as a source of oppression and discrimination, ethnicity is being specified as a source of meaning and identity, to be melted not with other ethnicities but under broader principles of cultural self-definition, such as religion, nation, and gender" (Castells, 1997, p. 53). Gilroy, on the other hand, sees a rise in racial consciousness especially in the oppressed Black communities of the most overdeveloped zones. "Identity, understood only as sameness," he says, "is once more lodged in and signified by special properties discernible in black bodies" and "leavened with New Age and occult themes" (Gilroy, 2000, p. 211).

A World View of Race performs three functions useful for today's racial discourse. First, Bunche complicates our definition of race and the diaspora. If the cultural grouping of the diaspora were to form a new unit of analysis for global politics, Bunche would remind us that the process of colonization left indelible footprints on the racial attitudes of both the colonized and the colonizer. In his critique of pan-Africanism, for example, Bunche states that "Pan Africanists ignore completely the class, tribal, religious, cultural, linguistic, nationalistic and other differences among black and white peoples" (Bunche, 1936b, 95). These differences emerge sharply around an issue such as reparations in which the interests of diasporian Blacks and Africans are not identical. Moreover, while pan-Africanism may or may not provide a coherent programmatic response to White domination, it lacks a theory capable of explaining or predicting empirical reality.

Second, postmodern fascination with cultural studies and textual interpretation has blurred the distinction between cultural history and the history of social and political thought. Adolph Reed Jr., for example, charges that the work of Henry Louis Gates attempts "to *redefine* political significance to give priority to literary expression and criticism as strategic action" (Reed, 1997, p. 150). In our discussions of globalization and the pervasiveness of Black or hip-hop culture, Bunche allows us to bring the political and economic back in. With Bunche, we cannot mistake some superficial acceptance of a "Black global culture" with real economic or political power. In fact, *World View* foreshadows the economic analysis of slavery found in the work of Eric Williams (1944), Bunche's student, and Walter Rodney (1972).

Darryl Thomas defines global apartheid as "a Structure of the world system that combines political, economic and racial antagonism." In this system, a minority of Whites occupies the pole of affluence, while a majority composed of other races occupies the pole of poverty. Thomas contends that this third world has shifted from the pan-pigmentationalism that Bunche railed against to the pan-proletarianism he advocated. Just after Bunche's death in the early 1970s, these forces pressed for the first special session of the United Nations devoted to economic issues rather than military concerns. More generally, third world nations advanced the notion of a New International Economic Order (NIEO). While this economic solidarity was soon undermined by a variety of factors, Bunche would have applauded Tanzanian president Julius Nyerere's statement that "ours is a kind of Trade Union of the Poor" (Thomas, 2001, p. 144).

Third, the combination of an historical with a comparative approach to the social construction of race provides a model for future research. Greg Moses, in attempting to locate a secular foundation to match the sacred foundation of the modern civil rights movement, focuses on Du Bois, A. Philip Randolph, and Bunche as the three key figures in its construction: *A World View of Race* is dedicated to the proposition that national distinctions and racial distinctions can only hamper our human quest to be free. For Bunche, there was one great global battle between the exploiting and the exploited before which all other distinctions fade. Thus, with Bunche we have a complex theory of global economics that incorporates the dimension of racism (Moses, 1997, p. 126).

Bunche was a young man when he wrote *A World View of Race*. His last writing over thirty years after his global analysis of racism might give us a better framework for predicting where Bunche would align himself on today's most pressing racial issues. Of course, it is always dangerous to project someone's views written nearly forty years ago into the present. Nonetheless, it provides a benchmark for examining what has changed and what remains the same.

In some cases we do not have to guess what Bunche would have said because he predicted what was likely to happen. In 1969 he said, "Modern man himself is now responsible for an incredible alienation of his environment by polluting it to such an extent that something akin to global suicide is in prospect if heroic measures are not soon taken" (Henry, 1995, p. 305). Today Bunche's view is commonplace, although some argue that it may be too late for even heroic measures.

Bunche also believed we should slow population growth, predicting that by the end of the twentieth century the world's total population would approximate over six and a half billion people (in July 2005, the world's population stood at approximately 6.4 billion people). "The population explosion," said Bunche, "brings in its train a crisis of inadequate food supply" (Henry, 1995, p. 308). He accurately predicted the vast majority of those suffering and dying from starvation would be mainly non-Whites in places such as Africa and Asia.

Both environmental degradation and the population explosion are linked to the biggest obstacle to world peace: "the great and dangerously widening gap between the haves and have-nots of the world" (Henry, 1995, p. 308). Bunche contrasted the per-capita national incomes of the fifteen poorest countries of the world—all non-White—to those of the wealthiest nations of the world. He then related this gap to chronic undernourishment, decreased life expectancy, and illiteracy. What is striking is that the gap has increased significantly since Bunche's death. Fellow Nobel laureate Joseph Stiglitz reports that over the last decade of the twentieth century, the actual number of people living in poverty increased by almost 100 million even as total world income increased by an average of 2.5 percent annually (Stiglitz, 2003, p. 5). Bunche believed that a racial divide—euphemistically called a North-South divide—was at the root of the wealth gap.

Harder to predict are the political scientist's views on domestic issues. He would not be taken in by the concept of color blindness. Recognizing that color blindness is a function of power, he would point out that the playing field is not now nor never has been level. What has changed is the maintenance of White supremacy through seemingly neutral policies and structures ranging from shrinking enforcement of civil rights laws to the "privatization" of public goods like education. Bunche would reject Black neoconservatives as shrewd and unprincipled hired guns for White supremacy. In 1969 he stated, "Being black is thinking black. But not for anyone. No white man can become a black man because, in fact, no white person can ever think black, lacking the indispensable racial background and experience to do so. But every Negro can become a black man if he begins to think black. By this definition, certainly, not all Negroes have as yet become black men, by any means" (Henry, 1995, p. 300). Unlike many of his generation of Black leaders, Bunche was able to accept Black power as politically necessary. It did not mean that Blacks who embraced what he called "Blackism" could not be racist, he said, but it was by no means synonymous with racism, as many claimed.

For Bunche, "Blackism" was an essential defensive reaction that had come to be identified with survival. Yet he rejected Black nationalist demands for a separate land base and called claims for reparations outlandish. The reparations cycle defined by the Nation of Islam and by James Forman in the late 1960s did call for separation. I think Bunche would be more receptive to today's reparations movement, which focuses more on economic and education programs to assist the Black poor more than separate development.

The government's response to Hurricane Katrina would have both horrified and enraged Bunche. The cries of Blacks standing on rooftops shouting "We are Americans" as flood waters raced beneath them would have broken his heart. His whole life was devoted to the inclusion of African Americans as full and equal citizens of the United States. The government's failure to provide for the most basic needs of its citizens in New Orleans—the right to survive—strikes directly at the notion of citizenship. It is a denial of the basic social contract between the individual and the state.

As a UN official who often dealt with refugee issues, Bunche would have quickly corrected those who labeled persons fleeing the hurricane "refugees." Technically, refugees are people who have fled their own country because of persecution based on race, religion, political opinion, or social group. People fleeing natural or human disasters such as floods or war are termed "internally displaced."

But what do you call internally displaced persons whose own country has fled them? What do you call internally displaced persons who, in some cases, received more aid offers from foreign governments than from their own government (Kunnie, 2005)? Yet perceptions of the government's response were also shaped by race. A variety of polls indicate that while a large majority of African Americans believed race played a role in the hurricane response, a majority of Whites did not (ABC/7News Poll, 2005; Pew Research Center, 2005; ABC/Washington Post Poll, 2005).

While social programs aimed at reducing the gap between the rich and the poor have been regularly cut by officials of both political parties since the end of the Great Society programs in the 1960s, most Blacks believed their government would not deny them basic emergency services. Given the reality of poverty in America highlighted by Hurricane Katrina and its aftermath, I believe Bunche might see current reparations efforts in a new light, that is, as an attempt to force White recognition of historical racial injustices that are still with us as a nation. In the face of color blindness, reparations discourse forces an acknowledgment of White privilege. Moreover, and this is the point Bunche would most agree with, it is a call for political community and human rights in the face of racial democracy. Democracy, Bunche would argue, is no substitute for human rights. The political fact that a majority can vote to deny a minority population social justice does not make it morally right or acceptable. More than poverty, Katrina revealed the enormous and increasing rips in our nation's social fabric. "Thus, the fateful alternative confronting mankind," Bunche would say, "is alienate and perish or harmonize and survive" (Henry, 1995, p. 307).

Notes

1. Sociologist Anthony Giddens defines globalization as "the intensification of worldwide social relations which link distant localities in such a way that local happenings are shaped by events occurring many miles away and vice versa." Political scientist and journalist Clarence Lusane identifies three effects globalization has on race relations: (1) it undermines progressive economic integration of marginalized racial groups as it destroys jobs, fosters competition, depresses wages, cuts worker's benefits, and limits opportunities; (2) it gives rise to new race-conscious political and social movements that attempt to resist racialized social assaults, policies of containment and imprisonment, and the elimination of the welfare state; and (3) it has a negative cultural impact as manufactured racist and negative images of racial and ethnic groups are projected to the world, which has little or no alternative framework for assessing the lives and cultures of these communities (Lusane, 1997, pp. 3–5).

2. Errol Anthony Henderson distinguishes between a worldview that is truly holistic, encompassing an entire belief system, and a paradigm that is more explicitly "scientific" and often aimed at providing the parameters of inquiry into a particular discipline (1995, pp. 3–4).

3. Bunche displayed his new anthropological skills in an insightful article, "The *Irua* Ceremony among the Kikuyu of Kiambu District, Kenya" in the *Journal of Negro History*, vol. 26, no. 1 (January 1941), pp. 46–65.

5. Political Science Educational Contributions

Integrating Theory and Practice

HANES WALTON JR.

From Ralph Bunche's later writing can be gleaned the nature, scope, and significance of his educational philosophy of the discipline of political science. Five major intellectual categories emerged from his writings and notes since 1940, whether those categories were original ones and/or whether they were modifications of categories already in existence. Both the original and secondary nature of these categories of Bunche's educational philosophy created a different perspective and vision for the discipline. Herein lays his great contribution.

Of the two conceptual motifs and frameworks that Lindsay set forth as the organizing principles of this book, the one referred to as "public intellectualism" will be used in this chapter as the basis for the exploration and analysis of Ralph Bunche's ideas about his academic discipline of political science. Sadly, Bunche's educational philosophy for the discipline as well as his contributions to it have been omitted and excluded from the sundry studies of the history of the discipline as well as from the official reports of the American Political Science Association (Walton & Smith, 2006). Yet none of the leaders of the profession have uttered a written word of protest. Inside Lindsay's conceptual landscape, one finds that Bunche's "public intellectualism" continues "very progressive, some would contend radical, views for addressing economic and sociopolitical inequities within the United States and in intellectual settings." Therefore, if one organizes Bunche's ideas and reflections about the political science discipline around Lindsay's conceptual motifs, one will immediately see why he insisted upon a specific educational philosophy and programmatic direction for his discipline. And his desired direction clashed with the rising behavioral thrust emerging within the discipline.

Embedded in Ralph Bunche's writings and organizational practices is a unique and exceptional conceptualization of political science as a discipline. This conceptualization and vision, which we shall call an educational philosophy, is not to be found in a single coherent and comprehensive document. Yet it can be gleaned from his writings during his wide-ranging career in diverse leadership roles in the Howard University department of political science, the presidency of the American Political Science Association, the U.S. Department of State, and the United Nations. His philosophy is also to be found in his four research memoranda for the Gunnar Myrdal report, *An American Dilemma,* and in his field research in South Africa (Edgar, 1992; Grantham, 1973). In these sundry works, Bunche left an intellectual record, and it is possible to delineate from that record of scholarship and field studies his conceptualization of political science as a discipline that challenges, contrasts, and diverges sharply with the dominant and consensus one now driving the discipline.

The Methodological Approach

Bunche delivered his presidential address to the American Political Science Association (APSA) in Chicago, Illinois on September 9, 1954, which just happened to be the fiftieth anniversary of the organization. Using this unique moment in time, as well as this historic occasion (of being the first African American to serve as president of the APSA), Bunche told the membership that the nation-state and the international community had certain problem areas that merited greater attention from the discipline of political science (Bunche, 1954a).

Among the problems that Bunche noted were "the problem of colonialism, particularly of colonial Africa"; the fear, intolerance, suspicion, and confusion emanating from racial demagogues; and the second-class citizenship emerging from racial segregation, White supremacy, and disenfranchisement (Bunche, 1954a, p. 969). In Bunche's view, these grave problems faced by the profession and society had been ignored by the discipline, and they threatened both freedom and democracy. But perhaps most important is not Bunche's identification of these problems but what they offer in terms of insights into the mind of a public intellectual who happens to be an African American political scientist. Undergirding his poignant remarks and suggestions is a vision of the discipline of political science that, while borne of the past and present, offers a course correction for the future.

To see this vision with its proposed reforms for an academic discipline and professional organization, this study will begin with a textual analysis of Bunche's post-1940 writings and delineate from those works and the appropriate secondary sources the seminal intellectual categories of his educational philosophy. From these categories of ideas and reflections, one can reconstruct a holistic portrait of Bunche's desired political science education. This study picks up the analysis of Bunche's intellectual ideas from Jonathan Scott Holloway's exposition in this volume of his early career. Holloway's essay shows the evolution and focus of Bunche's ideas, as well as their nature and significance. The present chapter reveals that Bunche's ideas and philosophy changed from the 1940s forward.

Political science from its inception to Bunche's presidential address has been exceptional in undertaking textual analyses of a wide variety of political thinkers and philosophers and reconstructing the pertinent concepts, ideas, and thoughts in the original texts so that they provide the readers with a comprehensive and systematic portrait of the writer's political philosophy and/or political theory. It has been done with Greek thinkers like Plato and Aristotle, with Roman thinkers like Machiavelli and Cicero, English thinkers like Hobbes and Locke, and French thinkers like Rousseau (Sabine, 1973). It has been done for African American political thinkers like Martin Luther King Jr., W. E. B. Du Bois, and Huey Newton (Jeffries, 2002; Reed, 1997; Walton, 1971). Therefore, this study of Bunche's educational philosophy about the nature, scope, and significance of political science as a discipline will model itself on those enduring studies in political thought and theory by taking their well-tested and logically developed techniques as the guidelines and frames of reference to organize and structure Bunche's ideas, visions, and perspectives. Thus, the methodology for this study is performing a textual analysis of Bunche's writings from 1940 to his last ones in the 1960s.

The Empirical Bases of Bunche's Five Intellectual Categories

Bunche's vision for a different type of political science arose from his empirically based field studies as well as from his experiential efforts, not from armchair speculation. By way of comparison, we can turn to another political scientist, who, like Bunche, rose to the top of the discipline by studying the same problem area—Southern politics—that was outside of the realm of the discipline. V. O. Key Jr. (1958), in his presidential address to the APSA titled "The State of the Discipline," suggested that political science had rarely considered the fundamental questions of how scholars go about pushing the limits of knowledge: "Method without substance may be sterile, but substance without methods is only fortuitously substantial. Technique and method in themselves perhaps may not generate many new ideas, but they are most handy for verification or, as occurs with melancholy frequency, disproof. And new techniques and methods often make it possible to raise new kinds of substantive questions" (Key, 1958, p. 967).

Not only did both men acquire national reputations from their studies of southern politics, both men used statistical methodological techniques to analyze their data and provide an empirical foundation for their political interpretation and findings. Yet, despite their commonality in methods, they would diverge in terms of the future course that they wanted the discipline of political science to follow, as we shall see.

Bunche's works, which we organize here into several basic categories (African American politics, southern politics, political parties, African politics and colonialism, and international organization and world politics), were born with empirical methods that allowed him to raise incisive and insightful questions about the particular and the unique as well as the nature of the discipline. He conducted field studies on African American and southern politics for the Carnegie Foundation study of America's race problem along with the Swedish economist Gunnar Myrdal. Bunche was contracted to prepare four memoranda for the study, which contributed to Myrdal's massive volume, *An America Dilemma*. One of the studies analyzed leadership, another Negro pressure groups; one looked at the political status of Negro politics in the North and South, while the fourth and final one probed the different ways that the Negro problem had been addressed and reflected upon the racial ideologies behind these conceptualizations. All were empirically based works that created the groundwork for Bunche's thought on African American and southern politics.

Next, Bunche conducted similar field studies on African politics, African colonialism, and South Africa. These African studies covered the differences in British and French colonialism on the continent, the White supremacy regime in South Africa, and the politics and liberation efforts of native Africans in these different systems of oppression and subjugation.

Then he conducted participant observations as part of his work in international organizations and world politics. Here his publications analyzed the role and function of the United Nations in the post–World War II world. When taken collectively, these intellectual categories sharpened Bunche's disciplinary imagination that spurred creative analyses and provided for bold new interpretations. Table 5.1 is a summary of the four major categories and their subareas.

First and foremost among Bunche's intellectual categories is the one derived from his fieldwork for his doctoral dissertation in 1934. This work on

Table 5.1. The five political science intellectual categories as developed by Ralph
Bunche: Origins and sources

Categories	New or Modified	Origin/Source
African American politics	New	Field studies
Southern politics	New	Field studies
Political parties	Modified	Field studies
Subcategory: African American Partisanship		
African politics & colonialism	New	Field studies
Subcategory: South African politics	Field studies	
World politics & international organization	Modified	Experiential

Source: Adapted from a textual analysis of his writings

African politics and colonialism focused on Togoland and Dahomey, but
his thinking was broadened, enriched, and enhanced with his field study of
South Africa in 1937 (Edgar, 1992). Both of these studies led to several articles
on African politics and colonialism and the problems that he encountered in
these political systems and processes. His observations appeared as remarks
in his presidential address of 1954 and shaped the suggestions he made to and
about the discipline. In fact, this body of work—which appeared in articles,
book chapters, and monographs—made him aware that the discipline of
political science had evaded, dismissed, and/or overlooked colonialism in
general, and African colonialism in particular, as a subject of concern.

Prior to his dissertation field studies, Bunche published two articles on
African American politics in 1928. These were studies of Negro politics in
Chicago. However, he did not return to this genre until 1935–36 and 1939–40,
that is, after he completed his dissertation. Bunche established his second
intellectual category of African American politics with the field studies that
he undertook for the Myrdal study, which were financed and backed by the
Carnegie Foundation. Bunche produced four of the forty-four monographs
that were commissioned for the study. Of these four, "The Political Status of
the Negro" consisted of 1,600 pages, nineteen chapters, and three appendices.
It thoroughly enriched and enlarged this budding new intellectual category.
Nothing of this scope and significance on the topic had surfaced in the dis-
cipline before. Bunche's work covered all of the major regions of the United
States—southern, northern, eastern, and western (Urquhart, 1993). Perhaps
Negro Politician, the study of Chicago politics by political scientist Harold
Gosnell, is the closest comparison to the depth and range of Bunche's work.

In addition to his pioneering contextual analysis about African American politics, Bunche's field studies for Myrdal laid the groundwork for the
intellectual category of southern politics (Walton, 1994a). Long before V.
O. Key Jr.'s classic *Southern Politics,* which appeared in 1949, many of the

concepts, themes, political institutions, and interpretative frames of reference were formulated, denied, and operationalized in Bunche's landmark
political status memorandum for the Myrdal study. Key's book not only
referenced Bunche but was in the final analysis significantly influenced by
him (Walton, 1994a).

His fourth intellectual category is that of political parties. It also emerged
during the field studies for the Myrdal study. Analysis of the 1936 presidential
election revealed that the African American electorate, a strong supporter of
the Republican Party since the 1856 presidential race, had realigned with the
Democratic Party. Although in several southern states after Reconstruction
a number of African American Democratic state legislators were elected, the
vast majority of officeholders in this period were Republicans. But what shook
Republican Party leaders was the vast realignment of the African American
voters with the Democratic Party in President Franklin Roosevelt's 1936 election. Such a critical realignment of the African American voter spurred the
Republican National Committee (RNC) to commission Bunche to undertake
a study of why the switch occurred and how they might regain this segment
of their partisan base (Walton, 1990).

Bunche probed the nature of African American Republican partisanship
and the factors that eroded that long-term relationship. Dominant among
the litany of factors, Bunche's study determined, was party policies and the
leadership around those policies. Since Republican Party public policies such
as the Thirteenth, Fourteenth, and Fifteenth Amendments and the 1875 Civil
Rights Act had drawn African American support in the first place, the aban-
donment of those polices had led to party detachment and weak partisan
ties. Simply put, the Republican Party did not strongly support the African
American community in the 1936 presidential election as it had done from
1856 until 1932.

In doing this study of the Republican Party, Bunche had the unprecedented
opportunity to see the formation of the African American alignment with the
Democratic Party at the mass base. Partisan alignment with the Democrats
had taken place at least at the elite level and then at a limited mass base level
prior to the Civil War; however, large-scale mass alignment at the presidential
level came during the Depression with the election of Roosevelt. About this
Negro realignment Bunche wrote, "This was a vote for Roosevelt, for relief
and for made-work, rather than an indication of any new Negro devotion
to the Democratic Party. The Negro Democratic vote in 1932 and 1936 was a
'bread and butter' vote." And then he advanced the reason why this African
American realignment might be an enduring one. He wrote, "It must be
clear that in politics one cannot successfully run with both hare and hound,

and the Republican Party will need to decide whether it prefers to court the dissident White vote of the Democratic South, through continuance of its lily-white programs and an obscure Negro policy, or really desires the Negro vote. It cannot seduce both" (Bunche, 1939, p. 10). With this "Confidential Report to the Republican Party," Bunche—working as a political consultant and scholar—establishes for the study of political parties the important of the race variable in not only shaping individual political party behavior but organizational party behavior at the national and regional levels. This study wrought for Bunche insights into political party behavior for both dealignment and alignment.

Although Bunche derived much of this intellectual category from a single study, he added a bit more to his writing on this area through his article on "Disenfranchisement of the Negro" (Bunche, 1941c), because the movement to deprive African Americans of their right to vote was a public policy sponsored by southern members of the Democratic Party. Other factions of the Democratic Party opposed this policy and assisted African American Democrats in overcoming disenfranchisement. African Americans' dealignment from southern Democrats was not nearly as detrimental in the long run as the Republican Party dropping of its support for civil rights policies. This category, like the others, had many intellectual insights to offer about the American party system and process.

Then came World War II, and Bunche moved from academia to the Office of Strategic Services. Later he joined the State Department and served as an advisor to the U.S. delegation to the San Francisco conference that drafted the United Nations charter (Walton, 1995). In 1946, he joined the UN Secretariat as head of the Trusteeship Department. Bunche's writings from this time until his death, with exception of his American Political Science Association presidential address, create his last major intellectual category: international organizations and world politics.

Several publications in this time frame created and expanded this category, and they essentialized his concerns with world peace and how the United Nations might serve to make world peace attainable. Seemingly, Bunche's domestic concerns in these years were superseded by foreign affairs. His last major publication on African Americans, in 1942, deals with the legal status of this group in America up until that moment in time. Then, when his intellectual focus shifts to world politics, his works were about African politics and colonialism. His last publication, a book chapter analyzing the problems in the Congo, appeared in 1965.

However, it must be noted that Bunche did make several major speeches after 1965, which are currently in his unpublished papers; some of these have been reprinted in an anthology of his writings edited by Henry (1995). Combining these unpublished speeches with some of his pre-1940 writings, one could argue that these works constitute another intellectual category called the civil rights movement. While potentially interesting, the current analysis does not organize this body of work into such a category. Most of the work for this possible category deals with intragroup politics and only indirectly with the larger political system and political science. Furthermore, his last unpublished speech is a reaction to not only the Black Power movement phase of the civil rights movement but specifically to some of his critics within that movement. The published and unpublished speeches are clearly personal, unlike the scholarly stance of his earlier works. Lastly, this potential category is excluded because it does not rest upon any systematic empirical bases like the other categories. While some of these speeches are logical and solidly reasoned discussions, Bunche did not collect any data nor perform any systematic data analyses. Even though this category is not formally developed, however, it is taken into consideration in the overall formulation of this study's effort to craft a holistic perspective of Bunche's educational philosophy.

In summary, Bunche developed out of his scholarly studies five distinct intellectual categories. The first three are from his empirical studies of the American political system and process: (1) African American politics, (2) southern politics, and (3) political parties. Then he developed two more from his field studies in Africa and his experiential efforts at the United Nations: (4) African politics and colonialism and (5) international organization and world politics. Bunche drew from these five distinct areas, as well as from his civil rights movement participation, that the academic discipline of political science was deficient in these subfields. Only the area of political parties had been heavily studied and analyzed. The other areas were either marginal to the discipline or omitted altogether. This meant to Bunche that the discipline was grossly incomplete both in its study of the American system and of the international system.

These five distinct intellectual categories allowed Bunche to craft a critique and reconstitute the discipline upon a different intellectual axis than was currently being attempted by individuals in political science who relied on evaluations and assessment of history and evolution (Farr, Dryzek, & Leonard, 1995; Somit & Tanenhaus, 1967). With the five subfields of study outlined, Bunche was seeing the discipline from intellectual ramparts that were not even in the range of vision of political scientists of the time. Simply put, these categories gave him a different perspective. And this perspective did not just rest upon these new intellectual ramparts (Walton, Miller, & McCormick, 1995).

The Experiential Factor

Bunche's vision of a discipline of political science did not rely solely upon empirically based research. Nor should we peg our analyses entirely upon his scholarly publications. That would be shortsighted. Bunche fashioned his vision also from his job experiences, and these experiences involved him in different problem-solving capacities. In the working world, he faced real-world problems in a variety of areas, which forced him to confront the strengths and limitations of his own discipline.

In his presidential address to the APSA, Bunche argued that political science needed not to be an abstract and isolated discipline, but could be one concerned with addressing real-world problems. On this matter, he stated, "The severest challenge to the political scientist, it seems to me, is . . . to find remedies for these potential fatal defects in political conduct" (Bunche, 1954a, p. 968). He further asked, "Are political scientists still too much attached to abstract formalism, to metaphysical and juristic concepts . . . to be of maximum usefulness to a world in dire distress?" (p. 968).

Visible in these remarks is a man concerned with his discipline playing a problem-solving role in both domestic and world affairs. Yet this was not typical of presidential addresses to the APSA. Contrasting Bunche's presidential address with that of V. O. Key Jr., a notable scholar in his own right, one immediately is struck by Key's focus on the need to generate knowledge from inside the discipline with better methodological tools and techniques. Key is concerned with how to expand the boundaries of the discipline and push back the knowledge frontiers. He is less concerned with the problem-solving ability of the discipline in real-life situations. Problem solving for Key is simply one of solving knowledge problems inside the discipline. To this end, he proffers a *unidimensional* perspective of the discipline: "The burden of my argument may be stated briefly and bluntly. It is that the demands upon our profession have grown more rapidly than has the content of our discipline . . . We must devote greater resources in manpower and ingenuity to the systematic analysis of the phenomena of politics" (1958, p. 970). Elsewhere in the address, Key amplifies this unidimensional vision by recommending that "a critical need of our discipline is for more, and far more rigorous, research training . . . A second area . . . is that of recruitment of . . . genuinely creative scholars to push back the frontiers of knowledge" (p. 970).

Clearly, Key's vision is quite different from that of Bunche. This is not to say that he did not have job experiences in the real world, because he did. He worked under his former Chicago mentor, Professor Harold Gosnell, at the Bureau of the Budget during World War II (Heard, 1977; Lucker & Key, 2001). From that experience he wrote an academic treatise (Key, 1940, 1942). He served in a political commentary role by writing for popular magazines and newspapers. He even served on President John F. Kennedy's presidential commission to study campaign financing (Lucker & Key, 2001). Yet, even with these real-world experiences, Key's main role and function was as a "scholar advancing political knowledge." This meant that in the end, Key's vision of the discipline, like so many of his predecessors, crafted a unidimensional perspective. About Key's vision, one of his leading students has written that "he was a most suggestive hypothesis maker, and he tested his deductions on a grand scale—through intuition, empirical historical knowledge, and carefully worked out quantitative measures . . . Key . . . wrote . . . a primer on statistics for political scientists." His success with these quantitative techniques and methods eventually "stimulated a quantum expansion of work of that type," and herein lies his great contribution (Havard, 1977)—thus the thesis of his presidential speech. Bunche, any way you perceive him, had an absolutely different perspective; that difference derives in part from his experiential knowledge and inheres his invaluable contribution to the discipline. This difference between Bunche and Key in terms of their vision for the discipline does not detract from either man's scholarly statute and/or contribution to the discipline. The difference is a matter of emphases, and it illuminates the fact that the discipline has followed the empirical emphasis of Key and not the programmatic policy concerns of Bunche. Clearly, however, the discipline needed to embrace both visions as valuable intellectual roadmaps.

Bunche's first experiential task was to find and then organize the department of political science at Howard University in 1929. He had to construct a political science curriculum for primarily African American students who found themselves disenfranchised in an entire region of the country and in limited areas in other parts of the nation (Bunche, 1941c). Bunche's challenge was to provide a professional education along with knowledge of how to solve the problem of lack of suffrage (Prestage, 1969; Walton, 1968). Establishing a department that met the special needs of this unique population was no mean task.

Next, Bunche worked on the Myrdal study and the RNC study. In these job experiences, he had to bring a variety of disciplinary research techniques to bear upon the problems of race relations in the nation and party partisanship of African Americans. These job experiences offered Bunche participant-observer status in the nation at large as well as its political party system. In both areas, democratic processes simply failed to function for an entire segment of the population—and had been failing for quite some time. Bunche was faced with making the democratic process in America work for the excluded.

From 1941 to 1945, Bunche worked for various sections of the nation's foreign policy–making bureaucracy. In these different roles, he was engaged in solving serious foreign affairs problems, especially those dealing with colonialism and burgeoning African nation states. These subjected people of color had to achieve self-determination and liberation in a postwar world. In addition, they had to acquire the resources with which to overcome the limiting conditions they had endured for centuries.

Finally, Bunche worked for an international organization, the emerging United Nations. In this job, he saw both African and Middle Eastern problems that needed immediate solutions. Problems here surfaced in the social, political, economic, and health realms. Eventually, conflict and civil wars in these areas forced Bunche into a peacekeeping role. A testament to his effectiveness can be seen in his winning the Nobel Peace Prize in 1950. Once again disciplinary knowledge of people, of conflict, and international paths to conflict resolution enabled him to work out acceptable, practical solutions. Using the United Nations to achieve peace, however, was a total new learning reality.

With these job experiences and his mental makeup, Bunche had to take theory and merge it with a practice that was as applicable and acceptable to the troubled societies, communities, and fledgling nation-states in which he found himself involved. In each and every circumstance, he had to fashion out of his political science education—largely self-directed—an answer to a crippling antidemocratic reality and assist democracy to emerge and prevail.

Such a career is vastly different from a pure academic one that provides an occasional foray into domestic and foreign matters. Bunche's path is first into an academic career and then into a career that is bureaucratic and organizational. Truly, each of these careers depends upon a political science education and experience. Political science, unlike the disciplines of history, sociology, and anthropology, trains its students about politics, political behavior, political organization, law, political conflict, and constitutions. This is the main focus of the discipline and not cognate areas. However, it was these experiential career roles that granted Bunche another dimensional view of his discipline of political science.

Therefore, in 1953 when Bunche was elected president of the APSA and by the time of his presidential address in 1954, he had crafted a *multidimensional* vision and perspective of the discipline. This vision enabled him to link theory and practice and place the discipline into both an intellectual and problem-solving mode. He asserted this in his presidential address, and this separates him from his predecessors. He had by now a different political science discipline in mind. It was a discipline with programmatic features.

The American Political Science Association Legacy: A Congressional Fellows Program

During Bunche's presidency, he created the APSA's Congressional Fellows Program that selected scholars from the academic and journalistic world and assigned them to different members of Congress, both the House of Representatives and the U.S. Senate. Yet assignments to member of Congress were not the only possibility. The selected individuals could also be assigned to work with standing congressional committees. Additionally, congressional fellows were asked to rotate their assignments during the second semester of the legislative year. This meant that one could participate with and observe members in the House of Representatives for one half of the year and then observe and participate in the Senate or with a standing committee for the other half of the year. Such rotating assignments would provide budding academicians and future journalists with a comprehensive portrait of Congress, a portrait not based on theory, modeling, memoirs, and secondary data alone but in conjunction with actual experiences—a real-life, insider view of representative government. This aspect of the program closely parallels Bunche's field studies.

From this group of participants have emerged vast numbers of publications in the form of books, book chapters, and journal articles and essays, as well as journalistic works and commentary. All the participants have a firsthand account of citizen legislators and the functioning of one of the three different branches of American government. Over the years, the APSA Congressional Fellows Program has expanded academic knowledge and led, in some circles, to some of the problem solving in this branch of government. With this program, Bunche gave the APSA a different view of the discipline, combining theory and practice. Unfortunately, the discipline has paid little attention to it (Utter & Lockhart, 2002).

For college students, the APSA in cooperation with Duke University sponsors the Ralph Bunche Institute, a summer program that takes top minority college juniors from all over the country and trains them in the nature, scope, and significance of the discipline so as to encourage them to join the profession. This summer training helps them gain entrance into some of the top graduate schools in the country. The program is essentially a manpower program designed to increase the number of minority scholars in the profession. It has been immensely successful in getting more minority scholars in the leading political science departments. Hopefully, as these young minority scholars emerge into the profession, some of them will address some of the problem areas that Bunche explored and directed the profession's attention toward.

In the final analysis, Bunche's major legacy lies in the rich benefit inherent in and flowing from the Congressional Fellows Program. Such a program readily exemplifies his innovative, creative, progressive vision for and perspective on political science. The program connects the academic scholar to real-world issues and the attempts at problem solving that the legislative branch of government undertakes to make democracy a reality in the American political system. With this program, the profession and the real world can effectively interact with each other. Through the Congressional Fellows Program, the APSA is performing its civic duty, thus achieving Bunche's multidimensional vision and perspective of the discipline.

Conceptualization of Political Science

Drawing upon his imaginative intellectual categories and his experience outside academia, Bunche was able to see his profession from different angles and see that the discipline needed far more than empirical research and a set of new research guidelines. Grooming new scholars was vital to Bunche's educational philosophy and important to the future development of the discipline, but it was not sufficient. American democracy was beset by a host of domestic and foreign problems that had to be solved. There was a role for the profession beyond the academy—the multidimensional facet of Bunche's vision.

But multidimensionality is just one of the cornerstones of Bunche's political science vision. Unlike Key, who spent a career trying to reorient political scientists toward the adoption and effective use of methodological techniques, Bunche's programmatic approach sought to reorient political scientists toward a real-world approach that combined theory and practice. Both approaches seek to retrain political scientists. And both approaches are still in existence today. Nevertheless, Key's methods and techniques approach is the dominant one. Bunche's Congressional Fellows program has a small impact among those who have an interest in Congress. Because the larger potential of the program gets subsumed under the task of observing Congress, the discipline fails to see the program beyond the congressional task. However, the participant-observer component is only one aspect of Bunche's conceptualization.

Bunche's intellectual categories and experience formed for him a very strong support of democracy. Initially, Bunche was a Marxist with a belief in the communist system as a solution to the plight of the masses in America (Bunche, 1936b; Henry, 1995; Holloway, 2002; Kirby, 1980). Even the budding New Deal program of the early Roosevelt years did not convince Bunche to give up his Marxist ideology. When World War II came and revealed the Nazi and Italian dictatorships, along with Stalin's dictatorship in Russia, the human rights and economic problems under these systems served as a personal eye-opener that these systems left a great deal to be desired. Bunche came to the realization that the problems facing African Americans might not get a resolution given the racist orientations of these dictatorial systems. The communist system would be infinitely harder to change.

By the early 1940s, Bunche moved to embrace a democratic system, and he supported democratic institutions at the international level. The prospect for positive and progressive change in a democratic system, as Bunche saw it, was rooted in the system's formative legal documents that respected human rights and offered a chance for self-determination, inclusion, and liberation. Democratic theory also held out for just such possibilities. Born from this set of concerns was a theoretical framework for Bunche's vision of the discipline.

For this political scientist, Bunche's work shifted theoretical perspectives. Democratic theory replaced Marxism and explained the relationship between the variables of humankind and its government better than the former. Theory had always underpinned Bunche's scholarship, but now democratic theory became the strategic framework. Thus, in the midst of the behavioral revolution in political science that placed quantitative analysis over theory and value neutrality over a systemic commitment (even when the system was democratic), Bunche made a commitment to the values and beliefs in democratic theory.

Many in his discipline during the Cold War committed themselves to a democratic system that was racially exclusive. They supported the American political system in the 1940s through 1970s despite its horrendous practice of segregation. Some supported the system because they believed in racial inferiority. Other claimed states' rights and the fiscal burden that minorities placed upon the system. Bunche did not waver. His democratic theory and beliefs were clearly inclusive in both the domestic and foreign spheres. Specifically, he committed himself to the American system with all of its imperfections because of its promise and future possibilities. This meant that Bunche had to criticize limitations of African American leadership and some of their ideologies and programs, which ranged from African American nationalism to African American cultural approaches and programs.

Such criticism, which he raised throughout his career, came back in the late 1960s to haunt him during the Black cultural revolution. Sadly, many scholars have seized upon this conflict between Bunche and the African American leaders of the cultural revolution, focusing upon the verbal fireworks between the contending parties as if it were Bunche's entire message. Therefore, they missed the larger issue of his democratic theory. Here was a democratic theory that was inclusive and not one defined by the reactionary radicalism of the cultural revolution. As he had done in developing his democratic theory, Bunche worked against the reactionary White right and left to shape and structure his theory. As a result, in the 1960s and early '70s, he was opposing those reactionaries on both the right and left.

Few members of his discipline faced the same ordeal. Surely, this type of conflict did not haunt Key, but Bunche's experiences ultimately enriched his theoretical perspective. This racial reality became a force that shaped his vision of political science. In the end, his disciplinary vision has a democratic theoretical base, a multidimensional focus, and an intellectual categorical foundation. When these components of his educational philosophy are linked, one sees a different view of political science in striking contrast to the consensus-based unidimensional one. Yet this difference comes at a great cost to Bunche in terms of the history and legacy of the discipline (E. Wilson, 1985).

The Cost of Imagination, Vision, and Race

It is not that scholars and students of political science have not promoted the unidimensional vision over the multidimensional version that Bunche developed (Dawson, 2000; Farr, Dryzek, & Leonard, 1995; Somit & Tanenhaus, 1967). Rather, they have promoted the behavioral approach over the applied approach that Bunche stood for and that the Congressional Fellows Program implies. In general, scholars have accepted low-level and middle-level theory over an inclusive democratic theory. Bunche's contributions and pioneering vision are all but omitted from the books that analyze the history and evolution of the discipline. Bunche is not seen as one of the preeminent political science scholars of the discipline despite the fact that his work was in the mainstream of the behavioral revolution even before it got underway, which set the criteria for laudatory assessments. Instead, Bunche has been relegated, if he is acknowledged at all, to little more than a competent political scientist who worked as Myrdal's assistant (Utter & Lockhart, 2002). The writers of the histories, biographies, and evaluations of the discipline might mention that Bunche is among a very few of the profession (the others are

President Woodrow Wilson and Henry Kissinger) to win a Nobel Peace Prize. Nevertheless, Bunche's legacy has been reduced to passing comments or extemporaneous footnotes (Baer, Jewell, & Lee 1991, p. 83). Few have taken the time to measure his contributions or probe his works for the fresh ideas he advanced. His concepts, frameworks, and theoretical and empirical models are all there. Most have stood the test of time (Walton, 1994a).

The textual analysis of this study has finally generated the first composite portrait of his political science education. Then, there is the matter of peacemaking and peacekeeping that the Bunche educational philosophy makes clear for the profession. However, the Bunche example and achievement model is little known and understood. It remains in an unclear intellectual limbo. Further focus on Bunche's work would be fruitful.

In closing, Bunche has had one avenue of influence that is visible today. Many political science departments, along with the APSA, consider the subfield of African American politics and/or race and politics. Bunche was clearly a founder of this intellectual genre and generated many of its intellectual concepts and theoretical foundations. It is possible that Bunche's contributions will continue to emerge and build a legacy in the discipline equal to his vision and perspective. Lindsay's conceptual motif about Bunche's "public intellectualism" has helped us to see how and why this African American scholar developed a unique vision and perspective for his academic discipline that challenges the hegemonic one, which embraces method and technique at the expense of inequities in its political democracy.

PART II

Educational Venues and Public Intellectualism and Diplomacy

6. Educational and Diplomatic Influences at Public Research Universities

BEVERLY LINDSAY

During the early 1950s, Bunche was being investigated by the congressional Committee on Un-American Activities (HUAC) for his alleged ties to the Communist Party and their endeavors in the United States. Simultaneously, Bunche's former colleagues from Howard University (such as historian John Hope Franklin) and students (such as psychologist Kenneth Clark) were preparing the historical, educational, psychological, and legal arguments for eliminating separate and equal public school systems for African Americans and European American students (Keppel, 1995; Henry 1999). The legal case that would be decided by the Supreme Court on May 17, 1954, was *Brown vs. Board of Education,* which declared that separate and equal were inherently unequal. In Congress during that same week in May 1954, HUAC cleared Bunche of alleged ties to the Communist Party.

By the end of that decade, various organizations and universities seeking his candidacy for executive positions had approached Bunche. One day my doctoral research assistant excitedly handed me a volume penned by Clark Kerr, the late University of California system president and nationally known educator. The information: Ralph Bunche had been considered for the chancellorship at UCLA.

Since there were a number of major changes occurring in the University of California system, questions began to surface when Kerr, during his tenure as president, initiated the search for a new chancellor of UCLA. What kind of chancellor would be needed? What should his (not likely "her" at that time) characteristics be? Would government, corporate, or international organization executives be considered? What would be the distinctions that could move UCLA forward in the research arena in the post-Sputnik era? He would have dynamic, intellectual leadership qualities and could lead the university into a more renowned world research institution.

During early stages of the national search for a chancellor, Kerr raised the possibility of whether Ralph Bunche, who was a fellow member of the Rockefeller Foundation Board, might be considered. After all, Bunche was an illustrious graduate who had entered UCLA on an academic and athletic scholarship, who had been awarded the Nobel Peace Prize—the latter certainly resonated with Kerr, a Quaker. Kerr stated, "Ralph had indicated to me in response to my inquiry that he might be interested" (Kerr, 2001, p. 337). Yet Kerr realized there would be obstacles to Bunche's candidacy moving forward, as a number of regents believe that his appointment would have been too advanced for the era. Notably, John Canaday, one of the Southern California regents who graduated in 1927, the same year as Bunche, and likely knew the Negro class valedictorian, wanted noncontroversial candidates.

We can speculate whether Ralph Bunche would have taken the position if it had materialized. We do have some insight into his perspectives regarding university leadership and roles for comprehensive research universities: his experiences as an executive assistant to the president of Howard University and United Nations undersecretary, the views expressed at Rockefeller Foundation Board meetings, his acceptance of a professorship at Harvard, and his writings in the *Journal of Negro Education* and elsewhere (Kerr, 2001). Providing astute intellectual leadership and moral courage as a chancellor at a foremost research university did not transpire. Bunche did not have the option of leadership, as he asserted in several *Journal of Negro Education* articles (Bunche, 1935a; 1936a; 1940b). Bunche advocated pushing universities toward the forefront in promoting social change to address adverse sociopolitical problems.

Despite the fact that Bunche did not become the chancellor of the University of California at Los Angeles, Kerr continued to consult with Bunche formally and informally on higher education, particularly pertaining to the University of California. Moreover, Theodore Hesburgh as president of University of Notre Dame conferred with Bunche for over twenty years on issues of American and international higher education. Hesburgh maintains that Bunche espoused university roles in enhancing opportunities for poor and minority students and addressing social problems. For then emerging nations such as Nigeria, universities would enhance national development. Cooperative endeavors by American universities would be vital to university building in new nations. Building the curriculum, constructing the academic structure, and addressing concrete problems were foci pushed by Bunche and others as Rockefeller Board members (Hesburgh, 2006).

This chapter provides a proxy overview of Bunche's educational and policy contributions particularly as they pertain to contemporary research universities.

Conceptual Frameworks

To begin our conceptual examination, we build upon the historical, sociological, and political science literature by and about Bunche (Bunche, 1941a; Henry 1999; Urquhart 1993; Keppel, 1995) and the nexuses between diplomacy and education (Clark, 1990; Lindsay 2003; Stromquist, 2002; Amin, 1997). Based upon tenets of these scholarly and diplomatic works, we ask: What components of Bunche's scholarly and diplomatic skills may be used to facilitate contemporary research university endeavors as they address pressing diplomatic and public policies after September 11 and ongoing crises in the Middle East and other hot spots?

In this exploration and two chapters following, facets of Bunche's life and career are presented that help explicate responses to questions that include, inter alia, (1) What are some of the roles for universities in addressing contemporary sociopolitical events which appear new to the United States; (2) What principles should undergird universities' examinations of global phenomena and thereby assist their students and faculty assume mantles of public engagement and leadership in ameliorating conditions; (3) What are some of the conceptual and programmatic features of university internationalization; and (4) What disciplinary motifs and university organizational structures might best facilitate proactive and reactive domestic and international initiatives? Such illustrative questions should help us begin our exploration and guide us during this intellectual and policy journey.

During his UCLA undergraduate career, Bunche excelled academically and made memorable speeches that portrayed his nascent interest in internationalization, founded upon a spiritual and idealistic basis, as witnessed by a quote from "That Man May Dwell in Peace": "May there not be evolved a universal political society, in which each nation would retain its individuality, its nationality, if you please; extensive freedom of action and autonomy within its own domain; yet maintaining, withal, an abiding consciousness of membership in the more significant international society? Essentially, the welfare of the world body must take precedence over nationalistic interest in periods of crisis" (Bunche, 1969c, p. 19). Quite remarkable for an undergraduate student reflecting upon events after World War I, and which, although unknown at the time, presaged his career at the United Nations. Hesburgh maintains that Bunche's concentration on peace still remained in the 1950s and 1960s regarding universities (Hesburgh, 2006).

As the founding chair of political science at Howard, Bunche's foremost concerns were building a sound curriculum, teaching classes, and encouraging the intellectual growth of students. These responsibilities cannot be separated from overall purposes of universities, he observed in his presentation "The Role of the University in the Political Orientation of Negro Youth" (1940b), just prior to the United States' official involvement in World War II. He asserted that university students were disoriented, placid, and smug products who were uninspired and ill-equipped with any ordered dynamics. He further asserted that universities have a great responsibility in trying times. Windows of truth must be at the center, yet he declared, "Too often our search for Truth becomes an escape device. We may come to conceive of the quest after Truth as an end in itself and fall in the *unconscious error of assuming that there is no connection between the Truth and the practical and that it is not academically respectable to tackle the practical*" (Bunche, 1969c, p. 222; emphasis added). Universities often produce BAs—which Bunche spelled out "babes in arms," who, failing to obtain insight, turn to radical and lunatic fringe organizations. It is absolutely necessary for any university to equip its graduates with skills for an intelligent comprehension of the world and its multiple forces, institutions, and ideologies (Bunche, 1969c).

Bunche's Harvard graduate study and his Howard career clearly evinced the espousal of nexuses between the life of university and the necessity of addressing and positing policy and programmatic solutions to pressing academic problems. His contributions to the monumental research publication *An American Dilemma*, headed by Swedish sociologist Gunnar Myrdal, articulated the salient connections between the presence of segregation and discrimination and the principles of democracy. From his undergraduate days to his diplomatic career in the United Nations, Bunche espoused and then implemented the integrations between concrete problematic challenges and the life of the academy and the scholar.

Methodology and University and Presidential Profiles

Bunche's diplomatic and pragmatic skills, combined with his conceptual and global policy perspectives pertaining to roles of research universities vis-à-vis societal challenges, can be built upon to initiate policies and programs for ameliorating contemporary international threats. Given the harsh consequences of September 11 and the ongoing war in Iraq, universities, in particular, have special roles to exert in preparing students for their careers and the mantles of leadership *and* simultaneously fostering conditions wherein faculty and administrators can develop students and themselves in solid interdisciplinary scholarship (Bunche, 1940a; Bunche, 1940b; Lindsay, 2003; Banks, 2004). To paraphrase Bunche, to what extent are these roles present and/or envisioned in contemporary research universities? Or as Hesburgh asked, how might current presidents learn from and build upon Bunche's educational views?

To begin answering this question, interviews and/or participant observation with the chief executives of two major public research universities provide the salient methodological components of case studies to ascertain how these institutions responded to and initiated policies and programs after September 11, 2001, and to Muslim and/or Middle East conflicts, particularly after the 2003 war began in Iraq. Case studies and presidential interviews were undertaken of several research universities and liberal arts colleges. However, this chapter concentrates on the analyses of interviews and observations from two sites—the University of Massachusetts at Amherst (UMass) and the University of Michigan at Ann Arbor—both nationally known flagship universities headed by women.[1] Both women were students when Bunche's international influence was still pervasive. Both earned their undergraduate degrees with honors and doctorates: the UMass chancellor in comparative literature *and* English from Michigan State University, and the Michigan president in biochemistry from the University of North Carolina at Chapel Hill. Prior to becoming the chancellor or president, both had spent much of the previous two decades in senior administrative positions where they were exposed to the vast array of scholarly and external issues affecting universities. One interviewee is an African American and the other is European American.

The University of Massachusetts at Amherst (headed by a chancellor who grew up in Bunche's home state of Michigan and was familiar with Bunche throughout her youth) is situated near the Berkshire Mountains in the western part of the state. Tracing its origins to 1864 and the endeavors of its third president, William Smith Clark, then Massachusetts Agricultural College by 1876 hosted students from throughout New England and international students from Brazil, Chile, and Japan. Several years later, President Clark concentrated on the concept of a "floating college" that would have citizens, students, and scholars engaged in learning and direct interaction with people throughout the world, which, though not realized in his lifetime, served as a strong impetus for the university's global reach and interactions with citizens in the commonwealth and abroad (Office of the Chancellor, 2004a). Today, the university is a comprehensive research institution with some of its 960 faculty being lauded as Nobel and Pulitzer Prize recipients. Undergraduate degrees are offered in nearly 100 areas and doctorates in fifty fields to 18,000 baccalaureate and 5,200 graduate students in ten schools and colleges.

It appeared logical to examine the University of Michigan, which is located only about an hour from Bunche's childhood home where his early life was influenced by a mixture of European American ethnic groups and African Americans in Detroit. The University of Michigan traces its origins to 1817 when the university was formed in Detroit by a Catholic priest and a Presbyterian minister who were heavily influenced by Jeffersonian ideas for a university and European educational concepts. Twenty years later the university relocated to Ann Arbor (University of Michigan, 2004).

Currently the university has a total enrollment of 38,972 students, of which 36,905 are undergraduate and 2,067 are graduate students. Undergraduate degrees are offered in 274 areas, doctoral degrees in 138 disciplines. Its 3,700 faculty are the recipient of Nobel and Pulitzer awards. In the early 2000s, the University of Michigan was featured in the media because of two legal cases brought before the Supreme Court—*Gratz v. Bollinger* (2003) and *Grutter v. Bollinger* (2003)—regarding the university's admissions policies designed to foster a diverse student body. The court ruled in the former case that the undergraduate admissions policies required altering, while the graduate admission procedures (highlighted in the latter case) could basically stand.

The interview protocol (see appendix A at the end of this chapter) began by building directly upon Bunche's seminal work, "The Role of the University in the Political Orientation of Negro Youth," written at the eve of World War II, wherein he asserted that "universities cannot divorce themselves from the tough and dangerous controversies in the domestic and international arenas" (Bunche, 1940b, p. 222). The questions for the interviews with Hesburgh are shared in appendix B.

Convergent and Emergent Motifs

Given the extensive data from the interviews, observations, and Web and/ or digital communication, we concentrate on salient themes: psychological and cultural motifs, public engagement and public intellectualism, influential Nobel laureates, and critical analysis and prototypic contributions to policies and action.

Psychological and Cultural Motifs

For Americans, unimaginable terrorist acts occurred on September 11. For those of us in the Washington, D.C., metropolitan area, the tragedies were very real as the plane struck the Pentagon and killed hundreds of individuals, including a local honor student en route to a science competition in California. Multiple individual perspectives immediately gave voice to raw emotions at universities and countless other venues across the nation.

Since Ralph Bunche's generation lived through the attacks on Pearl Harbor on December 7, 1941, which ignited fears that the continental United States would be bombed, many senior citizens compared that December day with September 11. According to the university chancellor, many on her campus were immediately touched because a favorite information technology employee was killed in a plane that struck the World Trade Center in New York. Disbelief gripped the campus because the event touched home. Immediately the chancellor began to walk the campus, to talk with individuals, and to hug those who could be comforted by an embrace, such as an extremely distraught student who could not locate her family. In hugging the student, she gently queried, "Will your university family do?" That night, as on many American college and university campuses, a vigil was held at the campus pond—a site which in the past had been used to demonstrate against American foreign policies—and the chancellor voiced these words: "Today is a day of deep, deep sadness . . . of profound human tragedy. There are no words to explain, no words to sooth, no words to comfort. . . . Tonight as we gather together in this crisis, let us remember that the grief of any one of us is the collective grief of all of us. As we grieve together, so must we remember to come together in our healing" (Office of the Chancellor, 2004b). She voiced more poignant expressions three days later on September 14: "On this day of remembrance we come together once again, with souls still buried beneath girders of grief, and healing still blocked by the debris of anxiety and desolation. Even now the howls of anguish and rage are ringing in our ears. How can we abide this grief . . . these multiple and conflicting emotions? Still burning deep with[in] each of are the fires of hopefulness and renewal and reconciliation" (Office of the Chancellor, 2004c).

In essence, a psychological prototype was evolving by her public behavior. But to sustain oneself and others, both the psychological and cultural must be immediately interrelated. The cultural landscape of the university should enable individuals to turn toward each other to address the issues that caused the massive acts of violence and to comprehend its effects on individuals while simultaneously trying to develop policies so such acts will not be repeated (Office of the Chancellor, 2004d). To begin the comprehension, the university initiated a series of university-wide panel presentations and discussions, which were also broadcast on the Housing Service Campus Network for those who could not attend. Throughout the year, topics included, inter alia, "The Nature of Terrorism," "Targets of Terrorism," "Liberty vs. Security:

Terrorism and Civil Rights," "The American Response to Terrorism," and "America Foreign Policy and Terrorism."

One year after September 11, 2001, at the alumni plaque dedication ceremony, the new president of the University of Michigan stated:

> There are no words for the magnitude of our loss. Even those of us who are newcomers are moved to share in this time of collective bereavement. These eighteen alumni were a microcosm of our whole community. . . . We must ensure that Michigan, as foster mother, as alma mater, of the eighteen we have lost, will go on nourishing all its children with the vital sustenance of knowledge. . . . We also find comfort in renewing the commitment we made one year ago . . . when a community 15,000 strong gathered on the Diag in an outpouring of concern, to reaffirm the highest ideals of our institutional and national purpose. (Coleman, 2002a)

Earlier that day, she stated, "Because we are part of a great center of learning, we must piece together the 'undone' words" (Coleman, 2002b). How to piece together the undone words becomes part of the cultural landscape of the university.

Prior to her arrival, her predecessor and other senior administrators had initiated a series of workshops and colloquiums to begin comprehending the phenomena of September 11. According to Vice Provost for International Affairs Michael Kennedy, violence, religion, and security may be the salient words for new cultural formations emanating from the attacks at the World Trade Center and the Pentagon (Kennedy, 2002). Thus in autumn 2001, the University of Michigan International Institute via cooperative campus-wide endeavors commenced a threefold focus on Islam in public culture, authorities' response to terrorism, and scholarly inquiry into violence (University of Michigan, International Institute, 2001). In the fall semester of 2002, Michigan students convened "The Palestinian Solidarity Conference." Located in the state with the largest concentration of Arab Americans in the nation, the president voiced her views that the university should provide a "safe space" for students and the university community to express views and to feel physically and psychologically safe. It could certainly be maintained that providing the safe space is an indispensable first step in ensuring a fair and open cultural dialogue.

Public Engagement and Public Intellectualism

Over seventy years ago, Bunche and his Howard University colleagues debated the critical significance of the university's relationship to President Franklin Roosevelt's New Deal and the war in the European and Pacific theaters (these topics are further discussed in chapters 3, 4, and 5). We could speculate that he would envision continuous roles for contemporary universities. But do current chief executives envision similar foci and if so, how would this manifest itself in the twenty-first century? The presidential responses to the first several protocol questions provide some insight.

Perhaps the most striking comments of the University of Massachusetts chancellor (who became quite familiar with Bunche's diplomatic triumphs during her undergraduate days) focused on the centrality of fundamental values that should provide the bedrock for the university community and all its endeavors. She concurred with Bunche's statement that universities have a critical role in preparing BAs who are not just "babes in arms." She began a program of the "living values initiatives," which became a hallmark of her tenure, concentrated on ensuring that principled values are as much a part of the university ethos as disciplinary tenets. Values are to provide constructive links to the challenges of the local, regional, national, and global communities. One prominent illustration was her invitation to Peter and Linda Biehl (the parents of American Fulbright graduate student Amy Biehl, who was killed by South Africans while she was researching in a Black township) to the university to discuss peace and reconciliation. Their daughter Amy was examining women's roles in the formation of the new South African constitution, and she was stoned and stabbed to death by youth who had just attended a pan-Africanist rally condemning Whites' involvement in perpetuating racial inequality. The Biehls forgave and befriended their daughter's killers; consequently they communicated with the young people to help them rebuild their post-incarceration lives. Two of the young people, in fact, worked with the Amy Biehl Foundation in South Africa. "Bunche's focus on BAs (babes in arms) is a value statement, that is, we prepare them; but we don't really prepare them," the university chancellor asserted. The Biehls' actions help the university community to grasp "that everyone is a member of the human race" and that the preparation of degree candidates is only part of the equation.

The quest for the truth is part of the intellectual formula wherein universities can least afford to be disconnected from the human responsibilities of the world. Raising tough questions, engaging in assessment, ascertaining what service means in various communities, and determining where to invest one's energies are basic components of university life. If the quest for truth is the sole objective, then one can be lulled into a euphoric state and not engage in pressing challenges, declares the chancellor.

Becoming a public intellectual is a vital role of university presidents and faculty. In the immediate aftermath of September 11, the chancellor told the faculty senate, "These times call for us to be public intellectuals in the best sense. . . . The public has entrusted us—not to do their thinking for them—but to enrich public conversation and to enable a larger and more diverse set of voices to join the dialogue" (Office of the Chancellor, 2004e). Being a public intellectual is developed over time along with one's disciplinary expertise. Thinking with the community—not for the community—and thinking out loud engages a multitude of voices to understand the challenges and begin formulating solutions. The public intellectual takes the lead in "thinking out loud" while listening diligently to community voices. Interestingly enough, the chancellor perceived distinctions between the public intellectual and the academician who narrows her/his focus to disciplinary truth. Being a public intellectual is responding to the public trust in the creation of new knowledge and its dissemination for the public good.

In further contemplating the meaning of university public engagement, the chancellor maintains that synergy should connect referential and relational linkages between disciplinary comprehension and acknowledgments of public responsibilities. Therefore the university develops, fosters, and enhances curriculum, co-curriculum, and scholarship for students, the university, and the larger community, which echoes Bunche's words (Bunche, 1940b).

Given the harsh devastation of September 11, the university must think out loud on several simultaneous planes. Attending to basic infrastructural components such as water, food, electricity, maintenance of laboratories and the like, addressing the psychocultural needs of the university and surrounding communities, and preparing contingency plans for disasters are illustrative of multiple-plane thinking. For example, the University of Massachussetts at Amherst is a "safe spot" if there is a nuclear disaster in the neighboring state of Vermont. That is, the university is part of the New England community and region.

According to the president of Michigan, universities have evolved considerably since the 1960s when she was an undergraduate in preparing students for the real world: higher education has moved noticeably beyond Bunche's statement that the "universities should do more than produce babes-in-arms." University of Michigan students can volunteer in social service agencies, public schools, and community clinics wherein they can connect their scholarly work with "the problems and issues of society." Students have opportunities to study abroad and be exposed to international communities. "These experiences are invaluable to students and . . . we are much better preparing students for what Dr. Bunche was talking about," she asserted. Medical school students can engage in rotations in underserved communities, while law students work in legal clinics with people who cannot pay for legal counsel. The challenges, according to the president, are to provide similar options in the traditional Ph.D. programs.

Engaging in public intellectual roles entails presidential participation in university-wide conferences as the president presided over the October 2003 conference, "The Destruction of Civilization and the Obligations of War." The causes of war, the consequences of war on human lives, and the loss or destruction of irreplaceable artifacts were central foci. Conference participants raised questions such as what conditions should exist before engaging in war, should nations enter unilaterally, and what the responsibilities of noncitizens and nations are in preventing genocide. The debate at such conferences should expand beyond the university campus to include citizens from the local region while the campus community plays a key role in raising the salient issues. Exerting a positive impact on the nation and the society by debating issues of social importance is part of public intellectuals' portfolios.

At the University of Michigan, its Institute for Social Research is conducting the "first ever survey of Arab Americans in the United States which will provide baseline data to know more about this population," the university president declared. The study will expand to include Caledonians who are Christians, not Muslims, and Arabs residents who have lived for decades in the United States. Public engagement encompasses vital partnerships with overseas partners in Chinese universities, for instance, on collaborative social science research to lend insight into Chinese in both nations.

In a sense, the public intellectualism continues via traditional course offerings and class endeavors. The Michigan president stated that after September 11, for example, there has been an enormous increase in courses on the Middle East, which "are jam-packed and various programs focusing on the Middle East and Islam are of great interest." The university has initiated special themes for the 2003–04 academic year: "Celebrating the 300th Anniversary of St. Petersburg" in the fall and the "50th Anniversary of *Brown v. Board of Education*" during the spring semester.

Influential Nobel Laureates

Nobel peace laureates represent the zenith of nonviolent solutions to overwhelming domestic and international violence. Some, such as the 2002 laureate, President Jimmy Carter, readily acknowledge how other laureates affected their analyses and actions in seeking peaceful resolutions to conflicts. In fact, President Carter's Nobel speech quoted extensively from Bunche's Nobel message by reiterating, "To suggest that war can prevent war is a base play on words and a despicable form of warmongering. The objective of any who sincerely believe in peace clearly must be to exhaust every honorable recourse in the effort to save the peace. The world has had ample evidence that war begets only conditions that beget further war" (Carter, 2002; Bunche, 1950a).

To continue this line of reasoning, the chief executives were asked their perspectives of President Carter's statement that "we must adjust to changing times and still hold to unchanging principles." Both the chancellor and president readily concurred with this statement and recognized the synergy between laureates Bunche and Carter. When the chancellor expressed her familiarity with other Nobel peace laureates, she cited Archbishop Desmond Tutu and former presidents Nelson Mandela and F. W. de Klerk of South Africa. She exclaimed that the several Nobel laureates were attempting "to make a step forward, to move together." Yet in troubled places, whether in South Africa or Northern Ireland, common ground needs to be identified while attempting to move forward, which, in essence, was her view of reconciliation. Peace is not the sole goal; rather it is the thriving that requires the action, the concrete steps of moving beyond disparate parts of the globe whether with Israelis or Palestinians or Catholics in Northern Ireland. When asked as a follow-up query about the "suicide bombers," she stated there is a profound irony since "the ultimate value is life, not death! Then it's misguided to give up the ultimate value at the beginning."

Giving up life at the front end does not present opportunities for reconciliation or for adjustment to changing times while holding fast to unchanging principles of life and freedom. Helping students to wrestle with such tough dilemmas is a constant challenge for university executives and faculty.

Both executives expressed similar views regarding how universities might recognize whether success has been achieved. One stated that the conversations on vital matters can never cease, as "part of the habit of being in the university is the interrogation, the continuous assessment, the seeking of solutions to thorny problems." The other declared, "I don't know if I will ever declare success. The challenges are many and we are called upon to help our country. We can't be successful if we do not cross the borders."

Prologues to Action

Much of the preceding analysis lend itself to a framework that Kennedy (2002) identifies as "prologues to action." That is, reflective analysis should lead to higher education policy development and/or alterations so that students are prepared to assume leadership responsibilities. A salient question lingers: how do we translate critical articulations by university chancellors and presidents into dynamic policy development and concrete program paradigms? Several fundamental propositions are posited.

First, the chancellor voiced the concept of "administrative proof." For example, there are key elements that are fundamental to the vitality of the organization that should be evident regardless of who occupies the position of university chancellor or president. Even if the chancellor, senior executives, and faculty change, fundamental values and programs or components thereof should be evident. International affairs and programs, diversity offices, and experiential or service learning are often downsized or eliminated when fiscal resources become scarce. Yet the commitment to internationalism and service learning should still be manifested in other university structures and curriculum. Particular administrative arrangements should continue the basic values of the institution as observed in international and service learning, where students can continue to examine global challenges. Hesburgh stated that similar views were expressed by Bunche in Rockefeller Foundation Board meetings (Hesburgh, 2006).

Second, one executive introduced the concept "infrastructure of the human spirit." Often professionals are concerned with the physical aspects of the organization—the buildings, the logistics, the administrative procedures, and the like. We must ensure that the human dimension or spirit is always foremost in our thoughts and actions, a focus Bunche would endorse (Hesburgh, 2006). Horizontal rather than vertical approaches, involving all relevant constituents, should characterize this infrastructure. As King has discussed, open or transparent processes would distinguish horizontal processes (King, 2003).

Third, "striving for excellence" is the raison d'etre for all university endeavors, maintains the chancellor and president. This means an operationalization of excellence, not just in the abstract but as a constant relating to basic fundamental principles of democracy and equity to ensure such conditions exist in the local and global community. Bunche attempted to mesh such propositions as a Howard University professor and executive assistant to the president wherein he pushed democratic principles in the domestic settings. Plus he examined alternatives for implementation in international venues as a member of the Rockefeller Board and as a diplomat. He advocated new and/or redefined multidisciplinary paradigms that are still applicable for today's students, scholars, administrators, and policymakers. The establishment of an endowed Ralph Bunche Chair at UCLA, designed to foster innovative models for addressing sociopolitical matters, provides contemporary credence for the importance of relationships between the academy and continuing challenges outside the university community. Pressing issues of the day force us to move forward with dynamic innovative modes for the welfare of the world body. As research universities succeed, Bunche's legacy, although he never became chancellor at UCLA, will continue to sustain solid foundations for current and future generations.

Appendix A

The protocol questions structuring the interviews included the following:

1. Prior to my letter and/or e-mail to you, how familiar were you with Dr. Bunche?

2. Dr. Bunche published a seminal piece titled "The Role of the University in the Political Orientation of Negro Youth" at the eve of the second world war. He would maintain that his points applied to universities in general. One "sound bite" was "We decorate them [students] in tinsel and glitter and turn them loose as B.A.'s—babes in arms," because the students are not prepared to face the real challenges of the world. What is your perspective of this statement by Dr. Bunche?

3. In a related vein, Dr. Bunche maintained that universities often have an "unceasing quest after that elusive concept 'truth' and too often our search for Truth becomes an escape device—whereby we can divorce ourselves from the tough and dangerous controversies of the world." How applicable do you view this statement in today's universities and in particular your role as a university chancellor/president? What is the relative importance of "values" in addressing challenges outside the walls of academe?

4. Dr. Bunche and his Howard University contemporaries often discussed their roles and that of the university as public intellectuals. Is public intellectualism still appropriate? If so, how? How does this relate to curricular and co-curricular endeavors?

5. Our contemporary term for Dr. Bunche's perspectives regarding one major role of the university or college is engagement or service. How does this concept apply to your university? What principles might guide universities/colleges' examination of global phenomena for public engagement?

6. Does your university mission and/or vision statement include a central role for the various facets of internationalization? If so, what are they? Are there key organizational structures and positions (dean/vice provost with tenured faculty and/or staff) and fiscal allocations for internationalization at your university? In today's tight fiscal times, how does internationalization fare with competing priorities?

7. What specific actions were taken after September 11, 2001, and before, during, and after the 2003 war in Iraq or other crises that faced your state and/or locale?

8. Are these endeavors still continuing? Have they become institutionalized?

9. How do universities prepare the students, faculty, administrators, and the community for unimaginable crises such as that of September 11 and some might say the war in Iraq? Who or which entity (entities) takes the lead and/or coordinating roles?

10. Since you are the chancellor/president of a public university, how do you balance these progressive perspectives of internationalization with those of elected officials (local, state, and federal) and corporate or "deep-pocket" sponsors who do not advocate or support such perspectives?

11. Are there "political" or direct engagement roles or nonpolitical roles for university presidents/chancellors regarding a war or a crises such as September 11?

12. Are you familiar with other Nobel peace laureates? If so, who are they?

13. How might you compare their peace endeavors with those of Dr. Bunche?

14. President Jimmy Carter, in accepting the Nobel Peace Prize in December 2002, paraphrased Dr. Bunche, stating, "To suggest that war can prevent war is a base play on words and a despicable form of warmongering. The objective of any who sincerely believe in peace clearly must be to exhaust every honorable recourse in the effort to save the peace. The world has had ample evidence that war begets only conditions that beget further war" (Carter, 2002; Bunche 1950a). What is your viewpoint of this perspective of Dr. Bunche and as reiterated by President Carter?

15. President Jimmy Carter, in his acceptance speech, quoted a teacher who stated, "We must adjust to changing times and still hold to unchanging principles." How or does this still apply to today's universities?

16. How can universities and colleges recognize whether we have been successful or unsuccessful in our endeavors to address contemporary sociopolitical events which appear new to the United States and to the world?

17. Are there any additional comments or remarks that you wish to share? Thank you for sharing your time and providing in-depth information.

Appendix B

Interview questions for Father Theodore (Ted) Hesburgh.

1. How did you initially meet Dr. Ralph Bunche?

2. In what capacity or capacities did you interact with him?

3. What critical/key issues emerged during your joint tenure on the Rockefeller Foundation Board?

4. How were agendas developed on the board?

5. How were different perspectives addressed?

6. Did you and Dr. Bunche discuss various issues affecting higher education? If so, cite some illustrations. Did these become part of the Rockefeller Board agenda?

7. Dr. Bunche expressed plans to address urban poverty/ghetto life in the USA. From that emerged the Rockefeller Foundation–funded MARC project. Do you have particular points or ideas you wish to share about the project?

8. Did you have discussions about the U.S. Commission on Civil Rights, of which you were a member, that you discussed formally or informally with Dr. Bunche?

9. How would you characterize Dr. Bunche's style?

10. I've read various articles, book chapters, and the like about your thirty-five-year presidency of Notre Dame. What would you cite as the highlights of your presidential tenure?

11. Are you involved in particular activities as president emeritus of Notre Dame?

12. Are there other points which we did not cover that you would like to address?

Thank you for your time and insightful comments.

Note

1. Women presidential perspectives are presented to help ensure that diverse viewpoints and policies are explicated, rather than those of men only. The next chapter concentrates on the explications of male executives.

7. Intellectual and Diplomatic Imprints at Liberal Arts Colleges

BEVERLY LINDSAY

When undertaking archival research as a senior visitor at Harvard University's Dumbarton Oaks in Washington, D.C., during 2004, I was struck by its magnificent architecture and landscape in tony Georgetown. Hundreds of varieties of flowers and plants dotted the landscape, a continuation of the interest of Mildred and Robert Woods Bliss, who conveyed the estate to Harvard University. The ambiance suited that of an exclusive American liberal arts college. Undoubtedly, the location, ambiance, and privacy contributed to the site being selected as the venue for the Dumbarton Oaks Conference, the forerunner to the San Francisco Conference where the United Nations was established.

James Bryant Conant, then the president of Harvard University, and Ralph Bunche were participants at the Dumbarton Oaks Conference. Conant sometimes literally sat at the table with the official representatives from the United States, China, Great Britain, and Soviet Union. As a professional from the Department of State, Bunche provided invaluable intellectual and technical insight and support. Both were unsurpassed intellectuals who recognized the contributions that they and peers could contribute to concrete domestic and international sociopolitical and economic challenges in a postwar era (Conant, 1942; Finch, 1945; Hudson, 1945; Dumbarton Oaks archives). Their roles in the diplomatic sphere, steeped originally in undergraduate liberal arts curriculums, raise a critical query concerning these scholars' lingering influence on liberal arts colleges.

During significant junctures in international affairs of the twentieth century, conceptual perspectives emerged concerning the public service roles of universities that can help us comprehend the foundations for twenty-first-century roles. Such views are expressed as components of university mission statements and by eminent scholars and policy executives. The initiatives of James Conant, who introduced a general education curriculum later emulated by numerous universities, provided comprehensive perspectives for students to incorporate an awareness of public service roles (Harvard Committee, 1945). Writing just prior to the American involvement in the second world war, professor and future Nobel peace laureate Ralph Bunche articulated public service roles for universities to prepare students to challenge adverse societal conditions in contrast to an attitude he feared was fostered by universities: "We may conceive of the quest after Truth as an end in itself and fall into the unconscious error of assuming that there is no connection between the Truth and the practical and that it is not academically respectable to tackle the practical" (Bunche, 1940b, p. 576). In the post–World War II era, Harvard University established the 1940s Salzburg Seminars where liberal arts students from formerly warring nations could interact, discuss sensitive topics, and begin developing solutions to postwar problems (Mead, 1947).

As we fast-forward to the late 1990s and the early 2000s, we note the shifting focus to the concept of public engagement rather than just public service. As emphasized in the 2004 conference of the American Sociological Association, "Public sociology should transcend the academy and engage wider audiences to be inclusive and democratic" by building bridges that connect multiple communities and civil societies (American Sociological Association, 2004). Eminent international scholars and policymakers such as Ireland's former president, Mary Robinson, provided addresses on public roles of universities including that of contributing to democracy and civil society. The 2006 conference theme of the American Education Research Association, "Education Research in the Public Interest," sought to emphasize the linkages between scholarly research and challenges facing public school and university students as they seek to contribute to fairness in various milieus (American Education Research Association, 2006). Similar perspectives were articulated by Bunche several decades earlier as discussed in earlier chapters in this volume. This chapter further explores Bunche's legacy at three liberal arts colleges in the United States and France.

Methodology and College and Presidential Profiles

Salient questions remain: To what extent do and might liberal arts colleges undertake public engagement endeavors and enhance public intellectualism among their faculty and students? Are there lingering direct or indirect influences of Ralph Bunche? Might the statements of and programs initiated by college presidents serve as models of public intellectualism as posited by Bunche?

To begin responding to these queries, in-depth interviews with the presidents of three distinctive liberal arts colleges and select campus observations were undertaken from summer 2003 to winter 2004. The interviews focused on ascertaining the influence of Bunche's perspectives, especially pertaining to public engagement or service; and institutional responses to September 11, 2001, and to conflicts in the Middle East and other international and domestic crises. The colleges analyzed are geographically dispersed liberal arts institutions—Middlebury College in Vermont, St. Mary's University in Texas, and American University in Paris. Each currently has or just had European American men with considerable expertise in international arenas as president. This group of interviews contrasts with the responses of women university presidents discussed in the previous chapter.

The presidents earned their doctoral degrees from renowned research universities: Oxford University, Harvard University, and University of Arizona. The presidents of Middlebury and St. Mary's have undergraduate degrees and/or minors in religion and philosophy and political science, while the American University president concentrated in history. Throughout their careers, they concentrated on international affairs in their roles as president: at Middlebury, which has a strong international and languages focus; at St. Mary's, which has salient concern with international affairs especially in developing regions and conflict resolution; at American University, which has an international study body and where the president built upon his experiences as the chief executive officer and publisher for the *International Herald Tribune*, known as the world's first global newspaper. Each has appeared on national television, testified before Congress, and published extensively in his field.

Middlebury College, founded in 1800, is known as a top-tier liberal arts college and regards Amherst, Williams, Colby, and Bates among its peer institutions. The current undergraduate student body of 2,350 benefits from a 1 to 11 faculty student ratio that allows considerable time for professors' direct interactions with students in foreign languages, international studies, environmental studies, and the sciences. Over 33 percent of the 230-plus faculty are women, and about 98 percent are European Americans. Today, women comprise 52 percent of the student body. Approximately 71 percent are European Americans, 7 percent Asian Americans, 5 percent Hispanics, 3 percent African Americans, 8 percent international, and 6 percent unknown (Middlebury, 2005a). About three decades ago, when the student body was under 2,000 people, and long before many other colleges and universities,

Middlebury initiated first-year seminars where faculty of various ranks—including the college president—taught students via an intensive writing component (Middlebury, 2005b). The Middlebury president also required students to read the *New York Times* long before the paper was routinely distributed to campuses.

Although Middlebury is primarily a liberal arts college with extensive overseas study and practicum options, undergraduate and graduate programs are offered in various areas with the well-known ones in languages. Its doctorate in modern languages (DML) is a nationally recognized program offered to about seventy students. DML matriculants concentrate in two languages to prepare as specialists in second-language acquisition, language pedagogy, linguistics, and literature. German and the Romance languages are the most-often-taught subjects that enable over half of the DML recipients to later pursue college and university careers.

The past president of Middlebury was the president and chief executive officer of the Salzburg Seminar. In 1947, a group of faculty and students from Harvard established the seminar to provide a venue where students from formerly warring nations and the United States could discuss critical topics and begin developing solutions to pressing matters (Salzburg Seminar, 2005a). One of the initial Salzburg Seminars was directed by renowned anthropologist Margaret Mead. The Salzburg Seminar missions seek to continue building bridges among young people, prepare the next generation of leaders, and convene professionals and policymakers to learn and share best practices in order to address domestic and international affairs (Salzburg Seminar, 2005b).

St. Mary's University traces its origins to 1852 when it was founded by French Catholic clergy on the banks of the San Antonio River. It currently enrolls about 2,290 undergraduates, nearly 180 masters students, 32 Ph.D. students, and 785 law students. Originally established to educate European American (Anglo) males often of middle-class or wealthy backgrounds, the institution first admitted male students of color during the early 1950s. Women were admitted in the mid-1960s. Today, nearly 54 percent of undergraduates are Hispanics, thus making it a Hispanic Serving Institution (HSI; federal government recognition that at least 25 percent of the students are of Hispanic background). Women comprise over 50 percent of the undergraduate matriculants. Anglo students comprise about 34 percent of the population, African Americans 3.7 percent, Asian and Pacific Islanders about 2.5 percent, international students about 3.6 percent, Native Americans about one-half percent, and the rest are unknown. St. Mary's is located in one of the nation's fastest growing metropolitan areas, and its students can pursue majors in over fifty baccalaureate programs, which often include urban service learning and/or internship options in San Antonio. Given its Catholic mission, the university has focused on public service to the community throughout its history, although the forms have altered and accelerated in recent years (St. Mary's University, 2005a).

Over 90 percent of the nearly 200 full-time faculty at St. Mary's hold doctorates or terminal professional degrees. Nearly 140 adjunct faculty also offer instruction. Thus students experience a 1 to 13 faculty-student ratio. For several decades, St. Mary's law school was known for producing some of Texas's most eminent attorneys, including one of Texas's current U.S. senators. The university's strategic goal is to become the preeminent Catholic university in the Southwest.

American University of Paris is the newest of these three liberal arts institutions, as it was established in 1962. Yet is the oldest American university in Europe. AU enrolls about 900 bilingual students who represent fifteen nations. Undergraduate students can concentrate in fourteen majors and twenty-five minors, while masters degrees are offered in international affairs, conflict resolution, and civil society development. As an American university, it is accredited by the Middle States Association of Colleges and Universities and is a member of notable American professional organizations such as the Council of Independent Colleges (which includes Middlebury, Amherst, and Northwestern University) as well as the Association of American Colleges and Universities (which includes regional institutions such as San Jose State University, Chicago State University, and College of William and Mary). About 80 percent of the forty-four full-time faculty and the sixty-one adjunct faculty hold doctoral degrees. The 1-to-18 faculty-student ratio permits continuous student interaction and mentoring by faculty (American University of Paris, 2005).

The conceptual framework for this chapter and the protocol questions for the three presidents continue those features explicated in chapter 6 and portrayed in appendices A and B. Protocol question 10 was modified to focus on issues facing presidents of private colleges and universities. The president of St. Mary's University responded from both perspectives because of that university's HSI status. He interacts continually with the city's mayoral office, city council, elected state officials, and congresspeople and senators.

Awareness of Bunche

Because the three presidents earned terminal degrees and/or spent much of their careers in international affairs, it was not surprising that they were familiar with Ralph Bunche. Their knowledge and immediate familiarity primarily revolved around Bunche's career at the United Nations, as exemplified by the Middlebury president emeritus's response: "I have great admiration for Bunche. His roles at the UN were unparalleled." The AU president indicated that Bunche's training and UN experiences certainly provide lessons for contemporary higher education.

During the interviewer discussions with the president of St. Mary's University, some unanticipated insights emerged. For example, Bunche's maternal grandmother exerted considerable influence during his youth that affected his lifelong ethical perspectives. According to the St. Mary's president, the president's maternal grandmother (whose parents shared information about the post–Civil War era) affected him by trying to instill views of fairness toward everyone. In the multiracial Anglo American, Mexican American, and African American environments in the first half of the twentieth century, perspectives of fairness were not the usual norms. Given that the president's grandmother and Bunche's were of similar generations, the president speculated on what sociopolitical factors influence grandmothers' abilities to impart ideas to their offspring. This idea is further explored in the final chapter.

Truth and Public Intellectualism

The three presidents concurred that colleges and universities have indispensable roles in preparing youth for societal challenges, although they were hesitant to make sweeping generalizations about the extent to which this is a reality in numerous college settings. Their statements and descriptions of the quest for truth—as espoused when Bunche voiced that universities have an "unceasing quest after the elusive concept 'truth' and too often our search for Truth becomes an escape device"—and public intellectualism provided different viewpoints.

The Middlebury president emeritus maintained that his institution had a reputation for encouraging internationalism and multiple language acquisition. The applicant pool and subsequent matriculants reflected and perpetuated worldviews. Yet he maintained that the "new generation of higher education scholars, like many in Congress, have never been abroad." Therefore how could they know truth from only one regional or perhaps national perspective, and how might they impart internationalism and truth to their students? Moreover, he asserted that on many campuses the idea of "public intellectualism is optimistic. A few [faculty] write articles for the *New York Times*, and *Atlantic Monthly;* we reward them and they become quasi-intellectual celebrities." In the Middlebury community, only a handful of faculty participated in the life of the community, for example, being elected to the school board or a similar civic group.

The president of St. Mary's says he is impressed by the scholarly insights that academics have regarding domestic and world problems, but he is less impressed by what they actually do. He stated, "The intellectual engages in very thoughtful reflection; but he takes action and is ensconced in the community. Bunche exemplifies this . . . he was in the public and in the world of ideas." Of especial note was the president's view that "public intellectualism and engagement are the same." As an example, he cited Martin Luther King's *Letter from a Birmingham Jail* wherein steps for direct action were articulated. Although it is not generally known, King regarded Bunche as one of his intellectual and civic mentors (A. Young, 2003). This response gives cause to further refine our definition of public intellectualism: *thoughtful analysis and reflection coupled with appropriate action characterize the public intellectual. The public aspects of the action may be undertaken directly by the actor and/ or by his or her role in ensuring that others do so.*

Public intellectual roles are critical for colleges and universities, maintains the American University president. Nonetheless, he states that "academics often retreat from public and address narrow special audiences. Academic thinking does not make its way into the public arena. The work would be better if it did." As a communication and media expert, the American University president recommends that the media "do a better job of covering what's in the intellectual world. Simultaneously, cloistered professionals who write in special journals need to reach out so that society is well-served." Publications in various outlets and presentations in public forums that Bunche (the professor) undertook with civic groups exemplify comprehensive channels for intellectual dissemination. As this occurs, "the quest for truth" will become reality rather than a mere quest. Thus the American University and the St. Mary's presidents concur that public intellectualism and public engagement are a hand-in-glove relationship.

The Nature and Illustrations of Public Engagement

Public engagement may be present to varying degrees on American campuses, but it is often hampered by faculty allegiance to their disciplines rather than the college, asserts the Middlebury president emeritus. He further declared that institutions are viewed as custodians of local culture; faculty views of their colleagues at comparable institutions are more important than local cultural pronouncements. Thus there may be tension when the college as a higher education institution attempts to advocate public engagement while the disciplinary norms do not reward public contributions. To help rectify this tension, the Middlebury president emeritus recommends that more congruence be established in the tenure, promotion, and raise processes so that public service or public engagement gets comparable weight to teaching and scholarship. That is, faculty would "not be continually rewarded for knowing more and more about less and less."

Globalization, maintains the former president of the Salzburg Seminar and Middlebury College, "is a comprehensive phenomena that assumes an impact on higher education." At two-year colleges (attended by about 11 million students compared to 6 million at four-year sites), international public awareness and engagement need to be enhanced because limited fiscal resources do not enable faculty and students to participate in globalization via international study and research. For example, Miami Dade Community College, one of the largest in the United States, has nearly 168,000 students with 6,000 faculty on eight campuses—all with somewhat limited international exposure. In contrast, students at select wealthy colleges such as Middlebury and Carleton take for granted that they may have an international experience. Hence the Salzburg Seminar plans to incorporate summer programs to enhance the knowledge base of two-year faculty so new curricular content on global issues can be disseminated to students.

Three salient illustrations of public engagement were discussed by the St. Mary's president: a master's program in international relations; the Campus Compact and Civic Engagement Project; and the Presidential Peace Commission. While it is not unusual for a university to offer a graduate degree in international relations, the matriculants' desired professional careers are in arenas involving very direct public engagement. A notable percentage of students desire to work in nongovernment organizations (NGOs) and/or civic organizations based in the United States and overseas. Identifying problems and devising plans and programs to ameliorate conditions via their NGO careers illustrate direct public engagement. The president further stated that for several years, the master's in international relations has been offered at Fort Hood near Killeen, Texas—where he estimated that approximately 35 percent of the soldiers have been deployed to Iraq, Afghanistan, and surrounding countries. Now some are on their second and third deployments. Since he taught several times at Fort Hood, the president knows many of the soldiers; he stated that one regularly communicates with him from Iraq. Certainly, a number of the soldiers are simply interested in earning a master's degree for military promotions or similar reasons; others are interested in civic careers after their military careers. For the on-campus and Fort Hood students, examining ethical and moral dimensions of organizational programs *and* individual professional actions are bedrock curricular dimensions. Ethical and moral decision making will consequently guide the graduates regardless of their career options and daily pursuits therein.

St. Mary's involvement with the Campus Compact and Civic Engagement Project is designed for students' direct involvement with the larger society. The Campus Compact, headquartered at Brown University, is composed of colleges and universities throughout the United States wherein students and student directors devise projects in light of local or international needs. Related to this endeavor is St. Mary's Civic Engagement Project, which specifically focuses on San Antonio's neighborhoods and neighborhood associations. The St. Mary's Association was the only college association, in a recent year, to receive a grant from the San Antonio mayor's office to plan and design activities to address concrete neighborhood problems. How to communicate effectively with civic and political leaders, provide services to homeless populations, and enhance after-school programs for teenagers are endeavors undertaken by the association.

The President's Peace Commission (PPC) seeks to foster an ethical commitment to participate in the establishment of world peace and social justice. The commission further encourages respect for human rights and dignity of all people. An annual PPC symposium provides opportunities for students, faculty, and staff to develop and/or enhance their activities in pursuit of peace and justice. Through the symposiums and other activities, the commission seeks to build within the St. Mary's community a greater awareness of the Roman Catholic and Marianist perspectives on peace and justice. The President's Peace Commission, which includes students, staff, and faculty appointed by the university president, elicits suggestions from the campus community and from local and national leaders and organizations (St. Mary's University, 2005b). Understanding components of the Middle East conflict, the Patriot Act, and voting rights and voters' participation by various demographic groups are areas covered by the PPC in its various symposiums. Extrapolating from Hesburgh's comments (Hesburgh, 2006), a PPC would likely have strongly resonated with Bunche since he was preoccupied with peace and justice.

The St. Mary's president hopes that ideas associated with peace and justice are not viewed solely in an external or public engagement fashion, although public engagement is critical. Peace and justice should be part of the campus community, especially at a Catholic university. Approximately sixty (about 30 percent) of the St. Mary's faculty have been trained and certified in peace and conflict mediation that can be used in various milieus, including the university community. A seamless transition between the university community and larger issues of public engagement through peace and conflict resolution should be evident.

The past American University of Paris president focused on several components of the curriculum and faculty scholarship and research in relation to public engagement. Since he was a former publisher of the *International Herald Tribune* and a professor of communication studies and journalism at Northwestern University, select public engagement illustrations focused on these areas. As cited previously, AU is a multinational university with students from over fifteen nations; therefore the composition of the student body provides a natural avenue for cross-cultural communications about contemporary events and challenges facing various nations. The nature of bilingual communication (usually in English and French in addition to their indigenous language) means engagement with students and professionals from various cultures. As the president stated, "Everyone is a foreign student; there is no prevailing national culture. Students are forced to be cosmopolitan." Within the curriculum, this can translate into class discussions and projects about distinct cultures and noting generic conditions and challenges.

Quite specifically, the former AU president discussed the international study options of Northwestern University students at AU, which has an institutional link. Undergraduate and graduate programs at AU for Northwestern students enable the American students to gain some of the multicultural and international exposure that resident AU students constantly experience. The Northwestern graduate journalism program enables students to work with electronic and print media and to spend time in France and other parts of Europe. A second graduate program in marketing, according to the AU president, "often consists of older students in their 20s and 30s who have not had previous international experience . . . which they can obtain in Paris and London." International professionals, in addition to regular AU faculty, lead afternoon and evening seminars and excursions. Coverage of the Iraq war and SARS (severe acute respiratory syndrome) and the media's responsibility in covering such grave topics are part of the AU program for Northwestern students.

The AU president, when speaking in his Northwestern professorial role, stated that faculty scholarship and instruction must expand to address major domestic and global challenges. For example, one Northwestern professor now regularly includes Al Jazeera, the Arabic satellite news channel located in Qatar, in his journalism and communication courses. The use of Al Jazeera provides an alternative perspective on events in the Middle East and other parts of the world that is significantly different from that seen in the American and Western European press. For students to be involved in public engagement, they must understand alternative perspectives, which entails incorporating concepts and paradigms from various social science disciplines so that cross-fertilization of ideas and subsequent programs occurs. He advocates integrating ideas into the public discussion, the public dialogue—that is, public engagement—to tackle challenging problems.

For the several presidents, there were very direct relations among student and faculty curricular and co-curricular endeavors, the aftermath of September 11, and the commencement of the war in Iraq. Addressing immediate psychological trauma was, of course, an immediate concern as some students were extremely frightened. In addition to formal services offered by the student affairs office, St. Mary's University, for instance, had a retired Marianist brother visit the student dormitories, cafeterias, and informal meeting places to comfort students. This particular brother was known for his rapport with students. At Middlebury and St. Mary's, ecumenical meditative and/or prayer services were held, which encouraged students and faculty from various religious and/or metaphysical views to participate. Conscious attempts were made, for example, to include speakers who were Christian, Jewish, Muslim, Buddhist, and so forth. In various symposiums and colloquiums, students and faculty struggled to understand why a group of men would take such drastic efforts on September 11. Comprehending the multifaceted nature of Islam after September 11 and the beginning of the Iraq war were key topics of special symposiums. The challenge is to incorporate such critical topics into the regular curriculum regardless of disciplines, declares the Middlebury president emeritus as he echoes Bunche (1940b). Only the incorporation of critical topics into the curriculum and co-curriculum programs will have a lasting effect since the student body changes every four to five years.

Lingering Effects of Nobel Laureates

It could be argued that the zenith of public engagement, regardless of the profession, would be receiving a Nobel Peace Prize. As explicated in chapter 6, President Jimmy Carter acknowledged the intellectual and diplomatic influence of Ralph Bunche in his Nobel address in 2002. The three college presidents were asked their perceptions of some of Carter's statements—for example, adjusting to changing times and holding to unchanging principles—and their awareness and knowledge of other Nobel peace laureates. All expressed the importance of ensuring that the principles undergirding Carter's statement should continue. The Middlebury president emeritus, for instance, readily agreed with Carter's statement and cited similar quotes by Thomas Jefferson (regarding unwavering principles), which are inscribed on the Jefferson monument in Washington, D.C.

The St. Mary's and AU presidents referenced other Nobel peace laureates, Martin Luther King and Aung San Suu Kyi, and nominee Mary Robinson.

The intellectual synergy between Martin Luther King and Bunche and their striving for peaceful solutions were voiced by the St. Mary's president. Since Mary Robinson has been nominated for the Nobel Peace Prize, the St. Mary's president cited her efforts (when president of Ireland) toward peaceful solutions in her country. Furthermore, her work with the United Nations High Commission on Refugees to promote humane conditions and treatment was mentioned. The AU president discussed Aung San Suu Kyi's nonviolent struggles in Myanmar (formerly Burma). The Nobel Prize selection committee stated that Aung San Suu Kyi used nonviolent struggle for the second independence of Burma (Nobel Prize, 2005). Her nonviolent struggles and attempts for conciliation among various regions and ethnic groups led to AU's awarding her an honorary doctorate degree in 1997. Because she was under house arrest, her husband delivered her doctoral acceptance speech wherein the AU president recalled her espousing peaceful solutions and advocating student involvement, that is, public engagement in their communities.

Dimensions of Public Engagement and Success

What is striking about the presidents' discussions was their perspective that public engagement should be as much a part of a college's raison d'etre as teaching and scholarship. Some distinctions emerged concerning the concept of public intellectualism and its relationship to public engagement. Indeed, to what extent can there be public intellectualism without engagement? Conventional wisdom indicates that public intellectuals espouse their views through various forms of the media, and they are generally known by significant parts of the public. Thus during the current era, Elie Wiesel (Boston University), Michael Eric Dyson (University of Pennsylvania), Cornell West (Princeton University), Jeffrey Sachs (Columbia University), Lani Guinier (Harvard University), Doris Kearns Goodwin (Harvard University), and Chinua Achebe (Bard College) might come to mind as illustrations of public intellectuals. Nobel peace laureate Wiesel would likely fit a wide conception of public intellectualism given his intellectual espousals, his direct involvement in public and civic affairs, and his several professorial positions. *The crucial aspect is the nexus between intellectualism and public engagement, whether by one's own direct actions and/or by direct influence on others.*

Decades ago, Bunche recognized the saliency of globalization and its effects on sociopolitical and economic conditions. Taking a global analysis of phenomena is indispensable for public service or public engagement. The three college presidents concurred that globalization must be integrated into the public engagement equation. As the presidents further maintained, developing modes for incorporating public engagement into the curriculum and reward structure will help bring about successful faculty public service by the college community. Creative domestic and international study and co-curricular options would be one illustration. Even then, how might such innovative actions be measured as successes? One illustration cited by the St. Mary's president was the last five student body presidents' direct involvement in the university's neighborhood association. A second illustration entails follow-up surveys with alumni and their involvement with civic and social affairs and organizations.

A tremendous measure of success is acknowledging that long-range solutions can produce enlightened transformative human leaders. Such leaders and their actions will enable them and others to undertake weighty challenges and develop solutions. A relatively unknown episode in Bunche's life explicates this point. Clark Kerr, the renowned chancellor of the University of California, consulted with Bunche (at the time a UN undersecretary) about higher education at Rockefeller Foundation Board meetings. The Rockefeller Foundation is one of the foremost philanthropic foundations that funds research on higher education; its board members would certainly be attuned to the issues affecting postsecondary education. Kerr discussed with Bunche the idea of advancing equality of opportunity. Kerr stated, "I had been most impressed with the argument of Ralph Bunche, also a member of the Rockefeller board, that the worst thing you could do was to start people up a ladder when they had little chance to reach the top, only to have them meet deep disappointment along the way. It was better to get them ready to start up the ladder with adequate preparation and with continuing encouragement and assistance as they climbed up step by step. The real test was not how many got on the first step but how many reached the top" (Kerr, 2001, p. 379). Hesburgh also expressed Bunche's concern that students from ghettos and impoverished backgrounds in the North or South would have opportunities to complete high school and successfully pursue liberal arts degrees (Hesburgh, 2006). Bunche's recommendations contributed to Rockefeller's funding of programs to include diverse groups in colleges and universities. Intellectual tenets articulated in board meetings and communications contributed to public engagement and the public good with little public role by Bunche.

8. An Early Vision of Education

Applying Knowledge to Social Engagement

LORENZO DUBOIS BABER
AND BEVERLY LINDSAY

In the contemporary era, rarely is the legacy of Ralph J. Bunche associated with higher education philosophy. Dr. Bunche's role as a public intellectual is highlighted by his critical work in the field of political science at Howard University, his Nobel-prizeworthy contribution to the United Nations, and his position as an elder statesman in the civil rights movement of the 1960s. Each of these positions offered Bunche the opportunity to comment on developing social phenomena and, particularly in his work at the United Nations, shape public policies and programs. But in refining the intellectual legacy of Bunche, it is important to consider that one of his first public speeches, the 1927 valedictorian address at the University of California at Los Angeles, considered the role of higher education in society. A twenty-three-year-old Bunche encouraged his fellow graduates to use the knowledge they gained during their four years for more than just individual pursuits. Bunche suggested that he and his peers had a special obligation to concern themselves with the unsettled issues in the international community (Bunche cited in Rivlin, 1990).

Viewed in concert with other writings and speeches during Bunche's illustrious career, it is easy to see how his speech of June 1927 can be justly marked as an early philosophical offering from an emerging public intellectual. However, considered on its own merit, Bunche's speech makes a significant contribution to the pragmatic perspective of higher education. Bunche gave the speech during a period when progressive educators, led by John Dewey, were criticized for devaluing academic rigor in pursuit of experience-based learning (Levine, 1986; Ehrlich, 1997).

Almost eighty years later, with civic-minded pedagogy being incorporated at various higher-education institutions through service learning initiatives, it is appropriate to revisit this contribution of Ralph Bunche. In considering Bunche's early vision of higher education, this chapter presents the context that helped shape his speech, focusing on Bunche's undergraduate experience at UCLA and events of the time. Next, Bunche's valedictorian speech is analyzed and compared with theorists familiar in the study of higher education. Finally, this chapter highlights an innovative service learning program at the University of Maryland at Baltimore County as a contemporary example of how Bunche's vision continues to remain relevant. The authors of this chapter, an emerging scholar and established academician, note that the characteristics Bunche recognized as vital to undergraduate education generations ago are being discussed again.

UCLA and Bunche

Had Ralph Bunche been born a generation earlier, he may not have been able to pursue postsecondary education, certainly not at an institution such as UCLA. For African Americans and other working-class citizens, opportunities in higher education were very limited during the late nineteenth century (Geiger, 1999). Despite the development of land grant and predominately African American institutions, the higher education structure in the United States remained an elite system. African American land grant institutions, particularly in the South, were created to maintain a segregated higher education system rather than provide African Americans equal access to established colleges. These institutions, along with private African American colleges set up to educate freedmen, often concentrated on vocational and technical training. The academic pioneers of color who secured access to predominately white institutions faced many obstacles, as illustrated in W. E. B. Du Bois's essay "A Negro Student at Harvard at the End of the Nineteenth Century" (Lewis, 1995).

Three critical trends moved the higher education system toward mass access (Geiger, 1986). Foremost, secondary school access and graduation rates improved, increasing the pool of eligible applicants significantly. From 1920 to 1930, the number of high school graduates increased from 231,000 to 560,000. Second, the first quarter of the twentieth century was a time of prosperity, so more families could send their children away to college for long periods of time. Lastly, as the changing economy created a demand for more educated workers and applicants, a postsecondary education became highly sought after.

The rapid increase in college enrollment coincided with the growth of cities in the United States (Mundt, 1998; Geiger, 1986). Just as land grant universities were established to serve agrarian society in the mid-nineteenth century, urban universities were founded with a primary mission of meeting the educational needs of the growing working class residing near the core of the city. Many urban institutions evolved from normal schools to two-year junior colleges for part-time, commuting students. Often a branch of the large state university, the curriculum tended to consist of practical and applied subjects. As enrollment in higher education continued to increase, junior colleges developed into four-year, bachelor-degree-granting institutions with particular focus on professional education and teaching (Geiger, 1999).

Junior college growth was particularly strong in California as the state population exploded at the turn of the century. Between 1880 and 1914, the population of Los Angeles grew from 11,000 to 350,000 (UCLA, 2005a). Until 1919, the highest postsecondary institution in the area was a branch of the state normal school. In 1919, the California state legislature created the first junior college in California, the "Southern Branch" of the University of California. Located on the site now occupied by Los Angeles City College, the institution maintained its teacher education tradition while adding instruction in letters and sciences. A four-year program was soon offered, and in 1925, the Southern Branch graduated 300 students in its first four-year class. In the fall of 1927, months after Ralph Bunche graduated, the school was renamed the University of California at Los Angeles and broke ground on its new campus in the Westwood section of Los Angeles.

Bunche's access to higher education was not solely due to the timing of his birth but occurred out of family insistence and personal perseverance. In recalling his formative years, Bunche states, "I was an apprehensive and not very confident youth. I had no burning desire to go to college. As a matter of fact, I was able to make good money as a carpet-layer. Actually, I came to the Vermont Avenue Campus that opening day in the fall of 1923, only because of the insistence of a very wise and determined maternal grandmother, for who I had the greatest love and respect" (Bunche, 1969b, p. 5).

At a time when most African Americans were tracked to vocational education in high school, Bunche's grandmother insisted that he take college preparation courses (Rivlin, 1990; Urquhart, 1993; UCLA, 2005b). He was the only African American in his graduating high school class, earning valedictorian status as a result of his academic effort. Although Bunche's high school record was excellent, because of his race he was denied membership into the Ephebians, a citywide honor society. This rejection left him disillusioned about pursuing higher education: "I was aimless, for there was not strong incentive for a black youth . . . to make the long and supposedly formidable sacrifices necessary to attend higher education" (Bunche, 1969b, p. 5).

Fortunately, Bunche's grandmother kept him on the path toward college, and he hit his stride once he landed on campus. Bunche became a varsity athlete in two sports, a respected debater and orator, served as an editor for the annual yearbook, and even earned money trimming the ivy on the old campus buildings (Bunche, 1969b; Urquhart, 1994). His athletic achievements started on the football gridiron before an injury forced him to switch to basketball, where he was a member of three straight conference champion-ship teams. He took part in oratorical contests at UCLA and across the city. He was the founding president of the Southern Branch debating team. "My zest for producing, for achieving, for seeking to excel, quickly sharpened at UCLA, as did my intellectual curiosity. I wanted to learn and enjoyed learn-ing" (UCLA, 2005b).

A small student body and accessible faculty and administrators supported a quality learning environment at UCLA during Bunche's undergraduate years (Urquhart, 1994). Bunche recalls, "Our student body was much smaller in those days, and it almost seemed as though all of us knew each other, though, of course, that was not actually the case. But we students were closely knit in rather cramped quarters because the area of the campus was limited. We came to know many of the professors very well, had a remarkable degree of freedom of access to them, and, for that matter, to top administrative officials as well, from the Provost and the Deans on down the line" (Bunche, 1966, p. 1).

Bunche selected political science as a major, and his civic interests evolved as he began to "look beyond the limited sphere of campus activities" (Bunche, 1969b, p. 5) and towards addressing local and global concerns. In 1926, in a speech entitled "That Man May Dwell in Peace," foundational themes begin to emerge, including opposition to imperialism and the idea that social edu-cation was necessary to generate the global will to achieve peace (Urquhart, 1993). In a particularly sharp oratory delivered to a predominately African American audience in early 1927, Bunche condemned a Los Angeles plan to set up a "colored only" swimming pool. His speech, entitled "Across the Generation Gap," called for all African Americans to boycott the pool. "Any Los Angeles Negro who would go bathing in that dirty hole with that sign 'For Colored Only' gawking down at him in insolent mockery of this Race is either a fool or a traitor to his kind" (Bunche cited in Urquhart, 1994, p. 80). It was apparent upon Bunche's graduation that the aimless, apprehensive youth who had been pushed on the campus in 1923 was gone forever. In his place emerged an idealistic thinker, confident leader, and emerging scholar.

The Fourth Dimension of Personality as a Vision for Higher Education

Upon earning the highest marks in his class at UCLA, Bunche had the opportunity to make a speech during the commencement ceremonies as valedictorian. He immediately consulted one of his favorite mentors, Dr. C. H. Rieber, for a suitable topic (Bunche, 1966). Dr. Rieber, a philosophy professor and dean of the College of Liberal Arts, gave Bunche a volume of poetry by American poet Edna St. Vincent Millay and advised him to "go down to the beach, lie on the sand, read the poems, and reflect" (p. 2). As a result of the inspiration of the poems, and perhaps the natural scenery that surrounded him, Bunche offered to his fellow graduates and their families "The Fourth Dimension of Personality." This speech contains a vision of education grounded in a belief in personal development, social engagement, and civic responsibility.

Personal Development

> Here this morning, after four arduous years of higher education, we confront a new world. If the mission of this education be filled, there is planted in each of us those seeds from which fourth-dimensional personality will spring . . . We need not be less intellectual, we need be more spiritual. We need not think less, only feel more. We shall not only have developed the intellect, we shall have education of the heart. (Bunche, 1927a, p. 222)

Bunche strongly believed that his experience at UCLA had not only expanded his mind, but also cultivated his moral and spiritual development. The campus's small enrollment, 3,500 students at the time of his graduation (Urquhart, 1994), and their status as the "small brother" to the flagship in Berkeley allowed for a more "holistic" experience for students. During this period, a new generation of institutional leaders rejected the conversion to German higher education model of academic specialization, research, and graduate education (Brubacher & Rudy, 1976; Geiger, 1999). One of the most aggressive leaders was William Rainey Harper at the University of Chicago. By 1930, Harper had professionalized student development services at his institution. He predicted that eventually "the individualization of higher education would be achieved by the appointment of special officers who will devote their attention to the students as men and women rather than as minds merely" (Rentz, 1996).

With World War I still fresh in people's minds, it is no surprise that higher education institutions moved toward a refocus on cultivating the personal development of students. Perhaps with memories from the Great War, Bunche borrowed from Rabelais, stating, "Science without conscience—*conscience*—is the depravation of the soul" (Bunche, 1927a, p. 221). In associating a fourth dimension of personality to vision—"that spark of self-development . . . which enables man to grow outwardly as well as inwardly"—Bunche suggests the educational process is not complete upon graduation but is merely the first phase of a lifelong journey of learning.

In 1924, just a year after Bunche arrived at UCLA, one of the first national organizations for student development professionals, the American College Personnel Association, was created (Rentz, 1996). In 1937, the organization released its first statement of purpose, echoing Bunche's comments from a decade earlier: "This philosophy imposes upon educational institutions the obligation to (assist) the student to reach his maximum effectiveness through clarification of his purposes . . . and through progression in religious, emotional, and social development and other nonacademic personal and group relationships" (American Council on Education, 1937).

Social Engagement

> Indisputably, society is essential to civilization. Each of us must be trained as a social being. This not so much an individual concern as it is that of the education systems of the world, the "training grounds" of society. If these institutions are to fulfill their proper obligations to society, they must develop and give to the world socially viable men . . . Since the beginning, the world has boasted sons who have attained the loftiest pinnacles of intellectual development. But with all its mental genius humanity . . . is still plagued by hatreds which lead inevitably to war. (Bunche, 1927a, p. 221)

Beyond a holistic education, young Bunche suggests that higher education produce individuals with an ability to link new knowledge with solving contemporary issues. This view of the social application of knowledge was a basic foundation of the pragmatic philosophy of education during the early twentieth century. Led most notably by Dewey, pragmatists believed students did their best learning not by sitting in class exclusively but through engagement with the social environment surrounding them (Erhlich, 1997). Through personal investigation in a community setting, students could test established ideas in their disciplines to confirm or discover solutions.

As more students demanded access to higher education, traditional educators such as Robert Hutchins challenged the pragmatic approach to higher education (Geiger, 1986; Erhlich, 1997). Traditionalists believed that the pragmatic approach was an attempt to satisfy everyone and that learning should be pursued for its own sake, independent from the practical issues of society. The "intellectual goods" that students gained "are good in themselves and good as means to happiness" (Erhlich, 1997, p. 232).

There is value in having isolated experiences with stimulating literature, exemplified by Bunche's reflective experience on the beach with the poetry of Edna St. Vincent Millay. However, when Bunche states that "man learns and knows but he does not do as well as he knows," he recognizes that knowledge that remains within the circles of the academy has only limited influence on society. Through closing the gap between thought, action, and consequence, graduates can be "purged with the foolish animosities which have caused the world much misery through the ages" (Bunche, 1927a, p. 222).

Bunche's outlook on social engagement brings to mind the work of Ernest Boyer and the scholarship of service (Boyer, 1996). Boyer argued for the need to integrate, communicate, and apply knowledge through service in the community. The ability to use experience to identify an issue, draw upon prior knowledge to search for a solution, and revise accepted practice based on results is necessary for any discipline. This strategy incorporates a construction of knowledge gained through problem-based pedagogy and moves higher education beyond the "ivory tower" concept of learning.

Civic Responsibility

> We know ourselves only as we know other selves. It follows that our one object in an institution of higher learning should be the development of a fully-grown personality—a socially valuable individual. Without such development we can have no broad and abiding sympathy; without it we are mere clansmen or tribesmen, or narrow members of a guild, trade union, or profession. We become self-contained recluses. (Bunche, 1927a, p. 223)

Building upon his principles for personal development and social engagement, Bunche promotes civic virtue for higher education, grounded in a global context. More than developing as a person, beyond engaging in community issues, Bunche suggests that graduates have a responsibility to promote cross-cultural understanding for the betterment of mankind.

This educational vision must have had special meaning for a young Ralph Bunche as an African American during the legalized segregation era in the United States. It is difficult to comprehend how Bunche, along with others of his generation, maintained an unwavering belief in others in a society that offered him only second-class membership for most of his life. Yet beginning with this speech in 1927, Bunche exhibited a strong commitment to democracy. He suggests that graduates become "large-hearted citizens of the Universal," viewing other countries as neighbors within the same society (Bunche, 1927a, p. 223). He concludes his speech with an optimistic cheer, "So much we have in common with the youth of all lands—as we go, so goes the world!"

The role of American higher education in engaging in civic virtue has been debated for centuries (Dewey, 1916; Kerr, 1963; Wolff, 1969). One perspective supports the objectivity of the university as necessary to maintain its autonomous nature. A clear boundary between higher education and societal values is essential to protect the pursuit of scientific research. An alternative view states that an institution both implicitly and explicitly expresses a set of core institutional values through the character of the student body, faculty, and staff. The question is not whether values are espoused, but what values are institutionalized and made normative.

In considering the contemporary global reality, Bunche's call for an international vision is especially poignant. "Citizens of the world," a term offered by Nussbaum (1997), is an important part, as higher education cannot afford to produce individuals who lack the skills to communicate and problem solve across different cultures. As Gutmann (1990) argues, the challenge for higher education is settling the tension between the value of individual freedom and civic virtue. In particular, Americans value the freedom to choose while simultaneously demanding the development of common social good. Gutmann offers a democratic alternative—a democratic theory of education. This perspective does not merely collapse civic virtue into individual freedom, or vise versa. In the spirit of diplomacy that defined Bunche, democratic theory of education offers public debate about an issue "in a way which is more likely to increase our understanding of education and each other" (p. 13)

In his typical humble manner, Bunche recalled his commencement speech in a 1966 letter: "I came up with a topic, a rather esoteric one, which seemed good to me, although to this day I cannot truthfully say that I really ever understood its meaning, and much less the substance of the speech I made under it. It was high-sounding and mellow enough" (Bunche, 1966, p. 2). An in-depth analysis offers plenty of meaning and substance in the speech, particularly for a recent graduate. Although his academic focus was political science and he established a legendary career in international diplomacy, in May 1927, a young Ralph Bunche established an early vision of higher education.

Bunche's Education Vision Reflected in Current Practice

Many would not associate Ralph Bunche with current professional practices occurring at higher education institutions. However, his vision is embedded in many co-curricular programs, most notably service learning initiatives. In various forms, service learning has been a part of postsecondary education as far back as the Morrill Act in 1862 when outreach extension became a part of the mission for state institutions (Campus Compact, 2005). As higher education institutions developed in concert with the population shift toward the city, outreach became particularly important (Maurrasse, 2001). Colleges and universities located in urban areas, such as UCLA in the 1920s, have traditionally maintained a strong connection with local neighborhoods through community outreach.

Similar to UCLA, the University of Maryland, Baltimore County (UMBC) was established as a response to the postsecondary enrollment growth in Maryland during the 1960s (Tatarewicz, 2004). Established in 1966 as commuter campus, UMBC helped ease the enrollment burden of the larger University of Maryland at College Park. Rapidly developing into a residential research institution, UMBC has an undergraduate enrollment of just under 10,000 students, 43 percent of whom belong to traditionally underrepresented ethnic groups (UMBC, 2005a). In 2002, UMBC ranked sixteenth in the country in NASA funding and 40 percent of its graduating students went directly to graduate or professional school.

A contemporary example of service learning in an urban environment is the Shriver Living-Learning Center (SLLC) at UMBC. Established in 1993 in honor of former ambassador Sargent Shriver and his wife, Eunice Kennedy Shriver, the mission of the center includes deepening students' sense of civic responsibility and broadening the meaning of scholarship to include not only research and teaching but the application of knowledge (Shriver Center, 2005). The center mission also urges faculty and students to link their academic work more effectively to urgent social issues and to advance the common good through applied projects and public advocacy (Hrabowski, Lee, & Martello, 1999).

The SLLC sponsors many programs in the city of Baltimore where students can offer their service. One initiative is the Choice Initiative Program, which targets adolescent truancy, delinquency, and school dropouts. Undergraduate students serve as mentors to over 1,100 adjudicated youth in the Baltimore area during each academic year. Students help provide support to the youth and their families thorough efforts that are community based and family centered (Hrabowski, Lee, & Martello, 1999).

In 2000, the SLLC and the Office of Residential Life at UMBC partnered to create the first living-learning center on campus (UMBC, 2005b). Students in the center lived together on a floor and took academic classes together.

The program is targeted to traditional first-year students, who are selected through an application process. Most students who are interested were highly involved in community service during their high school years. Their service commitment was about three to five hours per week and participation in service is noted on their transcript. The academic coursework includes a one-credit course in the fall, Sociology 396. The pass-fail course covers issues of changing American society and the ways that social structures influence the community in which their service sites reside. At the end of the fall semester, the students present to the provost and other university officials policy solutions to problems they have encountered at their service sites. For example, a group of students examined the state of Maryland's State Children's Health Insurance Program (SCHIP) and made suggestions, based on their examination of the program and their experience in the community, to adjust SCHIP in ways that would improve prenatal care for expectant mothers residing in underdeveloped areas (personal communication, 2004).

In many ways, the SLLC at UMBC represents Bunche's early vision of education. In separate interviews with two practitioners working with the program (one concentrating on the residential education component, the other focused on coordinating service sites), themes from their current practice consistently related to observations Bunche offered almost eighty years ago. Neither administrator knew much about Bunche prior to our discussion, and each were offered passages from his 1927 speech during the interview. As one administrator commented, "It's amazing that he was saying the kinds of things in 1927 that we, years later, are saying now" (personal communication, 2004).

Personal Development

In commenting on Bunche's call for higher education to cultivate the "fourth dimension of personality," the residential education practitioner stated, "Our whole goal is to teach how to interact with others in effective ways, how to set norms, and how to handle conflicts—the things that students will need to do when they leave UMBC and enter the community" (personal communication, 2004). He continued, "Development is a slow process. You plant a seed, but you are not sure how long it will be before it sprouts." Continuing with the same metaphor as Bunche, the practitioner's comments mirrored Bunche's vision. Offering resources for a holistic educational experience in hopes of seeing personal growth was one goal of the program. However, the practitioner offered that there is still a struggle to define "what a well-rounded person should look like."

Another interesting challenge in student development is offered by the second practitioner, who stated, "The challenge [will be] the cost of higher education. The competing demands on students may move [them] away from the idea that there is time to become that complete person through your education experience." Students are increasingly working more hours as they attend full-time, delaying postsecondary enrollment, or attending multiple institutions at the same time (Borden, 2004).

A third issue in attending to personal development is the struggle to quantify program effectiveness. As budgets at higher education institutions are increasingly stretched, departments are forced to justify funding through statistics that represent their success. While there is intuitive and anecdotal evidence of success, future student affairs practitioners must find ways to improve assessment techniques in order to continue the "education of the heart."

Social Engagement

Ernest Boyer served as the chair of the Shriver Living-Learning Center's founding National Advisory Board until his death in 1995, so the program is a living testimony to his work in social engagement. One practitioner commented, "It was Boyer who talked about the ivory tower notion of the university and what good is knowledge that is created on that campus and inside the wall of academe that isn't translated out to direct service to the population."

The "training grounds" (Bunche's phrase) the SLLC provides students are located in some of the most underserved areas of Baltimore. For example, students work at after-school programs at the College Gardens Community Center, located in a neighborhood suffering from urban poverty. Simultaneously, they are learning theories about social institutions and change in their class. One practitioner said, "They are taking the knowledge gained from the class [and] pairing that with the real life experiences they have at the site [to produce] a recommendation that policymakers and legislative members can take a look at."

The first practitioner talked about the benefits for students of dealing with real community issues. He stated, "It's a pretty big thing to wrestle with, but it forces them to examine why is it that I'm going to a site five hours a week that doesn't have enough books; what is the real reason behind this?" He continued, "They learn that there is no magic wand . . . public policy problems exist for very real reasons. What they really get out of this learning experience is they learn root causes of problems . . . making them more effective advocates and activists later."

Beyond developing the "socially viable" student, institutional social engagement is important because it maintains a social relevance with the local community. As a practitioner put it, "The challenge is understanding relevance in a time of fiscal hardships." As higher education competes with other government services, such as secondary education and law enforcement, the ability to prove social value becomes critical. While the Shriver program is primarily funded by sources outside the university, SLLC observers see a correlation between state funding decreases and foundation giving decreases, as national philanthropic organizations are less inclined to increase their burden as they observe a reduction of state support.

Civic Responsibility

There is a stereotype that young people are less inclined to embrace their civic responsibilities. However, as one practitioner concludes, participants in the SLLC seem to develop an "abiding sympathy" for addressing social issues although it may not necessarily manifest into democratic participation. "I think there is a sense to what their role is as a citizen. It doesn't necessarily result in more direct political engagement; sometimes students feel that traditional politics have [caused the blight conditions of the service site]." The practitioner continued:

> The initial quote you talked about ["We know ourselves only as we know other selves . . ."], people not seeing themselves as segments or fractions of a larger society . . . I don't know if that is the commonly held vision today. The notion of what values should guide it, what values should be espoused prevents many of us from reaching that place. Everyone probably would say that eliminating racism, poverty, and strife is good, but people have different views about how that ought to happen. Often people examine the program[s] we do at the Shriver Center and see them as part of a liberal agenda, so political ideology confounds (how others feel about our work).

Bunche's observation on the role of higher education in fostering civic engagement is especially critical in a period when public debate often reduces complex issues to two sides, fostering "self-contained reclusion" rather than in-depth interaction and thought. As University of Pennsylvania president Amy Gutmann recently stated, "We are living in a smash-mouth culture in which extremists dominate public debate to the point of hijacking it" (R. Jones, 2005). In contrast to Gutmann's observation, Bunche's vision reflects an optimistic nature so consistent throughout his illustrious career and should serve as inspiration for higher education practitioners as they seek to validate their work. The potential result—a society that is more selfless and less selfish, more inclusive and less stratified, more democratic and less elitist—is a goal worth pursuing even eighty years after Bunche's articulation of it.

Transitioning from Bunche's UCLA to Contemporary Urban Universities

If we examine a range of comprehensive urban universities such as UMBC, Duke University, and UCLA, we note in their strategic plans and institutional mission statements regarding service and social engagement with local urban areas. In our conversations with UMBC president Freeman Hrabowski, he stressed the important role urban universities serve in addressing continuing social inequities in American cities such as Baltimore. In her tenure, former Duke University president Nannerl Keohane encouraged social science departments and the Duke Medical School to create innovative programs that assisted disadvantaged residents in the Durham area. Both these presidents are attuned to the urban milieu that currently exists near their campuses.

If we review the emerging UCLA campus in the 1920s when Bunche was a student, we note that the institution grew in concert with the city of Los Angeles, moving from a two-year college to four-year university within a ten-year period. A comparative contemporary example is the development of UMBC and the expansion of Baltimore. A young Ralph Bunche was involved in the Los Angeles community, for example in his involvement against the development of a segregated pool. If we juxtapose Bunche's experiences in the 1920s against the current activities at the SLLC, we observe that UMBC students also engage directly with community issues rather than relying on secondary observations and assessments. Their academic courses enable them to build upon their experiences in co-curricular activities. Might these students be budding intellectuals? They may not all become valedictorians of their class, but they are armed with both scholarly and real experiences as they prepare to navigate the rough terrain of an ever-changing world.

When one compares the world of 1927 to today, there are comparable contexts within both society and higher education. Like the period after World War I, growing extremism and nationalism have created escalating tension in the international community. In the United States, as in the pre-Depression era, material obsession and excess highlight the growing gaps among socioeconomic groups. In postsecondary education, increasing access coupled with shifting demographics is causing a growth in the nontraditional student population. With these global, national, and institutional contexts, it is not difficult to see why Bunche's valedictorian speech remains relevant today.

As an emerging public intellectual, young Bunche was uninhibited in offering his observations, a characteristic explored earlier in this volume. Further, he offers a direction for his fellow students, grounded in their use of "the fourth dimension of personality." As this chapter demonstrates, a link between Bunche's thoughts as a young man and current practices in student affairs can be espoused.

In May 1969, forty-two years after his valedictorian speech, Bunche returned to UCLA for the dedication of a campus building—Ralph Bunche Hall—in his honor. In his remarks, Bunche stated, "UCLA was where it all began for me. In a certain sense, it was where I began, because college for me was the genesis and the catalyst" (Bunche, 1969b, p. 4). As Bunche's rightful place in American history continues to be restored, his early vision of higher education should be recognized, studied, and appreciated by students, professionals, and emerging scholars alike.

PART III

Diplomats
Articulating Diplomacy

9. Diplomat in Pursuit of the International Interest

EDWIN SMITH

Few remember that, along with other prominent and prolific colleagues at the Department of State, Ralph Bunche was "present at the creation" of the United Nations (Acheson, 1969).[1] As a member of the U.S. delegation (Urquhart, 1993) to the seminal San Francisco negotiations that formed the "United Nations Organization," Bunche participated significantly in the drafting of the foundational charter that remains in force to this day. Shortly after that, Bunche became one of the international civil servants that launched the bureaucracy that administered that charter.

Bunche's involvement in efforts to preserve international peace came at a time when most observers assumed that diplomats would conduct their standard discourse by using time-honored approaches involving predictable practices such as diplomatic immunity, formal exchanges of negotiating credentials, and ceremonial, status-based protocols of interaction. Little did the participants understand the scope of the tectonic changes to the international order that were underway. Ralph Bunche became intensely involved in those changes, receiving international acclaim for his efforts. However, scholars have appreciated neither the novel context within which he undertook those efforts, nor the ingenuity nor creativity with which he pursued his objective. Intuitively and resourcefully, Ralph Bunche helped to alter the approaches by which states and international organizations respond to threats to global peace and security.

Specifically, Ralph Bunche faced several novel elements in his effort to mediate the Arab-Israeli conflict of 1948. His attempt at mediation took place under the aegis of the United Nations (UN), an international institution recently founded through the cooperation of the preeminent powers of the international community. In addition, he found himself involved with the newly born state of Israel, a negotiating entity that was inaugurated by a vote of that same international organization. Third, Bunche undertook resolution of an ongoing conflict where neither the Arabs nor the Israelis had prevailed militarily; most prior settlements had followed practical ascendancy by one of the combatant adversaries. Finally, because the disputants still contested the issues, Bunche pursued only the cessation of battlefield conflict, holding the larger political settlement in abeyance. As a result, he was able to reach an armistice, but the conflict continues to this day, providing some early lessons on limited international conflict resolution.

As states and institutions confront the twenty-first century, new shifts in the global order cause new uncertainties. While diplomats still rely on many of the approaches adopted by foreign ministries and international organizations in the early years of the UN, the global political landscape has changed yet again. Transnational interdependence has increased, generating both positive and negative consequences for the world's population; the negative consequences have caused many to question the value of globalization. Partially in result, destructive and malevolent individuals and groups have caused sporadic havoc around the globe. The familiar practices of international diplomacy, dispute resolution, and peacekeeping afford only limited assistance in the current circumstances.

These changes in the global political and social landscape force new and creative techniques at conflict resolution. Governmental decision makers will be forced to address the interests of small groups with ambiguous formal legitimacy but great potential for mayhem and disruption. National law enforcement and domestic security forces will be required to consider global threats, requiring transnational cooperation for effective prevention and response. Military leaders will face the necessity of balancing precise application of lethal force with minimal consequences to noncombatants. Officials facing these considerations must adopt novel approaches as they seek to address new international turmoil and instability.

Modern scholars and diplomats may benefit from examining the approaches and innovations adopted by Bunche. By making a considered comparative evaluation of Bunche's situation and of contemporary circumstances and context, scholars can assist policymakers in fashioning responses to the daunting challenges of the evolving global political environment.

Traditional Negotiations

In order to understand the context of Bunche's accomplishment as mediator, we must briefly examine the traditional methods used by diplomats and statesmen in addressing international conflicts. Developed over hundreds of years, these diplomatic practices evolved into a formal choreography that enabled governments to communicate their perceptions of the relative importance of other governments through the manner and content of routine intergovernmental communications. This diplomatic praxis formed the background for Bunche's efforts to mediate the Arab-Israeli conflict of 1948–49. However, shifts in the international environment forced Bunche to improvise, adopting new techniques.

The city-states of northern Italy began the practice of exchanging resident diplomatic representatives in the fifteenth century (Hamilton & Langhorne, 1995). Those states initiated that practice prior to both the Reformation and the Peace of Westphalia (Nussbaum, 1954).[2] Although contemporary skeptics complained that diplomatic practice encouraged the voluntary admission of foreign spies, the sending and reception of diplomatic missions came to be widely adopted across Europe because of its utility in political interactions. That traditional diplomatic practice came to involve several identifiable dimensions.

First, the representatives of foreign princes that were assigned to reside at the seat of a foreign government served as formal representatives of the sending government. In earlier times, religious representatives had served on occasion as neutral messengers from one prince to another. In other contexts, respected merchants from one city had negotiated commercial arrangements in another city. Among the Italian city-states, formal diplomatic practice evolved into the designation of individuals who acted as the formal representative of the sending ruler to communicate with the receiving ruler.

Second, those new diplomats gained particular protections. Sending and receiving rulers acknowledged customary norms by which they treated each other as sovereigns possessing formal legal equality, in spite of obvious political and military discrepancies. Rulers acknowledged each others' representatives with a formality and ceremony consistent with the status of their sovereign principals. Ambassadors customarily gained protection of and immunity from the receiving sovereign in a manner analogous to the immunity received by a visiting head of state. The practices of diplomatic immunity became standard and expected.

Third, as the status of the ambassador as a representative of the foreign sovereign gained acceptance, those ambassadors became the solitary legitimate avenues of communication between sovereigns. Prior to that time, there were no formal international organizations and few international conferences of any sort. With the formal appointment of ambassadors, bilateral diplomacy could become the standard practice. If interaction with several states was required, that contact was most often conducted serially; this pattern allowed each sovereign to retain control over the process of negotiation. The practice of conducting diplomacy through international conferences arose at a later date (Kissinger, 1994; Hamilton & Langhorne, 1995).

Under these circumstances, diplomacy evolved to provide a reliable alternative means of conducting political interaction between sovereigns. It provided a less impassioned and more routine avenue of communication whose use did not signal an impending clash. Messages could be exchanged between monarchs in measured and calculated ways by interlocutors who used formal protocol and measured language to avoid unwanted controversy. Sovereigns could resort to coercion and violence when they thought it useful, and military power remained the final measure of relative status. However, the choice of the use of force became a means to political ends (Rapaport, 1982), not the inevitable result of disputes between kingdoms. In this limited manner, diplomacy mitigated the resort to violence. Further, disputants could enter diplomatic agreements to resolve and stabilize the circumstances arising after the cessation of military violence.

By the nineteenth century, some political actors came to believe that the principles and practices of governments and monarchs could be understood to reflect binding legal principles by which the future actions of states should be evaluated. International legal scholars had long maintained that states were bound by customary norms that could be inductively identified from the evaluation of patterns of state action. At the close of the Napoleonic Wars, the dominant powers of Europe formed the Concert of Europe to facilitate diplomatic settlement of disputes that could devolve into military conflict. That arrangement and the diplomatic relationships that it initiated served to prevent catastrophic war in Europe for a century (Kissinger, 1994). By the waning years of the nineteenth century, this combination of diplomatic practices and legal conceptions led to formal multilateral treaties intended to mitigate the horrors of modern war. Initially, some governments negotiated these agreements for pragmatic purposes to limit the means by which force was employed in wartime. By the beginning of the twentieth century, diplomats from many states were engaged in substantial efforts to reduce the calamitous effects of warfare (Roberts & Guelff, 2000). In addition, states reached agreements committing themselves to the use of peaceful means to resolve disputes (Instructions to the U.S. Delegation, 2000).

These agreements manifested diplomatic endeavors intended to establish principles and procedures for peaceful settlements and to minimize the destructive consequences when peaceful settlement efforts failed. Unfortunately, those conventions did not alter the power relationships that defined international politics. Those relationships crumbled catastrophically in 1914.

Diplomacy could not prevent either the threat of violence or the resort to violence, and treaties to mitigate warfare could not prevent the most devastating war that humanity had ever generated.

Nevertheless, diplomats responded at the conclusion of the carnage by negotiating the Treaty of Versailles, which established the League of Nations, the first permanent intergovernmental organization, "to promote international co-operation and to achieve international peace and security by the acceptance of obligations not to resort to war by the prescription of open, just and honourable relations between nations by the firm establishment of the understandings of international law as the actual rule of conduct among governments, and by the maintenance of justice and a scrupulous respect for all treaty obligations in the dealings of peoples with one another" (Instructions to the U.S. Delegation, 2000).

Some of the diplomats and leaders of the prewar movement toward the institutionalization of peaceful dispute settlement renewed their efforts, having been horrified by the waste of World War I. Other leaders sought mechanisms primarily to limit the possibility that any of the vanquished states could rise to military or political power again. The drafters of the Treaty of Versailles attempted to strike a balance between imposition of political retribution and institutionalization of preventive diplomacy. They created an enduring transnational multilateral forum that rested on a broader foundation than the intermittent and limited arrangement of the Concert of Europe of the preceding century. But while all diplomats and leaders stood aghast at the carnage of the first global war, they came to different conclusions as to the best mechanisms for ensuring future peace. As a result, the drafters of the Versailles agreement incorporated inherent contradictions between provisions for retrospective political retribution and mechanisms for prospective conflict prevention.

While many initially doubted the efficacy of the League of Nations as a forum for peaceful settlement and diplomacy, the outbreak of an even larger conflict provided irrefutable evidence of its failure. Between 1939 and 1945, tens of millions died in a conflict of immense dimensions. As World War II ended, diplomats and leaders initiated a new effort to build an effective international institution to prevent another descent into the abyss of war. This new institution, the United Nations, was structured to avoid the evident inadequacies of the League.

The drafters of the Charter of the United Nations implemented several specific arrangements to remedy the failings of its predecessor. First, they insured that the structure of the UN permitted politically powerful states to play a role commensurate with their status. Further, they created an institution with a membership broad enough to engage most of the political and social movements in the world. In addition, they began a process intended to eliminate the colonial domination of large parts of the globe's population by a few European powers. Finally, they crafted a detailed system for the application of coercive means to protect international peace and security. At the end of the second global clash, many leaders developed renewed optimism for the potential for the peaceful settlement of international disputes and were hopeful that the main enterprise of a new diplomacy would now use multilateral persuasion rather than bilateral intimidation.

New Negotiation Context

The drafters of the UN charter created a novel institutional structure built upon elements drawn from the earlier League of Nations. The charter established a select executive Security Council, which included the five indispensable victorious global powers. The Security Council was to have supreme authority on matters involving international peace and security. The drafters also crafted the General Assembly, a broad body including all member states of the United Nations that is authorized to address any matters not included on the Security Council's agenda. The charter architects also included a body to address economic and social questions and a global judicial forum to settle international disputes. Finally, these authors included a Trusteeship Council for oversight and development toward the independence of nonselfgoverning territories.[3] As the director of the staff of this body, Ralph Bunche's work intimately intertwined him in the Arab-Israeli dispute, a role that led to his receipt of the Nobel Prize.

Contemporary diplomats recognized that the Arab-Israeli dispute constituted a threat to international peace and security, but they quickly discovered that the instrumentality that they had crafted had serious limitations. Based on the infrastructure that they developed after World War II, the designers of the UN must have assumed that the principal dangers to international security involved the use of military force by one established state against another. The charter text indicates that they did not perceive themselves as sanctioned to inquire into the constitutional legitimacy or internal politics of any state. However, they did understand the charter as authorizing collective enforcement action against any state engaging in cross-border aggression against another state. The Arab-Israeli dispute involved violence against a newly formed entity by states that contended that the new entity lacked legitimate status. As a consequence, any national or organizational response to the crisis entailed significant political and legal implications for those responding.

In addition, at that point in its history the United Nations occupied a novel position on the international plane. Although international organizations had existed previously, earlier bodies had limited and technical mandates allowing them to control traffic on international rivers or exchanges of international mail. The authors of the charter gave the UN broad authorization to involve itself on the global scene in matters previously addressed only by states. The secretary-general, receiving administrative support in his endeavors from the UN Secretariat, performed many functions generally undertaken by a foreign minister. However, he lacked the clear legal and political imprimatur of a state for his endeavors, placing him and the officers of the Secretariat in a new and ambiguous role in international diplomacy. The new diplomatic game had new players occupying unfamiliar positions. After the assassination of Count Folke Bernadotte, the first UN mediator in Palestine (Urquhart, 1993, p. 158), the organization learned that these new roles could become fatal.

Finally, these diplomats encountered a geopolitical landscape that differed substantially from the terrain anticipated at Dumbarton Oaks and San Francisco. Allied leaders conceptualized the United Nations as an organization based upon the cooperation of states sharing a common goal of preservation of international peace and security. That conception germinated in the common struggle to overcome Axis aggression, a struggle that partially shrouded economic and ideological differences among the Allied powers. Those differences became more evident as the war ended. Just a few years after the war, political conflict between the former allies became thorny, forcing sober reconsideration of the optimistic plans for the UN. In addition, populations residing in European colonies in Africa and Asia pressed impatiently for self-determination in spite of the UN's trusteeship arrangements; some movements resorted to guerilla violence. These circumstances frustrated the evolution of the institutional infrastructure contemplated in the planning of the UN, forcing the new global body to improvise hasty responses in circumstances involving violence and instability.

In the midst of these broad global shifts, Ralph Bunche became involved in playing an unanticipated role in novel circumstances. He applied the available tools of negotiation and diplomacy artfully, receiving international acclaim as a consequence. However, while he succeeded in his immediate task, he did not address the fundamental causes of instability and violence that persist to this day. His inability may have resulted from the inappropriateness of the contemporary diplomatic and political tools for the novel situations and actors that he confronted. Bunche's efforts merit new examination under the present circumstances since present-day leaders and diplomats face disturbances arising from the current generation of unconventional actors and novel situations.

The Fortuitous Diplomat

Ralph Bunche did not plan to become a famous international mediator. He was called to the task because of an emergency: the UN needed to continue an effort to stop large-scale fighting, and the UN's first mediator had been assassinated. Although he had participated in diplomatic drafting conferences, Bunche had no formal training or practical experience as a mediator nor was he a representative of a powerful nation. Yet, despite his obstacles, he succeeded in reaching settlements in four separate negotiations within a six-month period, relying on his own determination, intelligence, and personal integrity to persuade violent opponents to settle their differences through mediation and negotiation rather than military domination.

Bunche came to this historic station because he did not fit into stereotypical positions. He brought distinctive academic training and a unique personal and cultural background to the task. His initial career was academic, teaching courses in political science. However, at each stage of his life, his interests broadened and he learned new and unique perspectives. His interests in political science combined with his African American heritage and life experiences led him to develop an expertise on African politics and development at a time when few others in the United States had any significant knowledge of the area. His academic background and his awareness of the politics of cultural differences led to broader research. The world-renowned scholar Gunnar Myrdal (1944) relied on Bunche to assist in researching his seminal study on African Americans in the United States. As World War II began and the strategic importance of the continent of Africa became obvious, his reputation as a researcher and an expert on Africa led the government to call on Bunche to assist in the war effort. When World War II ended, Bunche was delegated to participate in the creation of the new United Nations, an assignment that allowed his escape from the distasteful "Jim Crow" environs of Washington, D.C. (Urquhart, 1993, p. 135).

Ralph Bunche participated in the formation of the infrastructure of the United Nations at several different levels. He served the U.S. delegation in the negotiating conference at Dumbarton Oaks, during which representatives of the United States, the United Kingdom, China, and the Soviet Union hammered at many of the central principles for the planned United Nations (Finch, 1945; Hudson, 1945; Urquhart, 1993, pp. 111–114). Bunche also participated with the U.S. delegation in the final drafting of the UN charter at the San Francisco conference that adopted the charter; he made significant contributions to the drafting of the articles on UN trusteeship of nonselfgoverning territories (Urquhart, 1993, p. 116 *et seq.*). His drafting skills impressed the diplomats assembled at San Francisco, and he was assigned to the U.S. delegations to the preparatory conferences and to the first meeting of the General Assembly of the United Nations (Urquhart, 1993, p. 125 *et seq.*). Bunche's name again came to the fore when international diplomats considered personnel for permanent participation on the staff of the new organization. His superior performance motivated Trygvie Lie, the newly designated secretary general, to request Bunche's service as director of the Trusteeship Division of the Secretariat of the UN (Urquhart, 1993, p. 134). His colleagues and superiors recognized Bunche's promise as a valuable member of a new community of international civil servants.

Bunche left the state department when he was appointed director of the Trusteeship Division. The Trusteeship Council, one of the permanent organs of the new UN, was intended to facilitate the process by which colonies would become independent state members of the United Nations. Since Bunche had played a central role in formulating the trusteeship provisions of the UN charter, he provided a good foundation upon which to build the nascent bureaucracy. However, shortly after Bunche was selected for the directorship, the UN confronted the beginning of a problem that remains with us to this day. That problem involved the formation of the state of Israel and the status of Palestine.

The Arab-Israeli Conflict: The Initial Fighting

At the end of World War II, citizens and governments across the globe faced the undeniable evidence of the Holocaust perpetrated by the Nazis. The global dilemma generated by the need to provide for the Jewish survivors and refugees in Europe caused many to dream of a Jewish homeland, with significant Jewish and non-Jewish support existing for the Zionist dream to establish that homeland in Palestine (Instructions to the U.S. Delegation, 2000; Fromkin, 1990). The United Kingdom's resistance at first frustrated the realization of that vision. The UK, having acquired a mandate over Palestine and Transjordan[4] under the Versailles Treaty that settled the disputes of World War I, refused to allow unrestricted immigration of Jewish refugees in order to preserve the demographic balance between the indigenous Arab and Jewish populations. However, sporadic fighting and terrorist actions led the British to announce that withdrawal from the region was the United Kingdom's only option; they could not resolve the conflict between the Jewish and Arab populations of Palestine (Morris, 2001).

When the United Nations established a special committee to inquire into the situation in Palestine in May 1947 (G.A. Res. 106, 1947), Secretary-General Lie gave the task to the UN's trusteeship office, specifically designating Bunche to support the inquiry. In this capacity, Bunche got his first exposure to Palestine (Urquhart, 1993, p. 140). After visits to displaced persons camps in Europe and to Palestine itself, a divided committee favored a partition of Palestine between the Jewish and non-Jewish populations. Bunche wrote a report that captured all perspectives on partition. On November 29, 1947, the UN General Assembly adopted Resolution 181 over Arab objections, ending the British mandate in Palestine and authorizing partition of the area into independent Jewish and Arab entities (G.A. Res. 181, 1947).

Large-scale violence in Palestine followed the adoption of Resolution 181 as hostile terrorist groups traded attacks on the Jewish and Arab residents of Palestine, taking the dimensions of a Jewish-Arab civil war. British military and civilian officials also became popular targets for assault, causing the British to hasten their departure from their mandate. As the British prepared to depart, the Jewish shadow government moved to take over the governmental and economic infrastructure of Palestine while large numbers of the Arab middle and upper classes began to leave (UN Document S/743, 1948). As with the initial violence, governments, politicians, historians, and activists have engaged in bitter recriminations about the origins of the contemporary Arab Palestinian refugee problem.

As Jewish military forces succeeded in controlling a substantial portion of western Palestine, the surrounding Arab states mobilized military forces to resist. The civil war evolved into an interstate war when the Jewish shadow government declared the independence of Israel on May 14, 1948. The surrounding Arab states moved with force "to establish security and order instead of chaos and disorder" (Morris, 2001, pp. 215–218). Military units from Syria, Iraq, Lebanon, Jordan, and Egypt entered Palestine. After some initial setbacks, Israeli forces proved themselves to be capable and adequately equipped. In contrast, the Arab forces proved to be poorly trained and limited by weak logistical support; the principal exception to the generally poor Arab performance was the Jordanian Arab Legion (Morris, 2001, p. 221).

Although the Arab states all articulated the same intention to prevent the formation of a Jewish state in Palestine, those states actually pursued inconsistent objectives with radically different results. Jordan advanced only as far as the partition line established by the UN (Morris, 2001, pp. 221–222).[5] Since Jordan fielded the most professional of the Arab military forces, its restricted participation in the first Arab-Israeli War reduced the risks faced by the Jewish forces (Shlaim, 1988). While the fighting continued, King Abdullah had been conducting secret negotiations with the Jewish leaders over control of Palestine (Morris, 2001, p. 227).

Egypt, Iraq, Lebanon, and Syria undertook less extensive campaigns, and were less successful. Egypt occupied a stretch of the coast of Palestine and some portions of the Negev desert, but refused to take part in the planned offensive action toward Tel Aviv. Iraq engaged in some limited action covering the right flank of the Jordanian advance. Syria made a minor incursion into Palestine, while Lebanon made none at all (Morris, 2001, pp. 230–234).

By the end of the war, the Jewish irregular contingents had evolved into a formidable, coherent fighting force, strengthened by the immigration of experienced combat veterans from Europe and North America. Israel had seized control over many areas that had been allocated to the Arabs under the terms of Resolution 181. The Arab armies found themselves forced to face their own technological inadequacies and poor performance. Under these circumstances, a negotiated cease-fire became feasible.

Initial Settlement Efforts

To facilitate an end to the fighting, the General Assembly authorized appointment of a special mediator for Palestine (General Assembly Resolution 186, 1948). Count Folke Bernadotte was appointed special mediator by the UN Security Council on May 20, 1949; he began the slow process of negotiating a truce. Secretary-General Lie asked Ralph Bunche to meet Bernadotte in Palestine to assist in the mediation process.

Bernadotte and Bunche succeeded in mediating a cease-fire after substantial efforts on June 11, 1948; that cease-fire was scheduled to last for four weeks. Immediately on the end of the cease-fire, the parties resumed hostilities on a reduced scale in early July 1948. Bernadotte and Bunche renewed their efforts at settlement. Although a new truce was negotiated, Bunche and Bernadotte continued to pursue a more stable armistice; their continued efforts to quell repeated violations of the truce met with mixed success until September 1948.

On September 17, 1948, during a mediation trip to Jerusalem, Bunche and Bernadotte became separated, Bunche's flight to Israel having been delayed by mechanical problems. Count Bernadotte departed by car to Jerusalem, without Bunche and accompanied by a French observer, Colonel André Sérot. Before their arrival, their automobile was halted by a roadblock and Count Bernadotte and Colonel Sérot were assassinated by assailants disguised in Israeli army uniforms.

The Security Council, horrified by these events, appointed Bunche to continue the settlement efforts in the region. The council designated Bunche as the new acting mediator, and Bunche endeavored to honor Bernadotte by redoubling his efforts to find an enduring peaceful settlement. Renewed pressures imposed by the UN and powerful member states forced the parties in the conflict to consider participation in the mediation of an armistice.

The Acting Mediator

It would be tempting to conduct a detailed analysis of Bunche's historic accomplishments in the 1949 negotiations, but that task is beyond the scope of this discussion. However, one point must be made. In undertaking a search for an armistice to settle the Arab-Israeli War of 1948–49, Bunche confronted a myriad of obstacles. Some of these impediments would have been familiar to anyone engaged in negotiation, but a number of them were unique. Exploring these obstacles and his responses to them permits us to gain a deeper appreciation of the scope of his accomplishments. That exploration may encourage others to engage in more systematic study of the diplomatic history of those events.

First, as acting mediator, Bunche sought an immediate end to the violence in Palestine.[6] He knew that the immediate issues involved the military forces on the ground, and that those issues had to be resolved in order to halt the fighting. However, Bunche was also aware of the scope of underlying problems that led to the conflict (Urquhart, 1993, p. 194). He knew that the introduction of a substantial new Jewish population into Palestine would cause upheaval and resistance. Bunche also knew that resolution of issues raised by the new Palestinian diaspora would remain problematic regardless of any contemporary armistice. Clearly all of these issues required resolution in order to reach a permanent peace.

The military positions of the parties held significant implications for the resolution of broader issues in the conflict in Palestine. The new Israeli state wanted to preserve its acquisition of territory beyond the boundaries of the initial partition resolution. Israel also sought undisputed control over Jerusalem. The Arab states intended to prevent Israeli control over Jerusalem; in addition, they needed to maintain control over the coastal Gaza strip then occupied by Egyptian forces. The Arabs were concerned about the fate of Palestinian refugees, but the extent to which that concern mandated specific Arab responses remained unclear.[7] Bunche understood that these issues could endure as a smoldering source of difficulties in the region (Urquhart, 1993, pp. 194–195).

Bunche immediately improvised on the breadth of his mandate to initiate negotiations. In his role as acting mediator, he had authority under two Security Council resolutions. The first (Security Council Resolution 61, 1948) called on the parties to establish a truce and to establish negotiations between the parties, with the acting mediator to determine terms if the parties failed to agree. However, the resolution also established a Security Council committee to advise and assist the acting mediator. In contrast, the second resolution (Security Council Resolution 62, 1948) used more measured language in deciding to establish an armistice "in order to eliminate the threat to peace and to facilitate the transition to permanent peace in Palestine." Under this resolution, the parties could act either directly or through the acting mediator. The parties almost immediately used the differences in these resolutions to accuse each other of noncompliance (Urquhart, 1993).

Bunche's mandate involved even greater complexity. The General Assembly, a different UN organ, originally created the mediator's post in an earlier resolution adopted at the beginning of the Arab-Israeli War (General Assembly Resolution 186, 1948). That earlier resolution detailed explicitly the broad objectives to be pursued, and the approaches and reporting responsibilities to be fulfilled, in stabilizing a truce. The General Assembly gave its instructions to Bunche's erstwhile predecessor and superior, Count Folke Bernadotte. Subsequently, the Security Council, with primary authority under chapter 7 of the charter for response to threats to international peace and security, gave more flexible negotiation authority to Bunche as acting mediator in its two resolutions adopted after Bernadotte's assassination. On receipt of Bunche's major report after Bernadotte's death, the General Assembly adopted a resolution giving instructions to Bunche as its subordinate (General Assembly Resolution 186, 1948). The assembly continued to insist on excruciatingly detailed objectives, procedures, and reports. As acting mediator, Bunche served as principal advisor and negotiator for both of these bodies. He initiated truce negotiations with instructions contained in four key resolutions from two major organs of the United Nations, instructions in whose drafting he played a significant role. These instructions at least allowed consideration of all significant questions raised by the conflicts in Palestine. Unfortunately, much of Bunche's time was spent in balancing the competing demands and political agendas of different participant and influential nonparticipant parties. Bunche labored under the complex burden of reaching a proper balance among his multiple roles (Urquhart, 1993, p. 191). In consequence, many festering problems remained unresolved.

When the delegations of Israel, Egypt, Transjordan, Syria, and Lebanon finally signaled some willingness to negotiate, Bunche confronted many thorny decisions about the location and timing of proceedings. The island of Rhodes, selected by Bernadotte as the headquarters of his initial mediation effort, provided a neutral and Spartan location that facilitated the negotiation (Urquhart, 1993, p. 201). More complex dilemmas arose from the tactical manipulations of the situation by the parties prior to the start of negotiations. As Bunche made his October report to the General Assembly, Israel initiated Operation Ten Plagues to secure the dominant military position in the Negev Desert, changing the negotiating context (Urquhart, 1993, p. 187). By the time that the Security Council demanded a cease-fire, an Egyptian division had been cut off at Al-Falujah, north of Gaza (Urquhart, 1993, p. 188). The fate of this division became a major issue in the Egyptian-Israeli negotiations. Egyptian demands for the relief of the division, countered by Israeli reluctance to forfeit the advantage, engaged an inordinate amount of time and effort at the start of negotiations. The parties failed to make significant progress on any of the issues until minor positive movement toward settlement of the issue occurred after two weeks of negotiations. The Al-Falujah situation delayed progress on many central issues throughout the negotiations. The parties memorialized resolution of the issue in article 3 of the final agreement (Egyptian-Israeli General Armistice Agreement, 1949).

Bunche initiated the Egyptian-Israeli negotiations as his first order of business. He commenced those negotiations shortly after the agreement of the parties to a cease-fire in the Negev. In making that negotiation his priority, Bunche exploited a political opportunity. Bunche determined in this, as in many other many instances, that the timing of negotiations must be at least partially determined by the needs and opportunities afforded in response to pressing events. As his principal biographer stated, "There was no model and no precedent for the negotiation on which Bunche was about to embark" (Urquhart, 1993, p. 200). In acting under the auspices of the three-year-old United Nations, Bunche occupied a novel role, since he could not automatically rely on the power of a traditional state to support his positions and initiatives during the negotiation process. Even his legal status as UN acting mediator was ambiguous.[8] As a consequence, Bunche took advantage of the diplomatic pressure provided by more powerful international players to move intransigent negotiating parties in critical situations. Two examples illustrate Bunche's use of this negotiating influence of others.

During the negotiations, Egyptian delegates sought to have Israeli forces withdrawn from El Auja, a position they had recently occupied on the frontier with Egypt (Urquhart, 1993, pp. 205–206). Israeli delegates insisted on retention of that position as essential for defense purposes. Bunche submitted significant proposals to resolve disputes over El Auja and other matters. At that time, Bunche spoke to Mark Ethridge, a U.S. national appointed by President Truman to the UN Conciliation Commission. Ethridge explained that Truman had offered to apply pressure as needed (Urquhart, 1993, p. 206). Shortly thereafter, Secretary of State Dean Acheson delivered a message on Truman's behalf to Israeli prime minister David Ben-Gurion urging Israeli acceptance of Bunche's mediation proposals (Urquhart, 1993, p. 207). Ultimately, Bunche's compromise proposal was accepted by the Israelis and included in the final Egyptian-Israeli agreement as article 8 (Egyptian-Israeli General Armistice Agreement, 1949).

In another case, Israel adamantly refused to withdraw from the town of Beersheba, a significant crossroads east of the Negev. Egypt stubbornly insisted on Israeli withdrawal until the status of Beersheba became the only remaining point of disagreement. Bunche sent a cable to Secretary-General Lie in New York explaining the impasse and suggesting that Lie should explain the stakes of the dispute to Mahmoud Fawzi, the Egyptian foreign minister. While several members of the Egyptian delegation from Rhodes returned to Cairo for consultations, Lie met with Fawzi three times in three days (Urquhart, 1993, p. 210). When the Egyptian delegation returned from Cairo, they informed Bunche that they accepted his tentative agreement allowing Israel to maintain control over Beersheba (Bunche, 1949). In each of these cases, Bunche orchestrated the influence and persuasion provided by significant outside actors to overcome a difficult impasse in negotiations.

These cases provide a few examples of the skill and imagination that Ralph Bunche brought to the mediation of the Israeli-Egyptian settlement. Shortly after the signing ceremony, Bunche initiated a new mediation with the Israelis and the delegation from Transjordan. That settlement was quickly followed by one between Lebanon and Israel. The final settlement conducted under Bunche's guidance, although with much less of his direct participation, involved Israel and Syria. In each case, the parties understood that the purpose of the exercise was to bring a stable armistice that would reduce the risk of renewed fighting. Simultaneously, they were aware that the limited measures, put into practice to secure a cessation of violence, did not address the underlying causes of the conflict in Palestine. Even as his accomplishment was internationally acknowledged through the award of the Nobel Peace Prize, Bunche acknowledged the risk of renewed violence would remain until the underlying issues were addressed. In a letter to a correspondent friend in Cairo after the close of negotiations, Bunche stated, "The way I always saw the Palestinian affair (and still do) was that we had to try to make the best of a bad situation. That sort of approach rarely leads to a *good* result, but only to something *less bad*. That, apparently, is where things now rest. At least, I hope so. But the hapless refugees are still on the hook. They are the *real* victims of the affair" (Urquhart, 1993, p. 230). Bunche foresaw the anguish that would pervade the ongoing Arab-Israeli confrontation even as global leaders lauded his accomplishments (Jahn, 1950).[9]

The New Paradigm

Ralph Bunche engaged in the Arab-Israeli conflict from a constrained position with a limited primary objective and a novel mandate. As mediator, Bunche participated in the negotiations as an international facilitator with no independent base of political power or influence. He represented the United Nations in its neutrally motivated effort to bring about a mediated cessation of violence on the ground. Finally, all of the participants were cognizant of the specifically limited mandate that the Security Council had provided to Bunche. In combination, all of these factors put narrow constraints on the role that he could play as mediator, making Bunche's success even more remarkable. These same limiting factors reduced Bunche's capacity to contribute to the substantive resolution of the overarching Arab-Israeli dispute.

Bunche's circumscribed role resulted from the changed context within which diplomats addressed the occurrence of violent conflict. Prior to the formation of the United Nations, diplomats engaged in at least three types of activities dictated by the pervasive possibility of violent conflict. First, they endeavored to prevent hostilities that were inconsistent with their particular national interests. Second, they conferred with other states to form alliances or other arrangements in preparation for the possible outbreak of hostilities. Third, they negotiated post-conflict settlements dictated by the consequences of those hostilities that did occur. Under these circumstances, those evaluating negotiating positions could assume that the interests of that diplomat's state provided a reliable measure of a diplomat's bargaining objectives. They could also assume that the power and influence of the diplomat's state provided an indication of the viability of the diplomat's pursuit of those objectives. Under those circumstances, diplomats could come to a relatively clear understanding of the tasks that they encountered.

Ralph Bunche encountered a markedly different task as mediator of the Arab-Israeli dispute. His objectives were not determined by a single foreign ministry. Instructions came from the United Nations in order that the mediator should "promote a peaceful adjustment of the future situation of Palestine" (General Assembly Resolution 186, 1948). At every instance, all parties were directed to cease hostilities "without prejudice to the rights, claims or positions of the parties concerned" (Security Council Resolution 49, 1948). In other words, the mediating UN officials were given the sole objective of the cessation of hostilities, not the resolution of the underlying dispute. All of these parameters were determined before Bunche was thrust into the spotlight by the assassination of Count Folke Bernadotte in September 1948.

As acting mediator, Bunche was engaging in an unprecedented new enterprise. Neutral third parties had intervened to assist in resolving other international conflicts; President Theodore Roosevelt had received the Nobel Peace Prize in 1908 for exercising his good offices in helping to end the Russo-Japanese War (Gilbert, 1997). Bunche's situation was different from Roosevelt's for several reasons.

First, prior international mediation efforts had been undertaken with the clear imprimatur of a specific state or government. Previous mediations had been undertaken by statesmen who based their practices and procedures on time-honored traditions of diplomacy. Those statesmen relied upon the support of their governments to provide incentives for the disputing parties to resettlement. In the Arab-Israeli case, mediation was undertaken based upon the instructions of a new international entity, the UN Security Council, at the loose direction of a new international bureaucracy, the Secretariat. In one respect, Bunche was conducting a high-wire act without a net.

Second, Bunche initiated an equilateral mediation process with parties that continued to deny the legitimacy of their counterparts. The Arab antagonists in this dispute moved military forces into Palestine because they denied the legitimacy of the newly declared Jewish state of Israel. Those antagonists were forced to acknowledge the de facto jurisdiction of Israel over the western portion of Palestine because of their military defeats. However, those defeats did not dictate the political or moral acceptability of the state of Israel, and those Arab states continued to contest the legitimacy of the newly declared state. Bunche pursued a mediated agreement between parties who doubted each others' legitimacy.

Finally, the objectives sought in this mediation, while politically very narrow, contained inherent contradictions. Ralph Bunche understood that political settlement of the Arab-Israeli dispute was not immediately feasible; the principal purpose of the mediation was to establish a durable armistice, ending the military conflict. The principal parties for military conflict, Israel, Egypt, Transjordan, Lebanon, and Syria, were enticed into mediation in pursuit of the armistice. However, the Palestinians, a critically important participant in the region, played no role in the process. While the Arab states justified their military intervention on the plight of the Palestinians, those states retained exclusive control over the issues to be discussed during mediation, preserving for themselves the right to assert any relevant Palestinian concerns. As a result, it became clear at an early stage that the underlying Palestinian interests were not well served during mediation process. The core causes of the international conflict were not addressed.

Ralph Bunche left a legacy of public service that merits respect and admiration. Anyone who studies his accomplishments must come away with deep admiration and respect for the man. But we must also recognize, as Bunche himself did, that vast problems remain to be resolved. Our best tribute to his memory would be to continue the work for peace that he initiated.

Notes

1. The title paraphrases a famous biography by Dean Acheson, *Present at the Creation: My Years at the State Department* (New York: Norton, 1969).

2. The Treaty of Westphalia, signed in 1648, marked the end of the Thirty Years' War in Europe. The treaty was the product of more than three years of negotiations, which took place in both Munster and Osnabruck. With the exceptions of England and Poland, all of Europe was present at the negotiations. The treaty represents the first attempt to use international organization for the maintenance of peace. It remained the framework for European political organizations for over a century.

3. Trygvie Lie acknowledged Bunche's academic expertise in this area as well as his practical experience in the construction of the trusteeship infrastructure when he offered the UN position to Bunche (see Urquhart, 1993, p. 134–135).

4. Transjordan, an area east of the Jordan River, gained its full independence from the United Kingdom in 1946. Transjordan changed its name to Jordan in 1949.

5. The Arab Legion caused the greatest problems of the war for the Israeli forces during the fight for control of the road to Jerusalem.

6. The initial mandate of the mediator established this objective. General Assembly Resolution 186 (S-2), supra.

7. See, e.g., telegram from King Abdullah of Transjordan to UN Secretary-General, Press Release PAL/164 May 4, 1948, available at United Nations Information System on the Question of Palestine, http://unispal.un.org.

8. In one of its first cases, the International Court of Justice provided some clarification of the legal status of a UN mediator in a decision based on the situation surrounding Count Bernadotte's assassination. See Reparation for Injuries Suffered in the Service of the United Nation, Summary of Advisory Opinion of April 11, 1949, retrieved on May 2, 2005, at http://www.icj-cij.org/icjwww/idecisions/isummaries/iisunsummary490411 .htm.

9. In recognition of his contribution to the Arab-Israeli armistice, Ralph Bunche received the Nobel Prize in 1950. As described by Gunnar Jahn, "By exercising infinite patience, Bunche finally succeeded in persuading all parties to accept an armistice."

10. An International Legacy

The Middle East, Congo,
and United Nations Peacekeeping

PRINCETON N. LYMAN

The United Nations was involved in the Middle East in the aftermath of the negotiations of 1948–49 and again in 1957. The evolution of its role there can be contrasted with UN involvement in the Congo in the late twentieth and early twenty-first centuries. Bunche's leadership, especially in the first of these periods, represents the high point of UN responsibility and direction of Middle East diplomacy. Since then there has been a steady decline in the UN's role in that region to the point that it has been virtually a non-actor in some of the region's most turbulent recent history. How did this happen? By contrast, the UN's role in the Congo was reprised in the early twenty-first century, testing the lessons of Bunche's legacy.

The Middle East

Bunche learned quickly that diplomacy in the Middle East was fraught with charges of bias, with complicity by external players, and heavy handedness. In the first period of his Middle East diplomacy, 1948–49, Bunche was accused by Israelis of a pro-Arab bias, a criticism picked up by a broad array of American commentators, including W. E. B. Du Bois (Urquhart, 1993; Rivlin, ed., 1990). The interests of major powers, particularly Britain, would confound his mediating efforts. The U.S. position, still ambivalent on many of the points in question, was not yet as developed as later, but required special attention. Bunche also faced the continuing efforts of the parties to make facts on the ground, through military or other means. Yet Bunche was able to maintain his position as the central mediating party. Through dogged, six-week-long discussions at Rhodes in early 1949, Bunche hammered out the armistice agreement between Israel and Egypt. Agreements with Syria and Jordan would follow. For the moment, earlier accusations were forgotten and Bunche returned home a hero, praised by all sides. In 1950 he was awarded the Nobel Peace Prize.

In 1956–57, the UN was once again heavily engaged in the wake of the British, French, and Israeli invasion of the Sinai. But in this situation, the overriding influence of the United States was becoming evident. The decision of the United States to oppose the invasion, insist upon withdrawal of all three forces, and to back the UN in policing the subsequent peace agreement was critical to what Secretary-General Dag Hammarskjöld, Bunche, and their UN colleagues were able to achieve. What was significant at this point was the strong support of the United States for a substantial UN role. It was in this situation that UN peacekeeping was born, with the creation of the United Nations Emergency Force (UNEF), the first armed UN military force. Once again, Bunche found himself in the crosshairs of those accusing the UN of bias, in this case of being "slaves" to the Egyptians in the deployment of UNEF. Meanwhile, the Egyptians made life for the UN almost equally difficult (Urquhart, 1993). Nevertheless, UNEF came to be considered a success, as the warring sides settled down to yet another, albeit short, period of peace. Ominously, however, as perhaps signs of problems to come, Israel refused to allow UNEF to be posted on its side of the border.[1] Ten years later, Egyptian president Nasser would demand UNEF's withdrawal from Egyptian soil as prelude to the 1967 Six-Day War.

The Six-Day War marked the beginning of the end of a major UN role in the Middle East. In the run-up to the war, this time it was Egypt that accused Bunche of bias, to the point that the secretary-general, U Thant, was told that Bunche would not be welcome on U Thant's visit to Cairo. The precipitating issue was Egypt's sometimes elliptical call for the withdrawal—or in some communications "redeployment"—of UNEF. Bunche sought with all his might to dissuade Egypt from the request, arguing that the UN could not simply stand aside to allow war to resume. However, Bunche also conceded that Egypt had a sovereign right to demand withdrawal. Moreover, the commanders of two key units in UNEF, from Yugoslavia and India, announced that they would cede to Egypt's request.

As would often be the case in the future, the UN became the scapegoat for much of what followed. It was pilloried for withdrawing UNEF and thus opening the door to war. A London paper called it "U Thant's War." "What is the use of a fire brigade which vanishes from the scene as soon as the first smoke and flames appear?" charged the Israeli ambassador to the UN. Major American commentators took the UN to task along the same lines.

American diplomatic memoirs later maintained the charge, often distorting the facts. Egypt joined in the process by later claiming that it had not really intended to have UNEF depart in toto, contrary to the historical record (Urquhart, 1993).

Bunche was prescient in foreseeing the long-term damage that would occur to the UN's role in the Middle East. "A likely result of the current war in the Near East will be a sharp curtailment, if not a complete end, of UN peacekeeping in that area. UNEF is finished and it may seriously be doubted that UNTSO [the UN Truce Supervisory Organization] will ever regain the status and responsibility that it has had since 1949. The decline of UN peacekeeping cannot fail to affect adversely the standing and prestige of the UN itself" (Urquhart, 1993, pp. 407–414).

Another change was taking place that would hasten the decline in the UN's direct role. In 1948, UN membership stood at fifty-nine member states. In 1957 the number had risen to eighty-two as the impact of decolonization began to be felt. By the end of the 1960s, the number was 127, with the majority from the developing countries. The mood of the UN on the Arab-Israeli conflict changed in the process. Increasingly, the General Assembly focused blame on Israel for the continuing troubles in the region and championed the cause of the Palestinians. The high point of this movement came in 1975 when the General Assembly passed a resolution equating Zionism with racism. For those sympathetic with the struggle for Israelis' independence and the motivating force of Zionism in Israeli nationalism, this seemed an unjust affront and an attack on the very basis of Israel's existence. The UN no longer seemed capable of being a neutral party.

A respite occurred in the relationship in the early 1990s. In the aftermath of the first Gulf War and a promising resumption of the Israeli-Palestinian peace process, the General Assembly repealed the "Zionism is Racism" resolution. There was a reduction in anti-Israel resolutions and support for the peace process under way. Israelis began to be elected to some UN committees and bodies. But when the peace process turned sour in 1996, and with the election of a more intransigent government in Israel under Prime Minister Benjamin Netanyahu, relations again became hostile.

The isolation of Israel in the UN system has gradually extended throughout the system. For example, election to any major body in the UN—the Security Council, the United Nations Economic and Social Council (ECOSOC), and the like—comes through nomination by a regional bloc, each of which has been allocated so many seats. Denied membership in the regional bloc of Asian-Arab states to which it would normally belong, and refused entrée to the Western bloc by European opposition, Israel has been in effect denied membership on any of these major UN bodies. No other member state, no matter its actions, has been so treated. Iraq, in violation of numerous UN Security Council resolutions on its arms program, even rose to chairmanship of the UN Disarmament Commission on the eve of the 2003 Gulf War. Sudan was recently elected to the UN Human Rights Commission despite accusations of horrific human rights violations during its long civil war. Libya, where significant violations have been alleged, was elected chair. On the Human Rights Commission, a separate agenda item each year is reserved for the situation in the Israeli-occupied territories, with all other human rights situations—no matter how grave—grouped together in another single item. Resolutions condemning Israel were passed in United Nations Educational, Scientific, and Cultural Organization (UNESCO) and became contentious issues in numerous specialized UN conferences.

In essence, for reasons of solidarity with a liberation movement—the Palestine Liberation Organization (PLO)—and perhaps because Israel and the confrontation with Arab states has become a symbol in the third world's anti-imperialism and in its frustration over the continuing disparity in power in the global economic system—for whatever reasons, the UN has become for Israel and its supporters a hostile institution. During this same period, the United States acquired an increasingly central role both in defense of Israel and as the major player in Middle East negotiations. In that role, the United States found itself constantly confronting what it saw as anti-Israel attitudes within the UN, not only in the General Assembly but in the Security Council. From 1972 to 2003, the United States used its veto thirty-five times on resolutions related to Israel, far more than on any other issue and nearly half of all vetoes it cast (Kafala, 2003).

This chapter does not try to assess the balance or lack of same in the various UN actions and resolutions on the Middle East situation. Many reflected the ups and downs of the peace process. The point, however, is that as the UN became perceived as hostile to Israel, it became less acceptable as a neutral party, or even as a participant in the various peace efforts of the past thirty years. In the negotiations to obtain Israel's withdrawal from Lebanon in 1982, the U.S. negotiator, Philip Habib, suggested the idea of a UN buffer force. After all, he noted, the UN (in fact Bunche) had invented peacekeeping and a UN force already existed in Lebanon. Israel's reaction was so hostile that the idea had to be dropped. Israel pointed out that half the UN members had no diplomatic relations with Israel (Boykin, 2002). The UN was not at Oslo; not at Camp David. Bunche would have been sorrowful.

Secretary-General Kofi Annan began to reverse that trend, though with limited success. In a landmark visit to Israel in March 1998, Annan acknowledged that Israel had cause to view the UN with disdain after decades of lopsided resolutions and denunciations. He spoke out strongly against Israel's exclusion from election to any major UN organ, and he vowed to work for a new era in UN-Israeli relations. Annan did not flinch on the peace issue, telling the Israelis that "the great majority of the member states regard Israel as having been responsible for provocative acts" that contribute to the crisis in Israeli-Arab relations. But he became the first secretary-general to recognize the unequal treatment Israel had received in the international body and its effect on the UN's ability to play a role in the peace process (Barka, 1998).

Annan's visit to Israel and his many efforts since to establish the UN as a reliable partner in this region have led to a small step in returning the UN to a principal mediation role. The United States invited the secretary-general, the European Union, and the Soviet Union, a group known as the "quad," to develop the most recent peace plan, the "roadmap," produced in 2003. While the role of the quad in the actual process of negotiations is undefined and so far limited, the presence of the UN marks a slow return for the UN toward the role Ralph Bunche once played with such dominance and respect but that has not been replicated since.

The Congo

Ralph Bunche's principal dedication in the United Nations was to decolonization and to guiding the successful independence of states throughout Asia and Africa. He represented the UN at the independence celebration in Ghana in 1957 and was greatly moved. But three years later, he would be thrust into a very different independence situation, that of the Congo.[2] The Congo encompassed many facets of Bunche's legacy: the extent of the UN's commitment to "neutrality" in a civil war situation, the mandate for using force, and the implications for UN peacekeeping.

The Congo was the victim of the worst form of colonial exploitation. Made a virtual private possession of Belgium's King Leopold in the late nineteenth century, it had been ruthlessly mined of its copper, precious gems, ivory, rubber, and other riches through forced labor, intimidation, and brutality. Its independence came suddenly, without preparation, without even minimum levels of education for managing a modern state, and with mixed motives on the part of Belgium (Hochschild, 1998). All of these factors played into the situation that Bunche would face.

At first as the Congo came into independence, the UN was asked to undertake a traditional role of advice, training, and assistance. The request came from Congo's Prime Minister Patrice Lumumba, whose career and fate remain today a source of great emotion and controversy. Bunche foresaw an ambitious mission—again a foreshadow of later UN missions in the Balkans, East Timor, and elsewhere—that would include police trainers as well as military and a wide variety of skilled civilians to oversee the provision of basic services. But before the request could be acted upon, the situation rapidly deteriorated. Belgian troops occupied key parts of the capital, professing the need to keep order, and began supporting a secessionist regime in the rich province of Katanga. Lumumba was outraged and asked the UN for a military force to replace the Belgians. The UN acted with haste not known before or since. Within three days of UN Security Council approval, 3,500 UN troops arrived in the Congo. The stage was thus set for a debate that would rage for months over just what the role of this force should be.

This chapter cannot do justice to the complexities of this history. In the midst of a deteriorating security situation, the UN players were dealing with a host of conflicting motives and agendas. Belgium clearly had in mind emasculating the new Congolese government, or short of that, establishing itself behind an independent Katanga where much of Belgium's mining interests were located. The United States was concerned over the Cold War implications of the situation. Lumumba, in his desperation, and with strong Soviet support, threatened to request arms from the Soviet Union if the UN could not rid the country of the Belgians. That set off alarm bells in Washington and other Western capitals. The Congolese army, left without officers or clear orders, mutinied and became both a source of instability and a force between competing Congolese factions. Intrigue, deception, covert actions, violence, and near anarchy prevailed on all sides (De Witte, 2001; Nzongola-Ntalaja, 2002; O'Ballance, 2000; Urquhart, 1993).

Almost immediately upon its arrival, the United Nations Operation in the Congo (ONUC) came into conflict with Lumumba as well as with other actors. Lumumba grew impatient with the slow withdrawal of Belgian troops from the capital and from Katanga, and threatened to use the Congolese army for this purpose if the UN did not act more aggressively. Bunche saw tragedy in this idea. On the other side, the U.S. ambassador and one of the UN's military commanders, a British professional, wanted the UN to disband or at least disarm the Congolese army. Bunche found this suggestion equally unworkable and only angered Lumumba by suggesting it to him. Meanwhile the situation grew more chaotic. The Congo president, Kasavubu, and Lumumba became increasingly estranged. Pressures were brought on Kasavubu by the United States, Belgium, and others to dismiss Lumumba. Lumumba was eventually dismissed, then arrested, and, most shockingly, turned over to Tshombe's government in Katanga. There he was executed.

Several critical matters in this time frame are important in assessing Bunche's legacy.

(1) The first issue, one which has presented itself to the UN throughout its history, is to what degree the UN is the servant of the interests of the great powers, or for that matter any single nation or group of nations. One of the areas of controversy regarding the Congo is the UN's response to the threatened secession of Katanga, under its premier Moise Tshombe. As noted, Lumumba pressed the UN to move forcefully on Katanga, assure the departure of the Belgians, and end the secession. Secretary-General Hammarskjöld, however, felt that UN entrée into Katanga should proceed with Tshombe's agreement, lest there be armed conflict between the UN forces and Tshombe's. He thus embarked on negotiations with Tshombe to this end. The negotiations spun on for several months.

Critics contend that the UN was in fact looking askance at the Belgians' real intentions and acting in sympathy if not outright support of the United States and others who were opposed to Lumumba and sympathetic to Tshombe. They argue that Hammarskjöld was in perfect harmony with the Cold War aims of the United States and that he saw as part of his mission keeping the Congo out of the hands of Soviet influence or of its Congolese allies. Some argue that Bunche was similarly inclined, and in particular harbored a negative view of Lumumba. The charges are further fueled by findings that UN troops, which had originally provided Lumumba protection, stood by while he was arrested, later beaten, and ultimately executed (De Witte, 2001; Nzongola-Ntalaja, 2002).

(2) This leads to a second issue and an important element in Bunche's legacy: the role of UN military forces. Hammarskjöld and Bunche argued that UN peacekeepers should only use force in self-defense. Bunche used this argument to reject the Americans' appeals to restrain the Congolese army and disarm it, just as Hammarskjöld had used it to resist Lumumba's appeal for a forced entry into Katanga. Bunche argued that ONUC was a peace force, not a fighting force. The question, which has arisen time and again with UN peacekeeping, is how effective UN peacekeepers can be in a situation of chaos, violence, and flouting of UN resolutions, if they are only a "standby force."

Further, Bunche insisted that UN forces should not take sides in political disputes within the country in which they are serving. Bunche even argued to Lumumba that when UN forces did enter Katanga, they would not take sides in the outcome of any political issues between the central government and Katanga. This further infuriated Lumumba (Urquhart, 1993; Nicholas, 1963).

Bunche and the UN were forced to face both these issues again in 1961, however, when after Tshombe procrastinated on a peace agreement that would end the secession, UN troops, under aggressive commanders and with the encouragement of the UN representative in the province, pushed into Katanga and began routing Tshombe's mercenaries and armed forces. This time it was the United States, sympathetic to Tshombe, that took issue with the UN. Bunche was rushed back to the Congo to sort out the situation, but in effect he condoned the operation. In 1962, as Tshombe continued to procrastinate and clashes between UN and Tshombe's forces grew more frequent, the UN moved even more aggressively and eventually took control of key parts of the province. Shortly after, Tshombe, traveling under UN protection, arrived in the capital to reach agreement with the central government. The secession was over.

As in the Middle East, the UN went from hero to enemy in the eyes of the press and American observers. Praised in the beginning for its rapid deployment and apparent contribution to stabilizing the situation, the UN quickly became caught up in the conflicting motives and manipulations of the various parties. When Bunche finally returned home from his Congo duties, he found the UN attacked from both the right, for being too aggressive against Tshombe, and from the left, for seeming to facilitate the fall of Lumumba (Urquhart, 1993).

The controversy has not ended. Debate continues today about the UN's role in the Congo, its real aims, and Bunche's own sympathies (De Witte, 2001; Nzongola-Ntalaja, 2002; O'Ballance, 2000). Lumumba, for many, symbolized (and still symbolizes) the Congo's first real nationalist spirit and was seen as leading its only genuine nationalist movement. Opposition to him appeared to adherents and admirers as catering to Western imperialist aims, that is, to maintain the West's direct or indirect control over the Congo's riches, and to deny them to the Soviet Union. In this light, the UN's reluctance to confront Tshombe and his Belgian supporters with force when Lumumba was in power, but to countenance such forceful action when Lumumba was gone from the scene and the central government was in more conservative hands, appears to the critics as evidence of the UN's serving Western interests. Although he was acting with an explicit new UN Security Council mandate in November 1961, Bunche lent his support to UN peacekeepers becoming, in later jargon, "peacemakers"—that is, ready to use force—and clearly party to a political settlement fashioned at least in part by the United States and its allies. This seemed counter to the principles of neutrality and limited use of arms he had enunciated so forcefully earlier in the crisis.

The legacy thus remains in controversy, all the more so as the Congo has fallen once more into chaos and humanitarian crisis. The UN's stated objective, and Bunche's primary interest, was to preserve the Congo's territorial integrity. But the central government that the UN helped come to power, eventually taken over by Joseph Mobutu, proved to be corrupt and brutal. Civil wars continued to convulse the country. Outside intervention, no longer from the UN but by Western troops or others supported by the West, would be called upon on several occasions to restore order and preserve Mobutu's government (O'Ballance, 2000). After more than three decades in power, Mobutu was forced out in 1997. He left the country in poverty and caught up in the fallout from the genocide in neighboring Rwanda. There was, moreover, no respite once Mobutu had gone. Congo fell further into civil war. Nine neighboring African countries entered the war. The war has cost a staggering three million lives. Four million more are displaced. Congo is today one of Africa's most tragic failed states, and one of the world's greatest humanitarian disasters.

Surely, this sad history cannot be laid at the doorstep of the UN or of those who led the UN operation in those early days of the nation's independence. But for Ralph Bunche, for whom the independence of African nations was one of his principal preoccupations in the UN, this experience—his most intense involvement in one of those independence processes—does not provide a legacy of which he would today take pride or solace.

Bunche would not realize another of his prescient objectives in the Congo. His ambitious plans for "nation-building" in the Congo fell victim to the secessionist wars, the politics, and eventually to the decline of the UN's role. When UN forces departed Congo in 1963, the UN's other roles declined in favor of bilateral donors, whose objectives were at least guided as much by the politics of the Cold War as by the interests of development.

The Congo experience would leave other legacies. After the Congo, the UN would revert to more traditional peacekeeping operations. The question of how UN peacekeepers should respond to a military challenge was largely set aside. But in the 1990s, the debate over the proper role of UN peacekeepers would resurface in the Balkans, in Somalia, in Rwanda, and in the Congo itself. The issues that Bunche faced in the Congo in 1961–62 would confront his successors with even greater consequences. Unresolved from earlier years, they would shake the world's confidence in the UN system altogether.

Peacekeeping

In the wake of the British, French, and Israeli invasion of Egypt in 1956, UN peacekeeping was born. The idea to interpose an international peace and police force came from Canada's Prime Minister Lester Pearson. But it was Bunche who was charged with establishing the operation. The United Nations Emergency Force (UNEF) was the first armed UN force. Many of the principles that would guide UN peacekeeping were established in its operation. UNEF was deployed—after much negotiation—with the agreement of both sides and made its entrée peacefully. It occupied disputed territories but tried to stay neutral in the political aspects. Thus UNEF neither enforced free passage of Israeli ships through the Suez Canal, which Egypt was denying—one of the causes of the war—or facilitated Egyptian establishment of governance in the Gaza and other disputed areas. Its job was to police an agreement on such matters as troop withdrawals and border defense, and to help prevent a resumption of hostilities.

Since then the UN has deployed peacekeepers on more than twenty occasions. They have become a mainstay of peace processes in Africa, Asia, Europe, and the Caribbean. Some have been in operation for more than fifty years—in the Middle East, along the India-Pakistan border, and (going on fifty years) in Cyprus. Some lasted but a year or two. In 1988 UN peacekeepers were awarded the Nobel Peace Prize.

In the 1990s, however, UN peacekeeping suffered its most lamentable setbacks, even humiliations, and brought the entire UN into disrepute. The critical cases came in the Balkans and Rwanda, with echoes of the same issues later in Sierra Leone and the Congo.

Three crises arose in rapid succession that challenged the UN in the 1990s: Somalia, the Balkans, and Rwanda. In Somalia in late 1990, where the central government had collapsed and warlords were devastating the country, the United States intervened militarily to stop an impending famine. U.S. troops were soon supplemented by a UN peacekeeping force. As in so many other cases, outside forces found themselves unable to stay clear of competing political agendas and forces within the country. UN forces from Pakistan were attacked by one of the warlords. U.S. forces, staging an attack on the same warlord, were surrounded and eighteen men were killed, one dragged through the streets to the horror of the American public. Almost immediately, the United States withdrew its troops and turned the operation over to the UN, which withdrew some time later. Although the costly U.S. military action was a purely U.S. decision, the UN was tarred in the press and in much of the American public's mind by the disaster (Hirsch & Oakley, 1995).

The concept of peacekeeping was also a major casualty. The idea that the international community could enter into a situation even for purely humanitarian reasons, and operate without becoming involved in the politics of a deteriorating situation, was discredited. That made peacekeeping a much more risky commitment, one that major powers would now look upon with considerable resistance.

The Balkans added another dire dimension. Almost at the same time as the burgeoning crisis in Somalia, Yugoslavia began coming apart in Europe. The collapse of communism, the death of long time leader Josip Broz Tito, the bursting forth of long-suppressed ethnic nationalism, and sheer ambition and greed coalesced to lead one after another of Yugoslavia's federated states to move toward independence, touching off a war that became more brutal than anyone had seen in Europe since the end of World War II. As the war deepened, the international community hesitated, struggled, and experimented with various formulas to bring it under control. Inherent in these efforts was a desire to avoid military intervention. Into this mix the UN was drawn (Little & Silber, 1996; Ullman, 1996; Holbrooke, 1998; Report of the Secretary-General, 1999).

The first major effort to end the war was a plan advanced under European sponsorship by the former American secretary of state Cyrus Vance and former British foreign minister Lord David Owen. As part of a complex cease-fire and partition agreement, the plan proposed that a UN force be deployed to protect several "safe areas" where minority Muslim enclaves were surrounded by Serb-controlled territory. In the original plan, there would be a cease-fire, withdrawal of Serbian forces, and disarmament of militias. Thus in 1992 the United Nations Protection Force (UNPROFOR) was born. The other major UN intervention was the provision of humanitarian relief, largely through the United Nations High Commissioner for Refugees. UN peacekeepers were also charged with facilitating the aid delivery. The latter was a first for the UN, and the implications, in a hostile situation, were not well understood. UNPROFOR was lightly armed and not large enough to take on combat operations on any significant scale. The mandates for use of force were vague and inadequate to the situation it would soon face (Ullman, 1996).

The UN portion of the plan would prove disastrous, for thousands of Muslims and for the UN. UNPROFOR was deployed as a "thin blue line" between hostile populations, but neither the cease-fire nor other peace elements of the plan were implemented. There followed several years of continued fighting, diplomatic jockeying, and humanitarian crises. Provision of humanitarian aid was frequently blocked by contending forces, and the UN was hard pressed to keep a minimum flow going. The first major disaster, however, took place in July 1995, in the town of Srebreneca. While not initially designated as a "safe area," it was defended by 300 Dutch UN troops. When Bosnian Serbs marched on the town, the UN Security Council desperately declared it also a safe area. The Serbs marched in nevertheless. Outgunned and without reinforcements, the Dutch troops stepped aside. What followed was the slaughter of perhaps eight thousand Muslim men. Not long afterwards, the Bosnian Serbs marched into another safe area, Gorazde. Again, the UN was unable to protect this safe area. In May of that year, the UN suffered another humiliation. In response to NATO bombing of Bosnian Serbian positions, the Serbs captured 350 UN peacekeepers as "human shields," handcuffed them to trees and telephone poles, and had the scene televised around the world.

Much of the blame for these disasters belongs to the major powers and the failure to address the situation with either sufficient force or other means. For example, Secretary-General Boutros Boutros Ghali had asked for 34,000 additional troops to fulfill the safe haven mandates. He received only 7,000. Nevertheless, the UN was deeply hurt. As Gorazde came under attack, Croatian president Alija Izetbegovic wrote Secretary-General Boutros Boutros-Ghali:

> The so-called safe area has become the most unsafe place in the world. The organization you headed proclaimed the free territory of Gorazde a UN protected area almost a year ago. Security Council Resolutions 824 and 836 refer to this protected zone, but they have remained only empty phrases. Neither you nor your personnel have done anything to use the mandate of all those resolutions to protect the people of Gorazde and the credibility of the United Nations. . . . Secretary-General, my people hold you responsible for this situation. . . . If Gorazde falls, I think that a sense of moral responsibility would command you to leave the post of UN Secretary General. (Little & Silber, 1996, p. 331–332)

International outrage was general. At worst the UN looked hopeless, even cowardly. At best it seemed ineffective. One liberal senator told this author several years later, as I argued for paying the United States' overdue dues to the UN, that she "would never forgive the UN for Srebrenica."

Part of the UN's agony in Yugoslavia lay in the same issues that had arisen in the Congo. The UN commanders in the field were fiercely wedded to the concept of UN neutrality. They not only sought to negotiate each crisis with the oncoming Serbian forces, they were opposed to the use of NATO bombing to back them up in the impending crises. Sir Michael Rose, the UN commander in Bosnia, argued that frequent resort to air strikes would push UNPROFOR from peacekeeping to peace enforcement. As his position was described, "Peacekeeping required strict neutrality. It was not the job of a peacekeeping force to intervene to alter the course of the war in favor of one side. . . . He called the fine line between peacekeeping and peace-enforcement . . . the 'Mogadishu line,' after the disastrous consequences of the United States efforts to impose a peace settlement in Somalia" (Little & Silber, 1996. p. 326). The problem with this view was that, in a situation like that of Bosnia, the humanitarian disaster lies in not taking sides; the value of UN neutrality pales.

The UN would, however, suffer yet another disaster when its commander sought to confront this issue. That was Rwanda (United Nations, 1999; Leader, 2001; Gourevitch, 1998; Durch, 1996; Shawcross, 2000; Organization of African Unity, 2000).

Like most complex war situations, that of Rwanda has a long history. A former Belgian colony, Rwanda had suffered through several bouts of internal conflict largely between two competing ethnic groups, the Tutsis and the Hutus. Tutsis, once the dominant minority, were driven from power early in the country's independence, and through several conflicts many fled to neighboring Uganda and other states. In 1990, a Tutsi-led force, the Rwandan Patriotic Front (RPF), invaded from Uganda, touching off a major crisis. Painstaking negotiations led to the Arusha Accords, which called for a coalition government, new elections, and integration of the armed forces. The United Nations Assistance Mission for Rwanda (UNAMIR) was authorized in 1993 to help implement the agreement, in particular to monitor the cease-fire and assist in integration of the armed forces and the demobilization of the various armed units not to be integrated. UNAMIR was authorized with only 2,548 personnel. By early 1994, it was apparent that the implementation of the peace plan was in trouble. The coalition government was not in place, and there was evidence of strong opposition to the agreement within the Rwandan government. Hate radio used by Hutu extremists was raising tensions. On April 6, President Habyarimana's plane was shot down by members of his own armed forces. Almost immediately a campaign of horrifying genocide would begin against Tutsis and moderate Hutus.

The commander of UNAMIR, Canadian brigadier general Romeo Dallaire, suspected the outbreak of armed conflict and sent an urgent telegram to UN headquarters. Dallaire wanted authorization to take action against suspected leaders, including members of the government, and to commandeer weapon caches. His telegram never reached the UN Security Council. Rather, the more traditional UN mandate, not to take up arms against one side in the dispute nor to intervene, was reaffirmed by UN headquarters. When the violence broke out, Dallaire pleaded for more troops, convinced that swift action—even the knowledge that more UN troops were on the way—would have dissuaded the genocidaires. The UN Security Council took the opposite action. UN troops had been attacked in the early hours of the outbreak; ten Belgian soldiers were killed along with the Rwandan prime minister. Belgium announced that it would withdraw its contingent. Other nations were on the brink of following suit. The UN Security Council was given three alternatives by the secretary-general: enlarge the force and its mandate to impose a peace, mediate between the parties, or withdraw. On April 21, the council chose to reduce the size of UNAMIR and its mandate, almost a full withdrawal.

As the full scope of the genocide became clear to the world, the secretary-general asked the council to reopen the debate. A larger force, a humanitarian mandate, and this time authorization to use force as necessary in support of the mandate was approved. Notably, and as a measure of how unwilling the international community was to recognize the reality of what was happening, an attempt to include the word "genocide" in the resolution was unsuccessful. But it was impossible in any case to organize and deploy a new and enlarged force in time to make a difference. France organized a separate mission, "Operation Turquoise," which purportedly protected tens of thousands of Rwandans, but was accused by the RPF of in fact enabling many of the genocidaires and their supporters to flee to the Congo.

Before the RPF finally took control and the massacres were ended, as many as 800,000 people were killed. The international community had said after the Holocaust of World War II, "Never again." But genocide had been allowed to occur once again. Looking back on the performance of the UN, on the members of the Security Council, and the international community in general, there is shame and continuing recrimination over Rwanda. The UN was particularly hurt in Africa, where it once had exceptional prestige. Rwanda spurned the new UN peacekeeping operation created in the wake of the genocide, ending it in early 1996. The UN struggled, largely unsuccessfully, to play a role in containing Congo's descent into civil war. And its response capability was further restricted by budgetary restrictions described shortly.

Among the reasons for what happened in Rwanda was the changing attitude toward UN peacekeeping in the wake of Somalia and the unfolding situation in Yugoslavia. Rwanda threw light on a changing view of peacekeeping that had terrible consequences in this situation. Somalia had made the United States, in particular, wary of peacekeeping in civil war situations. As the Rwanda tragedy was beginning to unfold, the United States was in the process of developing a new doctrine on peacekeeping, Presidential Directive (PD) 25. In essence, the new doctrine was that peacekeeping should be undertaken only in select situations, where the prospect of success was fairly clear, where (for the United States) national interests were at stake, and where clear-cut exit strategies could be delineated. With particular reference to civil wars, there was a reluctance to become involved without a clear indication that "there was a peace to be kept."

Anthony Lake, the National Security advisor to President Clinton, summed up this approach in May 1994 as the Rwandan genocide was reaching its crescendo, "These kinds of conflicts are particularly hard to come to grips with and to have an effect from outside, because basically, of course, their origins are in political turmoil within these nations. And that political turmoil may not be susceptible to the efforts of the international community. So, neither we nor the international community have either the mandate or the resources or the possibility of resolving every conflict of this kind" (Durch, 1996, p. 375).

The debacles in Somalia, Yugoslavia, and Rwanda had a further effect. In the United States, the sudden rise in UN peacekeeping budgets in the 1990s, especially from Yugoslavia, along with the failures associated with them, fueled anti-UN sentiments within the Republican-controlled Congress. What began as a protest against these expenditures soon spread to other costs, so that soon the Congress was withholding more than $1 billion in U.S. dues to the organization and demanding sweeping reforms throughout. Congress was particularly hard on new or enlarged peacekeeping operations. Together with the conditions in PD 25, this attitude led the United States to try to hold down, restrict the mandate, or shorten the time frame of any new peacekeeping operations over the next several years. The UN peacekeeping budget fell by two-thirds from the early 1990s. Under pressure from the United States and others, the UN avoided sending peacekeepers to the Congo (Brazzaville), limited the size and time frame for a mission to the Central African Republic, downsized the mission in Angola in spite of dangers to the peace process, and hesitated to provide peacekeepers in sufficient numbers to the Congo. Budget restrictions on other parts of the UN imposed by the Congress restricted other conflict prevention, human rights, and political activities, as well as slowing UN response to developing crises.

The combination of peacekeeping setbacks and loss of confidence led to the first major reassessment of UN peacekeeping since it began. In 2000, Secretary-General Kofi Annan asked the seasoned UN diplomat Lahkdar Brahimi to lead a panel to examine the mandates, structure, funding, and organization of UN peacekeeping. The panel's recommendations address a wide spectrum of preventive diplomacy, peacekeeping and peacemaking, and post-conflict reconstruction activities.

One of the fundamental conclusions of the review, and indeed a conclusion that much of the international community had reached, was that there needed to be a distinction between peacekeeping and peace enforcement. Further, it was recognized that where the task was peace enforcement, traditional UN peacekeeping was the wrong vehicle. The lesson of Yugoslavia, and the lesson that would be learned later in Sierra Leone, Liberia, and East Timor, was that for such a purpose, a "coalition of the willing" was required. Such a coalition would be authorized by the UN but would be composed of those states with a sufficient interest and willingness to commit combat troops, to fund those troops, and to use force as necessary.

For the more traditional peacekeeping, the Brahimi Report recommended modifying the fundamental doctrinal issues that had dogged UN peacekeeping from the beginning: "Once deployed, United Nations peacekeepers must be able to carry out their mandates professionally and successfully and be capable of defending themselves, other mission components and mission's mandate, *with robust rules of engagement, against those who renege on their commitments to a peace accord or otherwise seek to undermine it by violence*" (Panel on United Nations Peace Operations, 2000, Annex III, paragraph 3; emphasis added).

Mindful of frequent gaps between the mandates and the resources of UN peacekeeping operations, the panel stated, "The Secretariat must tell the Security Council what it needs to know, not what it wants to hear, when formulating or changing mission mandates" (Panel on United Nations Peace Operations, 2000, Annex III, paragraph 3). Moreover, the panel sought to encompass the earliest concepts of Bunche in linking military operations to broader aspects of stabilization and nation-building. It recommended enhanced capacity for peace-building activities, electoral assistance, criminal codes, and human rights as integral parts of a peacekeeping mission.

The pendulum would swing once more. In the wake of the NATO mission in Kosovo, and the desire of the United States to shift the post-conflict burden of nation building there to the UN, U.S. support for UN peacekeeping began to pick up in the late 1990s and the early days of the twenty-first century. Following peace enforcement missions in Sierra Leone and Liberia by a coalition of West African forces, the Security Council approved substantial UN peacekeeping operations in each country, reaching as high as 17,000 at one point in Sierra Leone. The UN took over from an Australian-led coalition in East Timor, providing both peacekeepers and a major nation-building mission.

Slowly too, the UN Security Council has adjusted to the dangers of providing too few peacekeepers with too limited a mandate and equipment. Ironically, it was in the Congo, where Bunche first confronted the doctrinal issues of peacekeeping and enforcement, that the UN in 2003 found it had committed too few troops to prevent a massacre in the northeast region and indeed to carry out much of its mandate. Following intervention by a coalition of European and African forces to restore order, the UN Security Council tripled the authorized force for that mission and strengthened both its mandate and capabilities.

Bunche's legacy in peacekeeping has thus endured acclaimed successes and disastrous setbacks, indeed a history of trials by fire. But that was inevitable. Peacekeeping was not foreseen in the charter. It had to be invented, tested, adjusted, and redeemed. Bunche would have recognized that. That it has survived and become a mainstay of the international response to the challenges of peace and security is testament to Bunche's foresight.

Bunche and Contemporary Legacies for the UN

Ralph Bunche said in his Nobel Prize lecture, "If today we speak of peace, we also speak of the United Nations, for in this era, peace and the United Nations have become inseparable. If the United Nations cannot ensure peace, there will be none. If war should come, it will be only because the United Nations has failed. But the United Nations need not fail. Surely, every man of reason must work and pray to the end that it will not fail" (Rivlin, 1990, p. 227).

Bunche projected this belief, this essential world need, in all his undertakings for the United Nations. Because he could be neutral in principle but realistic and hard in negotiation, he won the confidence of parties that give little of it to mediators or each other. Because he was committed to racial equality and the end of oppression, he dared take on the most daunting of decolonization's challenges. Because he was an innovator, he gave the United Nations new relevance in a world where peace was daily under threat.

Few who have followed him have achieved this prominence for the United Nations. Times changed but also the spirit in which members and officials worked. The United Nations no longer sits at the center of some of the principal crisis points where Bunche stood so tall. Some whom he championed in the cause of decolonization failed to live up to their opportunities, leaving havoc in their wake. Using military force on behalf of peace proved almost too great a challenge for an organization devoted to peace.

Yet Bunche's legacy remains strong. He set the standards, pioneered the concepts, and fought the battles. It is up to his successors, and those in positions of power, to make his legacy a force in today's world, to make of their work a true testament to the ideals to which he dedicated his life.

Notes

1. India has taken a similar position with regard to the United Nations Mission Observer Group in India and Pakistan (UNMOGIP), which was established in 1949 to monitor the cease-fire in Kashmir. Since 1971, India, claiming that UNMOGIP's mandate has lapsed, has restricted UN observer activities on India's side of the line of control.

2. The Democratic Republic of the Congo was renamed Zaire in 1971. The original name was restored in 1997. In this article, the term "Congo" will be used throughout.

PART IV

Contemporary and Future Critical International Inquiries and Models

11. Complexities Abound

Paradigms for Future Public Intellectuals and Diplomats

BEVERLY LINDSAY

The life and career of Ralph Johnson Bunche carries multiple messages if we take time to heed them. No matter how famous or valuable a person's contributions, their examples can shrink and wither if we permit them. By the same token, if we commit to interacting with the past as we discover the present and try to foresee the future, lessons learned from Bunche can continue to live, inspire, and build. As I write the final chapter, current events continue to impress upon us Bunche's value.

Our volume commenced in the aftermath of 9/11 or September 11, was submitted to the University of Illinois Press just days after the "7/7" or July 7, 2005, bombings in London, and completed days after the spring 2006 suicide bombings in the Middle East and Sri Lanka. The horrific events in London transport us back to Bunche and his research sojourn at the London School of Economics. As a new Ph.D. scholar, Bunche continued research and intellectual exchanges at the London school to prepare for his second research residency in Africa, part of an effort to comprehend how the developing and developed worlds were shaping one another in a world in which distances were being shrunk by technology. Bunche interacted in London with scholars and students who would become future leaders in Africa, Asia, and other developing regions who were struggling intellectually to conceptualize the philosophical and social premises for future nations, envision economic and political plans for their future nations, and commence actions to move toward political and economic independence (Edgar, 1992; Urquhart, 1993). Such concerns continue as witnessed by the July 2005 G-8 summit, talks hosted by the British prime minister with presidents and prime ministers from seven other countries—Canada, France, Germany, Italy, Japan, Russia, and the

United States. When the London blasts occurred, the summit's attention had been focused on extreme poverty in Africa and other developing regions and the overwhelming debt relief needs of such nations. How might and can world leaders from industrialized and emerging nations address such problems? What are the relationship and the timing between 7/7 and the primary focus of the G-8 summit? In January 2006, the Palestinian elections resulted in Hamas receiving the largest number of votes. Hamas provides social services for local residents while simultaneously advocating the legitimacy of violent tactics to achieve its objectives against a sovereign state, Israel. How might world leaders address immediate dilemmas caused by a new government's refusal to employ state diplomacy for nonviolent solutions? Surely, the talents of Ralph Bunche types of leaders are needed for such massive challenges.

Our volume seeks to probe the life of Bunche; shed insight on relatively unknown but significant aspects of his scholarly writings and career; engage in in-depth discussions with university and college presidents to ascertain their perspectives on Bunche in relation to academic, administrative, and intellectual and public engagement matters; and examine his diplomatic career to glean relevance to today's complexities. What insights have been illuminated? What lessons remain as we ponder critical solutions?

Our final chapter synthesizes and postulates. As we undertake this synthesis, we are struck by the nature of complexities regarding Bunche and domestic and international problems. Hence we now discuss complexities in light of Ralph Bunche, the man; colleges and universities; bureaucracies and international organizations; and contemporary global sociopolitical matters that transcend specific boundaries. The intersections among the complexities, public intellectualism, engagement, and diplomacy are articulated.

Complexities of the Man

Accidental conversations can produce insight on fundamental, yet complex, phenomena that affect a person's life and career. During spring 2005, the Educational Testing Service (ETS) convened a national symposium on women's and girls' achievement in education and work. Seated beside me at dinner was a distinguished endowed professor emeritus of psychology from both Columbia University and Yale University. When sharing information about our forthcoming book on Ralph Bunche, he exclaimed, "I worked for Ralph Bunche when I was a student at Howard!" I asked if he was Bunche's research assistant. "No," he replied, "I was his houseboy hired by Mrs. Bunche." He was, in effect, a participant observer in intimate family settings, and could tell me about Bunche the man. Bunche was sober, reflective, and distant in his home environment, a somewhat different persona from that of the admired Howard University professor.

Later that spring, I had another chance conversation, with an attorney at the national meeting of the Council on Foreign Relations. The attorney said he had met Bunche "when I was about ten years old in knee pants." By then Bunche was the distinguished United Nations diplomat. While the attorney only had vague childhood memories of his interactions with Bunche, he remembered quite vividly that Bunche's son, Ralph Jr., was refused entrance to the future attorney's private school and several other schools in New York City. The exclusion was a hot topic at dinner tables of wealthy New Yorkers.

These two conversations couple with Keppel's discussion of some early childhood and young adulthood social phenomena that affected Bunche, the man. Bunche encountered support from his family via his grandmother (whose husband graduated from college in 1875), from local African American women and churches in Los Angeles, and from Howard University colleagues. Yet he constantly confronted prejudice and racism on individual, family, and social levels. Even in the somewhat cloistered environment at Howard University, he could not escape the realities of harsh segregation in Washington, D.C. Nor could he escape the segregated co-curricular and housing conditions when he journeyed to Cambridge, Massachusetts, to earn his Harvard Ph.D. Even after Bunche lived in New York and achieved acclaim at the United Nations, his son encountered racial exclusion from private schools. Working to promote social, economic, and racial equality did not exclude Bunche from personal and family discrimination. Maintaining equanimity and optimism in such settings, undoubtedly, was a complex task.

The Yale and Columbia professor emeritus's description of Bunche, the man at home, may be viewed in two modes: racial discrimination and the role of men in the family. Here sociological and feminist literature is helpful. During the 1930s, 1940s, and 1950s, American men (regardless of race, ethnicity, and socioeconomic status) were not expected to be overly involved in daily family life (Lindsay, 1983, Lindsay, 2005; Bernard, 1973). After all, Mrs. Bunche hired the houseboy, not Dr. Bunche. Of course, as the psychology professor emeritus stated, "Bunche's personality" could be seen; yet it could not be divorced from sociocultural milieu of African American professional men who could afford houseboys. The intermeshing of sociocultural phenomena produces complexities for Bunche, the man.

With hindsight, we can speculate about the strong maternal role of Bunche's maternal grandmother. His "Nana" kept the family intact and encouraged his enrollment at the University of California, Southern Branch. Nana, while proud of her African heritage, advocated viewing ethnic groups in a nonprejudicial manner. Her playing this matriarchal role is worthy of in-depth study to ascertain what traits might be used in today's families, which are increasingly headed by grandmothers. Such grandmothers are father, mother, and grandparent. Children's willingness to listen to and internalize a grandmother's teachings may be more acceptable than listening to parents, asserts Burton and others, who have compiled for the National Institutes of Health an intergenerational study of minority and poor families in major cities in the United States (Burton, Dilworth-Anderson, and Merriwether-deVries, 1995; Burton and Merriwether-deVries, 1991). The offspring may know they have no other viable parental choices when grandparents are providing considerable support.

Keppel's and Baber and Lindsay's chapters discuss the importance of mentors to Bunche while he was an undergraduate and during his early Howard University career. Certainly, it is expected that parents and grandparents will mentor their offspring. A young African American man finding a university dean as a mentor was a rare phenomenon. The UCLA dean steered him toward poetry and philosophical readings in preparing the valedictorian address and to broaden the perspectives of the young man. To what extent might contemporary European American deans mentor young African American men who enter colleges and universities with backgrounds similar to Bunche's? Might this be an alternative model of university engagement?

College and University Complexities

When teaching comparative and international policy studies to students at Pennsylvania State University, several doctoral students (who majored in political science and sociology) told me that they had never heard of Ralph Bunche. He was not covered in their undergraduate political science courses. "How could this be?" asked one. Another stated that neither his undergraduate nor graduate seminars had covered *An American Dilemma* or Ralph Bunche in any fashion. Henry (1999) remarks that students at UCLA stare blankly when asked about Ralph Bunche, for whom a major building is named (which houses international studies, area studies, and other social sciences). It is typical for students and faculty to be unaware of the significance of named campus buildings. For political science and sociology majors, however, the query is significant. In undergraduate political science, international relations, sociology, and area studies, Ralph Bunche may be mentioned in passing or a footnote, if at all. He may be overlooked because he is merely forgotten. Or, given his progressive views as a public intellectual and his race, he may be consciously overlooked at mainstream colleges and universities.

Several writers in this volume—Keppel, Holloway, Henry, Walton, and Lindsay—discuss Bunche's academic career, which would fit today's definition of a public intellectual. That is, a public intellectual has media and public exposure beyond the parameters of her/his discipline and professional position; Bunche spoke to various audiences during the 1920s and 1930s wherein he frequently stressed the necessity of intellectuals addressing concrete economic and social problems. He emphasized the interrelations between domestic and international phenomena, as lucidly noted in his analysis of race as a social and economic construct. Bunche's presentation at a 1969 conference, about two years before his death, explicated the interrelations between race and sociopsychological alienation: racism takes a demoralizing toll on people. His statements forewarned of environmental degradation and its impact on poor nations and people as resources become scarce.

Several university presidents, interviewed by Lindsay and Baber, expand the conventional definition of public intellectualism to include public and/or private involvement in public engagement. Bunche's academic career during the 1920s and 1930s fitted both the conventional and expanded definition of public intellectualism. Significantly, present-day college and university presidents make statements and implement programs that are congruent with Bunche's views (as a professor and Rockefeller Foundation Board member) regarding universities and public involvement. University leaders should implement and model public intellectualism and involvement (Hesburgh, 2006).

Today, the endeavors for university public engagement and public intellectuals are areas where professionals and university officials concur at a broad level (NASULGC, 2004; NASULGC Strategic Vision Committee, 2000; Green, 2005; Green & Siaya, 2005). How the endeavors become operationalized is the more complex matter. The perspectives, which Bunche expressed during his Howard University career, were avant-garde for his day at many European American research universities. We could contend that views expressing the salience of socioeconomic class analysis, racial dominance, global phenomena, and the like are not readily accepted: an American Council on Education Report (Green, 2005) indicates that only within the last three years have nearly 70 percent of research universities included internationalization and related topics in their mission statements. These mission statements may be lip service rather than real action, however. What Bunche advocated is more often observed in the curriculum of ethnic studies and African American studies, and in some historically Black colleges and universities and Hispanic Serving Institutions (HSIs).

Within the academic sphere, Bunche's contributions to new paradigms in political science (as explicated by Walton) are notable intellectual features that are often not acknowledged. Nor are his intellectual and public engagement contributions, for example, the American Political Science Association's Congressional Fellows Program, which Bunche began in the mid-1950s. Via this fellowship, the scholarly, political, and policy realms directly interact. His experience led to his meshing the applied with conceptual paradigms that he espoused originally at Harvard and Howard Universities. He pushed scholarship and engagement to an innovative higher plane.

Despite these contributions, Bunche was criticized by senior contemporaries such as W. E. B. Du Bois and Roy Wilkins from the 1930s onward, cultural revolutionaries and African American radicals in the 1950s and '60s, and white conservatives during various decades. Criticism culminated with his being called before the House Committee on Un-American Activities. It is no wonder that a human toll could be observed in his physical health and his sometimes reserved nature with friends and family.

Complexities of Bureaucracies and International Organizations

Universities and other projects with which Bunche was affiliated (for example, the Carnegie-funded *An American Dilemma,* 1944, and the Rockefeller Foundation Board) present various bureaucratic nuances and political realities. The shifting environments in bureaucracies such as the United Nations and international organizations are even more complex.

Smith and Lyman examine the challenges and complexities Bunche encountered in his extensive diplomatic career. Smith analyzes the historical routes of Western diplomatic formal and informal relations between nations. Considerable concern emerged during World War II regarding the establishment of a diplomatic organization that could help prevent wars and help quell disturbances before they escalated. The League of Nations had been unsuccessful after World War I. The Dumbarton Oaks Conference in Washington, D.C., and the San Francisco Conference led to the establishment of the United Nations. Diplomacy was to be the bedrock of the emerging United Nations. Yet, Bunche, as an international civil servant, was pioneering new ground, as Smith explains. Bunche responded to an international organization that was juggling the interests of Western powers, pressures of smaller nations, and demands for independence by colonies.

Lyman further analyzes the nature of Bunche's complex role as the membership of the United Nations expanded from fifty-one countries in 1945 to nearly 130 by the end of the 1960s. The superpowers would always have representation on the Security Council, the Economic and Social Council (ECOSOC), and other key councils with rotating membership for other nations. Maintaining what could be termed "co-equal" membership was a challenge since powerful nations are first among equals regardless of council composition. Hence national politics and internal UN politics complicated Bunche's negotiations in the Middle East, the Congo, and other regions.

Smith elucidates a critical diplomatic model used by Bunche: immediate solutions had to be enacted for hostilities that were killing hundreds of people. Solutions that address immediate devastating problems and causalities often do not address the fundamental causes or lead to long-term solutions. Thus Bunche was successful in negotiating cease-fires among four Arab nations and Israel, although Middle East problems with varying levels of violence continue today.

Comprehending the complex violent dynamics in the Congo and variations of the Middle East crisis is further explored by Lyman. Peacekeeping has been critical to UN operations from the mid-1950s to the present. Canadian prime minister Lester Pearson proposed a UN peacekeeping force with the resultant charge to Bunche to operationalize a peace force to which both sides of the conflict would agree. Yet the peacekeepers were not to use force to harm or kill individuals. As time elapsed during and beyond Bunche's tenure at the UN, peacekeeping forces have been attacked, driven from conflict regions, and killed. Maintaining a neutral humanitarian stance to prevent violence is increasingly difficult as various sides shift their stances and those parties not included in the peacekeeping agreements feel disenfranchised.

American and other national superpower legislatures have been reluctant to authorize funds to support UN operations when inefficiencies and disasters have been the apparent results. A distinction was offered between peacekeeping and peace enforcement, wherein the UN force could use weapons that might subsequently alter the course of conflict in favor of one group. During the 1990s, the U.S. Presidential Directive (PD) 25 proclaimed that force would be used when the prospects of success were fairly clear, American interests were at stake, and an exit strategy could be outlined. Even this directive became difficult to implement since multiple parties and nations had varying political objectives. Albright (2003) maintains that the United States and the United Nations tried to apply PD 25 inappropriately in tailoring the proposals for UN responses in Rwanda. UN peacekeeping still exists today, which built upon the operational and logistical plans of Bunche, via coalitions among nations and regional bodies such as the Africa Union. Countries are to be willing to participate through their troops, funds, and advisors to maintain or develop peace building via principles articulated by Bunche.

Contemporary Challenges and Complexities

We return to the July 2005 G-8 summit, which was punctuated by bombings in London, and the January 2006 Hamas election victories. These two events and the summer 2006 war between Israel and Hezbollah,[1] based in Lebanon, highlight contemporary challenges and complexities as the nature of nation to nation, region to region, and non-formal groups to nations and regions changes tremendously. We conclude by identifying some complexities and by seeking to gain insight from the life and career of Bunche.

First, there are continuing complexities when working in comprehensive international bureaucracies. Transcending from one work environment to another and, indeed, multiple environments presents challenges for even the most scholarly and politically astute professionals (Arndt, 2005; Haass, 1999). To whom is the diplomat loyal: the UN, the host country, or the donor nations? Bunche's role as an international civil servant provides numerous illustrations as he sought to devise and implement UN diplomatic solutions while being cognizant of host country goals that should ultimately meet universal standards of human rights and social justice.

Second, shifting concepts of diplomacy emerge in light of new forms of communication. When Bunche began his diplomatic career, radio and newsreels at movie theaters were the main forms of electronic communication. Such news was disseminated days or even weeks after critical events had commenced. Today, electronic communication occurs as the international events are unfolding. To paraphrase one former senior American diplomat, it is like trying to remodel the plane in the midst of the flight. What would once have been private candid discussions are reported on the Internet; numerous Web sites and blogs enable the general public to analyze international and domestic events as they unfold.

Third, nations and emerging regional blocs do not always recognize the legitimacy of or involve key actors. When Bunche began the 1949 armistice discussions between the Arab nations and Israel regarding cease-fires and the state for Palestinians, Palestinians were not at the Rhodes negotiations. In hindsight, it is understandable that the armistices reached then would be temporary agreements. Bunche recognized that Palestinians were not represented; however, the immediate need to create and maintain a cease-fire overshadowed long-term solutions integrally involving all actors.

Fourth, a contemporary challenge is identifying who should be involved, especially when the violent acts are not committed on behalf of a formal state. Or which entity will be the formal state, as Lyman discussed with the example of the emerging state of Congo after the Belgium administrators departed?

Incorporating the perspectives and policies of regional entities such as the European Union, the Africa Union, or the League of Arab States poses new challenges. Transnational movements or groups such as Al Qaeda present another gargantuan challenge, as demonstrated in April 2006 when Osama bin Laden called upon Muslims in the Middle East to violently resist any UN peacekeeping forces that might be sent to Darfur in the Sudan (CNN, 2006).

Fifth, what are the roles of public intellectuals and diplomats in identifying and devising concrete solutions to problems with multiple layers of complexities? Here Bunche's early scholarly work, which he used to transition into the world of diplomacy, proves useful. Several college and university presidents outlined modes for blending public intellectual roles with engagement as they cited the relevance of Bunche's academic and diplomatic accomplishments to contemporary problems. Indeed, some presidents contend that intellectualism and engagement roles cannot be separated, although they are not always evident in the academic community given the reward structure of the traditional faculty tenure and promotion system. With progressive board members such as Bunche at the Rockefeller Foundation, philanthropic bodies can further advocate academic and public engagement linkages.

Finally, to what extent might universities and national governments engage in partnerships so that cultural and educational diplomacy become integral components of international relations? One illustration is the Ralph Bunche Center at Howard University (initially established as only one of ten Centers of Excellence in the United States funded by the Kellogg Foundation) that assumed its current mission in 1996 at formal ceremonies that included speeches by UN secretary-general Boutros Boutros-Ghali. The Howard University Bunche Center is to help develop vital international affairs knowledge and models to prepare individuals to make sound contributions to national and international challenges (Howard University, 2006). That is, soft power that employs various models and posits new paradigms for diplomacy (Arndt, 2005; Nye, 2004) can be used to ameliorate international conditions. If this materializes, then the effects of Bunche's academic and scholarly careers as a public intellectual and international diplomat will still continue.

Note

1. Hezbollah (Arabic for "Party of God") is an umbrella organization based in Lebanon of various Islamic Shi'ite groups that receive notable financial and philosophical support from Iran. Hezbollah's security apparatus operates in Europe, North and South America, East Asia, and other parts of the Middle East, and it is believed to be responsible for a number of other terrorist attacks in various regions (MIPT Terrorism Knowledge Base, http://www.tkb.org/Group.jsp?groupIF=3101, accessed May 22, 2007).

Bibliography

ABC/7 News Poll (2005). Broadcast, September 7.

ABC/*Washington Post* Poll (2005). Broadcast, September 28.

Acheson, Dean. (1969). *Present at the creation: My years in the State Department.* New York: Norton.

Albright, Madeline. (2003). *Madam Secretary: A memoir.* New York: Miramax Books.

American Council on Education. (1937). The student personnel point of view: A report of a conference on the philosophy and development of student personnel work in colleges and universities (American Council on Education Study, Series 1, Vol. 1, No. 3). Washington, DC: Author.

American Education Research Association. (2006). *2006 annual meeting theme: Education research in the public interest.* Retrieved April 13, 2006 from http://www.aera.net/annualmeeting/?id=694.

American Sociological Association. (2004). *2005 ASA conference theme.* Retrieved December 28, 2004 from http://www.asanet.org.

American University of Paris. (2005). *Facts at a glance.* Retrieved June 17, 2005 from http://www.aup.fr/main/about/facts.htm.

Amin, Samir. (1997). *Capitalism in the age of globalization.* London: Zed Books.

Anderson, James. (1988). *The education of blacks in the South, 1860–1935.* Chapel Hill: University of North Carolina Press.

Ani, Marimba. (1994). *An African-centered critique of European cultural thought and behavior.* Trenton, NJ: Africa World Press.

Appadurai, Arjun. (1996). *Modernity at large: Cultural dimensions of globalization.* Minneapolis: University of Minnesota Press.

Appiah, Kwame. (1990). Racisms. In D. T. Goldberg (Ed.), *Anatomy of racism.* Minneapolis: University of Minnesota Press.

Aptheker, Herbert. (Ed.) (1985). *Against racism.* Amherst: University of Massachusetts Press.

Arndt, Richard T. (2005). *The first resort of kings: American cultural diplomacy in the Twentieth Century.* Washington, DC: Potomac Books, Inc.

Asante, Molefi. (1990). *Kemet, Afrocentricity, and knowledge.* Trenton, NJ: Africa World Press.

Baer, Michael, Jewell, Malcolm, & Sigelman, Lee. (1991). (Eds.). *Political science in America: Oral histories of a discipline.* Lexington: University Press of Kentucky.

Banks, James. (2004). *Educating citizens in a multicultural society.* New York: Teachers College Press.

Barka, Jeff. (1998). UN chief sends tough message. *Jerusalem Post.*

Barrera, Mario. (1979). *Race and class in the Southwest.* Notre Dame, IN: University of Notre Dame Press.

Bernard, Jessie. (1973). *The future of marriage.* New Haven, CT: Yale University Press.

Blauner, Robert. (1972). *Racial oppression in America.* New York: Harper & Row.

Borden, Victor. (2004). Accommodating student swirl. *Change, 36*(2), 10–18.

Boyer, Ernest. (1996). The scholarship of engagement. *Journal of Public Service and Outreach,* 1(1), 11–20.

Boykin, John. (2002). *Cursed is the peacemaker: The American diplomat versus the Israeli general, Beirut 1982.* Belmont: Applegate Press.

Boyle, Kevin. (2004). *Arc of justice: A saga of race, civil rights, and murder in the jazz age.* New York: Holt.

Brereton, Pat. (2001). *The Continuum guide to media education.* New York: Continuum.

Brown, Ronald E., & Hartfield, Carolyn. (2001). *The Black Church and politics in the city of Detroit, Working Paper Series No. 5.* Detroit, MI: Center for Urban Studies, Wayne State University.

Browne, Vincent. (n.d.). Foreign affairs scholars program 1963–1969: Final report. Washington, DC: Moorland Spingarn Research Center, Howard University, Vincent J. Browne Papers Box 1.

Browne, Vincent. (n.d.). Ralph Bunche: Teacher and political scientist. Washington, DC: Howard University, Moorland Spingarn Research Center, Howard University, Vincent J. Browne Papers Box 2.

Brown v. Topeka Board of Education (1954). 347 U.S. 483.

Brubacher, John S., & Rudy, Willis. (1976). *Higher education in transition: A history of American colleges and universities, 1639–1976.* New York: Harper & Row.

Bunche, Ralph J. (1903–1971). Papers. Los Angeles: Papers of Ralph J. Bunche, Department of Special Collections, Young Research Library, University of California.

Bunche, Ralph J. (1926). That man may dwell in peace. In C. P. Henry (Ed.) (1995), *Ralph Bunche: Selected speeches and writings* (pp. 17–20). Ann Arbor: University of Michigan Press.

Bunche, Ralph J. (1926–1927). Across the generations. In C. P. Henry (Ed.) (1995), *Ralph Bunche: Selected speeches and writings* (pp. 21–26). Ann Arbor: University of Michigan Press.

Bunche, Ralph J. (1927a). The fourth dimension of personality. In B. Rivlin (Ed.) (1990), *Ralph Bunche: The man and his times* (pp. 220–224). New York: Holmes & Meier.

Bunche, Ralph J. (1927b). *The fourth dimension of personality.* Box 126. Los Angeles: Papers of Ralph J. Bunche, Department of Special Collections, Young Research Library, University of California.

Bunche, Ralph J. (1935a). A critical analysis of the tactics and programs of minority groups. *Journal of Negro Education*, 4, 308–320.

Bunche, Ralph J. (1935b, September 9–11). French and British imperialism in West Africa. Speech for Association for the Study of Negro Life and History. Los Angeles: Papers of Ralph J. Bunche, Department of Special Collections, Young Research Library, University of California.

Bunche, Ralph J. (1935c, March 2). Some observations of a faculty member on universities in general and Howard in particular. Speech for Howard Club of Philadelphia, Charter Day Dinner. Los Angeles: Papers of Ralph J. Bunche, Department of Special Collections, Young Research Library, University of California.

Bunche, Ralph J. (1935d, November 13). Education and minority group citizenship. Speech for Miner Teacher's College. Los Angeles: Papers of Ralph J. Bunche, Department of Special Collections, Young Research Library, University of California.

Bunche, Ralph J. (1935e, November 22). Academic freedom. Speech for Capitol City Forum. Los Angeles: Papers of Ralph J. Bunche, Department of Special Collections, Young Research Library, University of California.

Bunche, Ralph J. (1936a). *A critique of New Deal social planning as it affects Negroes. Journal of Negro Education*, 5, 59–65.

Bunche, Ralph J. (1936b). *A world view of race*. Washington, DC: Associates in Negro Folk Education.

Bunche, Ralph J. (1936c, 24 May). Politico-economic analysis of the politics of race in the U.S. Detroit Civic Rights Committee. Los Angeles: Papers of Ralph J. Bunche, Department of Special Collections, Young Research Library, University of California.

Bunche, Ralph J. (1936d, July). Education in black and white. *Journal of Negro Education*, 5(3), 351–358.

Bunche, Ralph J. (1936e, October 27). Some implications. Speech for Princeton School of Public Affairs. Los Angeles: Papers of Ralph J. Bunche, Department of Special Collections, Young Research Library, University of California.

Bunche, Ralph J. (1939). Confidential to Program Committee: *Report on the needs of the Negro*. For the Republican Program Committee, July 1.

Bunche, Ralph J. (1940a). The role of the university in the political orientation of Negro youth. Paper presented at the Howard University Summer School Conference on the Needs of Negro Youth, Washington, DC.

Bunche, Ralph J. (1940b). The role of the university in the political orientation of Negro youth. *Journal of Negro Education*, 9.

Bunche, Ralph J. (1941a). The Negro in the political life of the United States. *Journal of Negro Education*, 10, 567–584.

Bunche, Ralph J. (1941b, January 31). Some observations on black and white thinking on the Negro problem. Speech for third annual conference of adult education and the Negro. Los Angeles: Papers of Ralph J. Bunche, Department of Special Collections, Young Research Library, University of California.

Bunche, Ralph J. (1941c). Disenfranchisement of the Negro. In S. Brown, A. Davis, & U. Lee (Eds.), *The Negro caravan*. New York: Dryden Press.

Bunche, Ralph J. (1945). Trusteeship and non self-Governing territories in the Charter of the United Nations. *Department of State Bulletin*.

Bunche, Ralph J. (1949). Brian Urquhart collection of material about Ralph Bunche, Box 4, Files 3 and 6 ("Palestine, January-February 1949"), Department of Special Collections, Library, University of California, Los Angeles.

Bunche, Ralph J. (1950a). *Nobel Peace Prize acceptance speech.* Retrieved February 11, 2004, from http://www.nobel.se/peace/laureates/1950/bunche-acceptance.html.

Bunche, Ralph J. (1950b, June 16). *1950 UCLA Commencement Address.* Retrieved June 18, 2005 from http://www.library.ucla.edu/bunche/ucla.html.

Bunche, Ralph J. (1952). Gandhian seminar. In Charles Henry (1995), *Selected speeches and writings.* Ann Arbor: University of Michigan Press.

Bunche, Ralph J. (1954a). Presidential address. *American Political Science Review, 47.*

Bunche, Ralph J. (1954b). Nana lit the beacons. In E. R. Murrow's *This I believe.* Box 60, Folder 60.

Bunche, Ralph J. (1964, October 3). Letter to the fourth graders at Briarwood Drive, N.Y. Box 126, Folder 9. Los Angeles: Papers of Ralph J. Bunche, Department of Special Collections, Young Research Library, University of California.

Bunche, Ralph J. (1966, April 21). Letter from Ralph Bunche to Ronald W. House, editor of the *Daily Bruin.* Retrieved from http://www.library.ucla.edu/bunche/ucla.html.

Bunche, Ralph J. (1969a, September). My most unforgettable character. *Readers Digest,* 45–49.

Bunche, Ralph J. (1969b, May 23). *Remarks at UCLA dedication of Ralph J. Bunche Hall.* Retrieved June 18, 2005 from http://www.library.ucla.edu/bunche/ucla.html.

Bunche, Ralph J. (1969c). Race and alienation. In Charles Henry (1995), *Selected speeches and writings.* Ann Arbor: University of Michigan Press.

Burton, Linda M., Dilworth-Anderson, Peggye, & Merriweather-deVries, Cynthia. (1995). Context and surrogate parenting among contemporary grandparents. *Marriage and Family Review,* 20(3/4), 349–366.

Burton, Linda M., & Merriwether-deVries, Cynthia. (1991). The challenges and rewards of rearing grandchildren for African-American grandparents. *Generations,* 25(3), 51–54.

Campus Compact. (2005). *History of service learning.* Retrieved June 18, 2005 from http://www.compact.org/students/2002review.html.

Carmichael, Stokely & Hamilton, Charles V. (1967). *Black power.* New York: Vintage.

Carter, Jimmy. (2002, December). The Nobel lecture given by the Nobel Peace Prize Laureate. Retrieved from http://www.nobel.no/eng_lect_2002b.html.

Castells, Manuel. (1997). *The power of identity.* Cambridge, MA: Blackwell.

Clark, Kenneth B. (1990). Ralph Bunche: The human being and the international statesman. In Benjamin Rivlin (Ed.). (1990), *Ralph Bunche: The man and his times.* New York: Holmes & Meier.

Cmiel, Kenneth. (1999). Sandra Vogelgesang. (1980). American dream, global nightmare: The dilemma of U.S. human rights policy. The Emergence of Human Rights Politics in the United States. *The Journal of American History,* 86(3). http://www.mtholyoke.edu/acad/intrel/cmiel.htm.

CNN (Cable News Network). (2006). UNICEF "sounds alarm" for Darfur's children. Retrieved April 26, 2006, from http://www.cnn.com/2006/WORLD/africa/04/26/sudan.UNICEF.reut/index.html.

Coleman, Mary Sue. (2002a, September 11). *President Mary Sue Coleman: Alumni Plaque Dedication Ceremony.* Retrieved from http://www.umich.edu/pres/speeches/020911/alumplaq.html.

Coleman, Mary Sue. (2002b, September). *Remembering 9/11.* Retrieved from http://www.umich.edu/pres/speeches/index.html.

Conant, James Bryant. (1942). *Our fighting faith: Five addresses to college students.* Cambridge: Harvard University Press.

Cox, Bette Yarbrough. (1996). *Central Avenue: Its rise and fall.* Los Angeles: BEEN Publications.

Crocker, Chester A., & Hampson, Fen Osler. (1996). *Managing global chaos: Sources of responses to international conflict.* Washington, DC: United States Institute of Peace.

Crocker, Chester A., Hampson, Fen Osler, & Aall, Pamela. (Eds.). (1999). *Herding cats: Multiparty mediation in a complex world.* Washington, DC: United States Institute of Peace.

Dawson, Michael. (2000). Slowly coming to grips with the effects of the American racial order on American policy preferences. In D. Sears, J. Sidanius, & L. Bobo (Eds.), *Racialized politics: The debate about racism in America.* Chicago: University of Chicago Press.

Dawson, Michael, & Wilson III, Ernest. (1991). Paradigms and paradoxes: Political science and the study of African American politics. In W. Crotty (Ed.), *Political science: Looking to the future,* Vol. 1. Evanston: Northwestern University Press.

deGraaf, Lawrence Brooks. (1962). Negro migration to Los Angeles, 1930–1950. Unpublished doctoral thesis. University of California Los Angeles.

Dewey, John. (1916). *Democracy and education.* New York: Macmillan.

De Witte, Ludo. (2001). *The assasination of Lumumba.* London: Verso.

Diop, Cheikh A. (1979). *The cultural unity of Black Africa.* Chicago: Third World Press.

Durch, William J. (1996). *UN peacekeeping: American policy and the uncivil wars of the 1990s.* New York: St. Martin's Press.

Edgar, Robert. (Ed.). (1992). *An African American in South Africa: The travel notes of Ralph J. Bunche.* Athens: Ohio University Press.

Egyptian-Israeli General Armistice Agreement. (1949). *Reproduced in corrigendum to cablegram from the acting mediator to the Secretary-General.* Retrieved May 5, 2005 from http://domino.un.org/unispal.nsf/181c4bf00c44e5fd85256cef0073c426/9cc4a33 2e2ff9a128525643d007702e6!OpenDocument.

Ehrlich, Thomas. (1997). Dewey versus Hutchins: The next round. In R. Orrill (Ed.), *Education and democracy* (pp. 225–262). New York: College Bound.

Elster, Jean Alicia. (2003). *I'll do the right thing.* Valley Forge: Judson Press.

Farr, James, Dryzek, John, & Leonard, Stephen. (1995). (Eds.). Political science in history: Research programs and political traditions. New York: Cambridge University Press.

Farr, James, & Seidelman, Raymond. (1993). (Eds). *Discipline and history: Political science in the United States.* Ann Arbor: University of Michigan Press.

Finch, George A. (1945). The United Nations Charter. *The American Journal of International Law,* 39(3), 541–546.

Fromkin, David. (1990). *A peace to end all peace: The fall of the Ottoman Empire and the creation of the modern Middle East* (p. 276 et. seq.). New York: Avalon Books.

Geiger, Roger. (1986). *To advance knowledge: The growth of American research universities. 1900–1940.* London: Oxford Press.

Geiger, Roger. (1999). The ten generations of American higher education. In P. G. Altbach, R. O. Berdahl, & P. J. Gumport (Eds.), *American higher education in the twenty-first century: Social, political, and economic challenges.* Baltimore, MD: Johns Hopkins University Press.

General Assembly Resolution S/RES/49 (S/773). (1948). Retrieved May 28, 2005 from http://domino.un.org/unispal.nsf/9a798adbf322aff38525617b006d7/259b669e67c00f6 e852560ba006f7203!OpenDocument.

General Assembly Resolution 106. (1947). (S-1), U.N. GAOR, 1st Special Session, U.N. Doc. A/286. Retrieved May 28, 2005 from http://domino.un.org/unispal.nsf/0/f5a49e 57095c35b685256bcf0075d9c2?OpenDocument.

General Assembly Resolution 181. (1947). (II), Future government of Palestine, A/ RES/181(II)(A+B). Retrieved May 28, 2005 from http://domino.un.org/unispal.nsf/0/ 7f0af2bd897689b785256c330061d253?OpenDocument.

General Assembly Resolution 186. (1948). (S-2), Appointment of terms of reference of a United Nations mediator in Palestine, A/RES/186 (S-2). Retrieved May 3, 2005 from http://domino.un.org/unispal.nsf/9a798adbf322aff38525617b006d7/a9a8da193bd46c 54852560e50060c6fd!OpenDocument.

General Assembly Resolution 194 (III). (1948). Retrieved May 28, 2005 from http:// domino.un.org/unispal.nsf/9a798adbf322aff38525617b006d88d7/c758572b78d1cd00 85256bcf0077e51a!OpenDocument.

Gilbert, Martin. (1997). *A history of the 20th century.* Vol. 1, *1900–1933.* New York: Avalon.

Gilroy, Paul. (2000). *Against race: Imagining political culture beyond the colorline.* Cambridge: Belkap Press of Harvard University Press.

Gist, David P. (1990). Interview with John B. Jackson: Oral history program of the University of California, Los Angeles.

Goldberg, David Theo. (1993). *Racist culture: Philosophy and the politics of meaning.* Cambridge, MA: Blackwell.

Gosnell, Harold. (1935). Negro politicians: The rise of Negro politics in Chicago. Chicago: University of Chicago Press.

Gossett, Thomas F. (1997). *Race: The history of an idea in America.* New York: Oxford University Press.

Gourevitch, Philip. (1998). *We wish to inform you that tomorrow we will be killed with our families.* New York: Picador USA.

Grant, Stephanie. (1976). *Confidential report of Stephanie Grant on Ronald Palmer's visit to the International Secretariat.* Retrieved from Amnesty International http://www:// mtholyyoke.edu./acad/intel/cmiel.htm.

Grantham, Dewey. (Ed.). (1973). *The political statues of the Negro in the age of FDR.* Chicago: University of Chicago Press.

Gratz v. Bollinger. (2003). 539 U.S.

Green, Madeleine F. (2005). *Measuring internationalization at research universities.* Washington, DC: American Council on Education.

Green, Madeleine F., & Siaya, Laura. (2005). *Measuring internationalization at liberal arts colleges*. Washington, DC: American Council on Education.

Green, Marshall. (1990). *Indonesia: Crisis and transformation 1965–1968*. Washington, DC: Compass Press. See also Gardner, Paul F. (1997). *Shared hopes separate fears: Fifty years of Indonesian relations*. Boulder, CO: Westview Press.

Greenberg, Melanie C., Barton, John H., & McGuinness, Margaret E. (Eds.). (2000). *Words over war: Mediation and arbitration to prevent deadly conflict*. Lanhamm, MD: Rowman & Littlefield.

Greene, Harry. (1946). *Holders of doctorates among American Negroes*. Boston: Meador.

Gruber, Sibylle. (2000). *Weaving a virtual web: Practical approaches to new information technologies*. Urbana: National Council of Teachers of English.

Grutter v. Bollinger. (2003). 539 U.S.

Gutmann, Amy. (1990). Democratic education in difficult times. *Teachers College Press, 92*(1), 7–20.

Haass, Richard N. (1999). *The bureaucratic entrepreneur: How to be effective in an unruly organization*. Washington, DC: Brookings Institution.

Hague Conventions of 1907. Reprinted in A. Roberts & R. Guelff (Eds.), *Documents on the laws of war* (3rd ed., p. 67 et. seq.). Oxford: Oxford University Press.

Hall, Mary Harrington. (1969). A conversation with Ralph Bunche. *Psychology Today*, 49–58.

Hamilton, Keith A., & Langhorne, Richard. (1995). *The practice of diplomacy: Its evolution theory and administration*. London: Routledge.

Harvard Committee. (1945). *General Education in a Free Society*. Cambridge: Harvard University Press.

Havard, W. (1977). K. O. Key, Jr.: A brief profile. In V. O. Key Jr. (Ed.), *Southern politics: In state and nation*. Knoxville: University of Tennessee Press.

Heard, Alexander. (1977). Introduction to the New Edition. In V. O. Key Jr. (Ed.), *Southern politics in state and nation: A new edition*. Knoxville: University of Tennessee Press.

Henderson, Errol A. (1995). *Afrocentrism and world politics*. Westport, CT: Praeger.

Henry, Charles P. (1995). Abram Harris, E. Franklin Frazier, and Ralph Bunche: The Howard School of Thought. In M. Holden Jr. (Ed.), *National Political Science Review*, 5.

Henry, Charles P. (1999). *Ralph Bunche: Model Negro or American other?* New York: New York University Press.

Henry, Charles P. (Ed.). (1995). *Selected speeches and writings*. Ann Arbor: University of Michigan Press.

Hesburgh, Theodore. (2006, March). Telephone interview with Dr. Beverly Lindsay.

Hildebrand, Robert C. (1990). *Dumbarton Oaks: The origins of the United Nations and the search for postwar security*. Chapel Hill: University of North Carolina Press.

Hirsch, John L., & Oakley, Robert B. (1995). *Somalia and Operation Restore Hope: Reflections on peacemaking and peacekeeping*. Washington, DC: United States Institute of Peace Press.

Hochschild, Adam. (1998). *King Leopold's ghost: A story of greed, terror, and heroism in colonial Africa*. Boston: Houghton & Mifflin.

Holbrooke, Richard. (1998). *To end a war*. New York: Random House.

Holloway, Jonathan. (2002). *Confronting the veil: Abram Harris Jr., E. Franklin Frazier, and Ralph Bunche, 1919–1941.* Chapel Hill: University of North Carolina Press.

Howard University. (2006). Ralph J. Bunche International Affairs Center. Retreived May 8, 2006, from http://www.howard.edu/rjb/.

Hrabowksi, Freeman A., Lee, Diane M., & Martello, John S. (1999). Educating teachers for the 21st century: Lessons learned. *Journal of Negro Education,* 68(3), 293–305.

Hudson, Manley O. (1945). An approach to the Dumbarton Oaks proposals. *The American Journal of International Law,* 39(1), 95–97.

Hutchinson, Earl. (1994). *Blacks and reds: Race and class in conflict, 1919–1990.* East Lansing: Michigan State University Press.

Instructions to the U.S. Delegation to the International Peace Conference at the Hague. (2000). Available at the Avalon Project, Yale Law School, http://www.yale.edu/lawweb/avalon/lawofwar/hague99/hague99–03.htm.

Jacobson, Matthew F. (1998). *Whiteness of a different color: European immigrants and the alchemy of race.* Cambridge: Harvard University Press.

Jahn, Gunnar. (1950). Presentation speech by Gunnar Jahn, Chairman of the Nobel Committee. Retrieved May 27, 2005 from http://nobelprize.org/peace/laureates/1950/press.html.

Janken, Kenneth. (1993). *Rayford Logan and the dilemma of the African American intellectual.* Amherst: University of Massachusetts Press.

Jeffries, Judson. (2002). *Huey P. Newton: The radical theorist.* Jackson: University Press of Mississippi.

Jennings, Hartford. (1977). *Foreign affairs scholars program 1964–1977.* Washington, DC: Joint Center for Political and Economic Studies.

Johnson, Charles. (1938, June). A world view of race: Review. *Journal of Negro Education,* 7(1), 61–62.

Johnson, Ethel. (undated typescript). Tribute to a crucified mother, Box 126, Folder 16. Los Angeles: Papers of Ralph J. Bunche, Department of Special Collections, Charles Young Research Library, University of California.

Johnson, Nelle. (1953). Record of the Johnson Family written in 1953. Box 126, Files 16–17 (no author listed on this single-spaced typescript but the finding aid for the Bunche papers indicates that Nelle Johnson wrote this history at Bunche's request).

Jones, Howard Palfrey. (1971). *Indonesia: The possible dream.* New York: Harcourt Brace Jovanovich.

Jones, Ryan. (2005, May 26). At Wesleyan, Gutmann trumpets respect. *Daily Pennsylvanian,* Retrieved from http://www.dailypennsylvanian.com.

Kafala, Tarik. (2003). The veto and how to use it. *BBC News Online,* http://www.bbc.co.uk.

Karabel, Jerome. (2005). The chosen: The hidden history of admission and exclusion at Harvard, Yale, and Princeton. Boston: Houghton-Mifflin.

Keller, Morton, & Keller, Phyllis. (2001). *Making Harvard modern: The rise of America's university.* New York: Oxford University Press.

Keller, Phyllis. (1982). Getting at the core: Curricular reform at Harvard. Cambridge: Harvard University Press.

Kennedy, Michael D. (2002). Religion, security and violence in global contexts. *The Journal of the International Institute,* 9(2), 8–9.

Keppel, Ben. (1995). *The work of democracy: Ralph Bunche, Kenneth B. Clark, Lorraine Hansberry.* Cambridge: Harvard University Press.

Kerr, Clark. (1963). *The uses of the university.* Cambridge: Harvard University Press.

Kerr, Clark. (2001). *The blue and the gold.* Berkeley: University of California Press.

Key, Valdimer Orlando, Jr. (1940). The lack of budgetary theory. *American Political Science Review, 34.*

Key, Valdimer Orlando, Jr. (1942). *Politics, parties and pressure groups.* New York: Thomas Y. Crowell.

Key, Valdimer Orlando, Jr. (1949). *Southern politics in state and nation.* New York: Knopf.

Key, Valdimer Orlando, Jr. (1958). The state of the discipline. *American Political Science Review, 52.*

King, Joyce. (2003). Reflection on executive leadership. American Council on Education Conference: Educating All of One Nation, Atlanta, Georgia.

Kirby, John. (1980). *Black Americans in the Roosevelt era: Liberalism and race.* Knoxville: University of Tennessee Press.

Kissinger, Henry. (1994). *Diplomacy.* New York: Simon & Shuster.

Krenn, Michael L. (1999). *Black diplomacy: African Americans and the state department 1945–1969.* Armonk, NY: M. E. Sharpe.

Kugelmass, J. Alvin. (1962). *Ralph Bunche: Fighter for peace.* New York: Julian Messner.

Kunnie, J. (2005). "Wars in the Gulf: Who cares about poor black people in New Orleans?" Africana Studies, University of Arizonia.

LaRoche, Cheryl J. (2004). *On the edge of freedom: Free Black communities, archaeology, and the underground railroad.* Ann Arbor: UMI.

Leader, Joyce. (2001). *Rwanda's struggle for democracy and peace, 1991–1994.* Washington, DC: Fund for Peace.

Lee, Enid, Menkart, Deborah, & Okazawa-Rey, Margo. (Eds.). (1998). *Beyond heroes and holidays: A practical guide to K–12 anti-racist, multicultural education and staff development.* Washington, DC: Network of Educators on the Americas.

Lekha Sriram, Chandra, & Wermester, Karin. (Eds.). (2003). *From promise to practice: Strengthening UN capacities for the prevention of violent conflict.* Boulder, CO: Lynne Rienner Publishers.

Levine, David O. (1986). *The American college and the culture of aspiration, 1915–1940.* Ithaca, NY: Cornell Press.

Lewis, D. L. (1995). *W. E. B. Du Bois: A reader.* New York: Henry Holt.

Lewis, David L. (2000). *W. E. B. Du Bois: The fight for equality and the American Century, 1919–1963.* New York: Henry Holt & Company.

Lindsay, Beverly. (1983). *Comparative perspectives of Third World women: The impact of race, sex, and class.* New York: Praeger.

Lindsay, Beverly. (2003). *Insights from Ralph Bunche: University-wide policies on internationalization to ameliorate diplomatic and socio-political realities.* Invited Presentation at 2003 Comparative and International Education Society Annual Conference, New Orleans, Louisiana.

Lindsay, Beverly (2005). *Senior university executives and special professorships: The realities for women.* Invited Presentation for the ETS Symposium: Addressing achievement gaps: The progress and challenges of women and girls in education and work, Princeton, New Jersey.

Lindsay, Beverly. (Ed.). (2004). The legacy of Ralph J. Bunche and education: Celebrating the centenary year of his birth. *Journal of Negro Education* 73(2).

Lipset, Seymor Martin, & David Riesman. (1975). *Education and politics at Harvard.* New York: McGraw-Hill.

Lipsitz, George. (1998). *The possessive investment in whiteness: How white people profit from identity politics.* Philadelphia: Temple University Press.

Little, Allan, & Silber, Laura. (1996). *Yugoslavia: Death of a nation.* New York: TV Books.

Locke, Alain. (1925). *The New Negro.* New York: Atheneum.

Locke, Alain. (1935, February 1). Letter to R. Bunche. Bunche Papers, UCLA.

Logan, Rayford. (1943, February 11). Logan diary. Logan Papers, Library of Congress.

Logan, Rayford A. (1969). *Howard University: The first hundred years.* New York: New York University.

Lucker, Andrew, & Key, Jr., Valdimer Orlando. (2001). *The quintessential political scientist.* New York: Peter Lang Publishing.

Lusane, Clarence. (1997). *Race in the global era: African Americans at the millennium.* Boston: South End Press.

Malcolmson, Scott L. (2000). *One drop of blood.* New York: Farrar, Straus & Giroux.

Martin, Gilbert. (1997). *A history of the twentieth century: Volume one 1900–1933,* pp. 110–111. New York: Avon.

Maurrasse, David J. (2001). *Beyond the campus: How colleges and universities form partnerships with their communities.* New York: Routledge.

Mead, M. Margaret. (1947). *The Salzburg Seminar on American civilization.* Retrieved December 15, 2004, from http://www.salzburg.org.

Middlebury College. (2005a). *Factbook 2004.* Retrieved June 21, 2005 from http://www.middlebury.edu/administration/instres/factbook2004/.

Middlebury College. (2005b). *Quick facts.* Retrieved June 16, 2005 from http://www.middlebury.edu/about/quickfacts.

Miller, Loren. (1935, April 16). Mail order dictatorship. *New Masses,* 95.

Mills, Charles W. (1997). *The racial contract.* Ithaca, NY: Cornell University Press.

Mills, Charles W. (1998). *Blackness visible: Essays on philosophy and race.* Ithaca, NY: Cornell University Press.

Morris, Benny. (2001). *Righteous victims: A history or the Zionist-Arab conflict 1881–2001.* New York: Knopf.

Moses, Greg. (1997). *Revolution of conscience: Martin Luther King, Jr., and the philosophy of nonviolence.* New York: Guilford Press.

Mundt, Mary H. (1998). The urban university: An opportunity for renewal in higher education. *Innovative Higher Education,* 22(3), 251–264.

Myrdal, Gunnar. (1944). *An American dilemma.* New York: Harper & Brothers.

NASULGC (National Association of State Universities and Land-Grant Colleges). (2004). *A call to leadership: The presidential role in internationalizing the university.* Washington, DC: National Association of State Universities and Land-Grant Colleges.

NASULGC Strategic Vision Committee. (2000). *Expanding the international scope of* universities: *A strategic vision statement for learning, scholarship and engagement in the new century.* Washington, DC: National Association of State Universities and Land-Grant Colleges.

Nicholas, Herbert. (1963). UN peace force and the changing globe: The lessons of Suez and Congo. *International Organization, 17*(2).

Nobel Prize. (2006). Alfred Nobel's will. Retrieved May 23, 2007, from http://nobelpeaceprize.org/eng_com_will2.html.

Nussbaum, Arthur. (1954). *A concise history of the law of nations.* New York: MacMillan.

Nussbaum, Martha. (1997). *Cultivating humanity: A classical defense of reform in liberal education.* Cambridge: Harvard University Press.

Nye, Joseph S., Jr. (2004). *Softpower: The means to success in world politics.* Cambridge, MA: Perseus Books Group.

Nzongola-Ntalaja, Georges. (2002). *The Congo: From Leopold to Kabila.* New York: Zed Books.

O'Ballance, Edgar. (2000). *The Congo-Zaire experience, 1960–98.* New York: St. Martin's Press.

Office of the Chancellor. (2001a). *Past chancellors and presidents on the Amherst campus: Marcellette Williams—Chancellor remarks at campus vigil.* Retrieved February 4, 2004 from http://www.umass.edu/pastchancellors/williams/September11/vigil-williams.html.

Office of the Chancellor. (2001b). *Past chancellors and presidents on the Amherst campus: Marcellette Williams—UMass community remembrance remarks.* Retrieved February 7, 2004 from http://www.umass.edu/pastchancellors/williams/September11/remembrance/rem-williams.html.

Office of the Chancellor. (2001c). *Past chancellors and presidents on the Amherst campus: Marcellette G. Williams—Understanding the Unthinkable.* Retrieved February 7, 2004 from http://www.umass.edu/pastchancellors/Williams/September11/forum.html.

Office of the Chancellor. (2001d). *Past chancellors and presidents on the Amherst campus: Marcellette G. Williams—The renewed commitment of the land grant research university.* Retrieved February 7, 2004 from http://www.umass.edu/pastchancellors/williams/announcements/ facultysenate0920.html.

Office of the Chancellor. (2004a). *Past chancellors and presidents on the Amherst campus: William S. Clark.* Retrieved February 7, 2004, from http://www.umass.edu/pastchancellors/clark.html.

Omi, Michael, & Winant, Howard. (1986). *Racial formation in the United States.* New York: Routledge & Kegan Paul.

Organization of African Unity. (2000, May). Report of the International Panel of Eminent Personalities to Investigate the Genocide in Rwanda. Available at http://www.africa-union.org/official_documents/reports/Report_rowanda_genocide.pdf.

Palmer, Ronald D. (2003). *Ralph Bunche: The influence of a role model.* Presented at the Fulbright Association 26th annual conference, Washington, DC.

Panel on United Nations Peace Operations. (2000). Report of the Panel on United Nations Peace Operations, A/55/305, S/2000/809. Available at http://www.un.org/peace/reports/peace_operations/.

Papp, Ilan. (1994). *The making of the Arab-Israeli conflict 1947–1951.* London: I. B. Taurus & Company.

Personal Notes of Ralph Bunche. (1949). Acting mediator, armistice negotiations—Rhodes (Egypt-Israel), p. 33. Los Angeles: UCLA Charles Young Library Brian Urquhart Collection of Ralph Bunche Materials (Box 8, Folder 3—copy on file with author).

Pew Research Center (2005). *Two-in-three critical of Bush's relief efforts.* Retrieved November 1, 2005 from http://people-press.org.

Plummer, Brenda Gayle. (1996). *Rising wind: Black Americans and U.S. foreign affairs, 1935–1960.* Chapel Hill: University of North Carolina Press.

Pomona speaker places first in oratory contest. (1926, April 15). *California Grizzley,* p. 1.

Powell, Colin L. (2002). *Remarks at a ceremony for the presentation of the Ralph J. Bunche Award to former secretary of state George P. Schultz,* 3–4. Washington, DC: Association of Diplomatic Studies and Training.

Prestage, Jewel. (1969). *Report of the conference on political science curriculum at predominantly Black institutions.*

Ralph Bunche Centenary (2003–2004). *Ralph Bunche Centenary Commemoration Committee.* Retrieved from http://www.ralphbunchecentenary.org/textcommittee.html#RBCCC.

Rapaport, Anatol. (Ed. & Trans.). (1982). *Carl von Clausewitz on war* (3rd ed., Bk. I, Ch. I, p. 119). London: Penguin Classic.

Rasmussen, Cecilia. (2001, January 28). L. A. then and now: Ralph Bunche spent a lifetime battling bias, seeking peace. *Los Angeles Times,* B3.

Reed, Adolph L., Jr. (1997). *W. E. B. Du Bois and American political thought: Fabianism and the color line.* New York: Oxford University Press.

Rentz, Audrey L. (1996). A history of student affairs. In A. L. Rentz (Ed.), *Student affairs practice in higher education* (pp. 28–53). Springfield, IL: Charles C. Thomas.

Report of the Secretary-General. (1999). The fall of Srebrenica. UNGA A/54/549, November 15.

Rivlin, Benjamin. (1990). The legacy of Ralph Bunche. In B. Rivlin (Ed.), *Ralph Bunche: The man and his times* (pp. 3–27). New York: Holmes & Meier.

Rivlin, Benjamin. (Ed.). (1990). *Ralph Bunche: The man and his times.* New York: Holmes & Meier.

Roberts, Adam, & Guelff, Robert. (Eds.). (2000). *Documents on the laws of war* (3rd ed.). Oxford: Oxford University Press.

Robinson, Mary. (2004). Human rights and ethical globalization. Retrieved December 20, 2004, from http://asanet.org.

Rodney, Walter. (1972). *How Europe underdeveloped Africa.* London: Bogle L'Ouverture Publications.

Roediger, David R. (1991). *The wages of whiteness.* New York: Verso.

Rotberg, Robert I. (Ed.). (2003). *State failure and state weakness in a time of terror.* Washington, DC: Brookings Institution Press.

Sabine, George. (1973). *A history of political theory,* 4th edition. New York: Holt, Rinehart, Winston.

Salzburg Seminar. (2005a). *Biography of Dr. Olin Robison.* Retrieved June 16, 2005, from http://www.salzburgseminar.org/orcomments/bio.cfm.

Salzburg Seminar. (2005b). *Our mission, our work.* Retrieved June 19, 2005, from http://www.salzburgseminar.org/2005Vision.cfm.

Security Council Resolution 49. (1948). S/RES/49.

Security Council Resolution 61. (1948). Retrieved May 28, 2005 from http://domino .un.org/unispal.nsf/9a798adbf322aff38525617b006d88d7/ebadfb9d20944088852560c 2005d187e!OpenDocument.

Security Council Resolution 62. (1948). Retrieved May 28, 2005 from http://domino .un.org/unispal.nsf/9a798adbf322aff38525617b006d88d7/1a2b613a2fc85a9d852560c2 005d4223!OpenDocument.

Senate of the United States. (1969). United States security agreements and commitments abroad: The Republic of the Philippines. Hearings Before the Subcommittee on United States Security Agreements and Commitments Abroad of the Senate Foreign Relations Committee, United States Senate, Ninety-First Congress, First Session, Part 1, September 30, October 1, 2, and 3. Washington, DC: GPO.

Shawcross, William. (2000). *Deliver us from evil.* New York: Simon & Schuster.

Shelley, Cara L. (1991). Bradby's Baptists: Second Baptist Church of Detroit, 1910–1946. *Michigan Historical Review*, 17, 1–33.

Shlaim, Avi. (1988). *Collusion across the Jordan: King Abdullah, the Zionist movement, and the partition of Palestine.* New York: Columbia University Press.

Shriver Center. (2005). About the Shriver Center. Retrieved from http://www.shrivercenter .org/.

Smith, Joseph Burkholder. (1976). *Portrait of a cold warrior.* New York: Putnam.

Somit, Albert, & Tanenhaus, Joseph. (1964). *American political science: A profile of the discipline.* New York: Atherton Press.

Somit, Albert, & Tanenhaus, Joseph. (1967). *The development of political science.* Boston: Allyn & Bacon.

St. Mary's University. (2005a). *University profile.* Retrieved June 16, 2005 from http://www .stmarytx.edu/profile/pdf/University%20Profile%202004.pdf.

St. Mary's University. (2005b). President's peace commission. Retrieved June 20, 2005 http://www.stmarytx.edu/ppc/content/2000_10vid.html.

St. Petersburg Declaration Renouncing Exploding Projectiles of 1868. Reprinted in A. Roberts & R. Guelff (Eds.), *Documents on the laws of war* (3rd ed., p. 53 et. seq.). Oxford: Oxford University Press.

Steele, Claude. (1997). A threat in the air: How stereotypes shape the intellectual identities and performance of women and African Americans. *American Psychologist.*

Stiglitz, Joseph E. (2003). *Globalization and its discontents.* New York: Norton.

Stromquist, Nelly P. (2002). *Education in a globalized world.* Lanham, MD: Rowman & Littlefield.

Sullivan, William H. (1984). *Obliggato 1939–1979: Notes on a foreign service career.* New York: Norton.

Tatarewicz, J. N. (2004). UMBC founders oral history project. Retrieved at http:// userpages.umbc.edu/~tatarewi/founders/history.htm.

Thomas, Darryl C. (2001). *The theory and practice of third world solidarity.* Westport, CT: Praeger.

Ullman, Richard H. (1996). *The world and Yugoslavia's wars.* New York: Council on Foreign Relations.

UMBC (University of Maryland, Baltimore County). (2005a). *Office of Institutional Research Databook.* Retrieved June 18, 2005 from http://www.umbc.edu/oir/.

UMBC (University of Maryland, Baltimore County). (2005b). *What Is the Shriver Living Learning Center?* Retrieved June 18, 2005 from http://www.umbc.edu/sllc/whatis.html.

UN Charter, art. 2(7) (1945).

UN Charter, art. 11(2) (1945).

UN Charter, art. 24 (1945).

UN Charter, art. 62(1) (1945).

UN Charter, art. 92 (1945).

UN Charter, chap. VII (1945).

UN Document S/743 (1948).

United Nations. (1999). Report of the Independent Inquiry into the Actions of the United Nations during the 1994 Genocide in Rwanda. December 15, http://www.un.org/news.ossq/rwanda_report.htm.

University of California at Los Angeles. (2005a). *A brief history of UCLA.* Retrieved June 18, 2005 from http://www.ucla.edu/about/history.html.

University of California at Los Angeles. (2005b). *A centenary celebration of Ralph J. Bunche.* Retrieved June 18, 2005 from http://www.library.ucla.edu/bunche/intro.html.

University of Michigan, International Institute (2001). *Religion, security, and violence in global contexts: 2001–2002 activities.* Retrieved March 15, 2005 from http://www.umich/edu/~iisite/events/religion_security_violence_2001_2002.html.

University of Michigan (2004). *An encyclopedic survey: History of administration.* Retrieved March 15, 2005 from http://www.hti.umich.edu/u/umsurvey/.

Urquhart, Brian. (1993). *Ralph Bunche: An American life.* New York: W. W. Norton.

Urquhart, Brian. (1998). *Ralph Bunche: An American odyssey.* New York and London: W. W. Norton.

Urquhart, Brian. (1994). The higher education of Ralph Bunche. *Journal of Blacks in Higher Education, 4,* 78–84.

Utter, Glenn, & Lockhart, Charles. (2002). *American political scientists: A dictionary.* Westport, CT: Greenwood Press.

Vance, Cyrus. (1983). *Hard choices: Critical years in America's foreign policy.* New York: Simon & Schuster.

Vidal, Dominique. (1997). *The expulsion of the Palestinians reexamined. Le Monde Diplomatique.* Retrieved February 16, 2004 from http://mondediplo.com/1997/12/palestine.

Walton, Hanes, Jr. (1968). African and Afro-American courses in Negro colleges. *Quarterly Review of Higher Education Among Negroes, 36.*

Walton, Hanes, Jr. (1971). *The political philosophy of Martin Luther King, Jr.* New York: Greenwood.

Walton, Hanes, Jr. (1990). Black presidential participation and the critical election theory. In L. Morris (Ed.), *The social and political implication of the 1984 Jesse Jackson presidential campaign.* New York: Praeger.

Walton, Hanes, Jr. (1994a). Black southern politics: The influences of Bunche, Martin, and Key. In H. Walton Jr. (Ed.), *Black politics and black political behavior: A linkage analysis.* Westport, CT: Praeger.

Walton, Hanes, Jr. (1994b). Review of Ralph Bunche: The man and his times. *National Political Science Review, 4,* 318–319.

Walton, Hanes, Jr. (1995). *Black women at the United Nations: The politics, a theoretical model, and documents.* California: Borgo Press.

Walton, Hanes, Jr. (Ed.). (1994). *Black politics and black political behavior: A linkage analysis.* Westport, CT: Praeger.

Walton, Hanes, Jr., Miller, Cheryl, & McCormick II, Joseph. (1995). Race and political science: The dual traditions of race relations politics and African American politics. In J. Farr, J. Dryzek, & S. Leonard (Eds.), *Political science in history: Research programs and political traditions.* New York: Cambridge University Press.

Walton, Hanes, Jr., & Smith, Robert. (2007). The race variable and the American Political Science Association's *State of the Discipline* reports and books, 1907–2002. In Wilber Rich (Ed.), *African American perspectives on political science.* Philadelphia: Temple University Press.

Washington Tribune. (1935a, November 29). Cops break up alleged red meeting.

Washington Tribune. (1935b, December 6). Bunche's talk police halted, rescheduled.

Wells, Ida. B. (1969). *On lynchings: Southern horrors, a red record, mob rule in New Orleans.* New York: Arno Press.

Wilkins, Roy. (1934, September 19). Letter to Walter White. On the draft of the report by the committee on future plan and program. NAACP Papers, Library of Congress.

Williams, Eddie. (1994). Oral history interview. Washington, DC: Foreign Affairs Oral History Program, Lauinger Library, Georgetown University.

Williams, Eric. (1944). *Capitalism and slavery.* Chapel Hill: University of North Carolina Press.

Wilson, Ernest. (1985). Why political scientists don't study black politics, but historians and sociologists do. *PS: Political Science and Politics.*

Wilson, William Julius. (1978). *The declining significance of race.* Chicago: University of Chicago Press.

Wolcott, Virginia W. (1993). Defending the home: Sweet and the struggle against segregation in 1920s Detroit. *Organization of American Historians Magazine of History, 7*(4), 4.

Wolff, Robert P. (1969). *The ideal of the university.* Boston: Beacon Press.

Yale Law School, Avalon Project. (2005). *Hague Convention (1) for the Pacific Settlement of international disputes of 1907.* Retrieved May 27, 2005 from the Avalon Project Web site, http://www.yale.edu/lawweb/avalon/lawofwar/pacific.htm.

Yale Law School, Avalon Project. (2005). *Peace Treaty of Versailles, preamble to the covenant of the League of Nations.* Retrieved May 27, 2005 from the Avalon Project Web site: http://www.yale.edu/lawweb/avalon/imt/parti.htm.

Yale Law School, Avalon Project. (2005). *The Balfour Declaration, Letter from Arthur James Balfour to Lord Rothschild Nov. 2.* Retrieved May 28, 2005 from the Avalon Project Web site: http://www.yale.edu/lawweb/avalon/mideast/balfour.htm.

Young, Andrew. (1996). *An easy burden: The Civil Rights Movement and transformation of American.* New York: HarperCollins Publishers.

Young, Andrew. (2003). Communication at the national meeting of the Council on Foreign Relations, New York.

Young, James O. (1973). *Black writers of the thirties.* Baton Rouge: Louisiana State University Press.

Contributors

LORENZO DUBOIS BABER is a doctoral candidate in higher education at Pennsylvania State University. Prior to arriving at Penn State, he served as assistant director of the Student Development Center at the Mount Vernon campus of George Washington University. Baber has university administrative experience in residential life, multicultural affairs, and undergraduate admissions.

JOHN HOPE FRANKLIN is the James B. Duke Professor Emeritus of history at Duke University and the John Matthews Manly Distinguished Service Professor Emeritus of American history at the University of Chicago. He is a recipient of the Presidential Medal of Freedom. A former president of the American Historical Association and the United Chapters of Phi Beta Kappa, he has received dozens of major awards and more than 100 honorary degrees. He is perhaps best known for his study *From Slavery to Freedom: A History of African-Americans*, now in its eighth edition. His other works include *Racial Equality in America; Race and History: Selected Essays 1938–1988; The Color Line: Legacy for the Twenty-First Century;* and *Runaway Slaves: Rebels on the Plantation.* Franklin has taught at a number of institutions, including Brooklyn College of the City University of New York, Fisk University, and Howard University.

CHARLES P. HENRY is a professor of African American studies at the University of California at Berkeley. He is a former presidential appointee to the National Council on the Humanities. Former president of the National Council for Black Studies, Henry is the author/editor of seven books including *Ralph Bunche: Model Negro or American Other?* Before joining the University of California in 1981, he taught at Denison University and Howard University. In 2002–3, Henry was a Distinguished Senior Fulbright Chair in Italy and France and is a former National Endowment for the Humanities postdoctoral fellow and American Political Science Association congressional fellow.

JONATHAN SCOTT HOLLOWAY is a professor of African American studies, history, and American studies at Yale University. He is the author of *Confronting the Veil: Abram Harris Jr., E. Franklin Frazier, and Ralph Bunche, 1919–1941.* He also annotated and edited Ralph Bunche's previously unpublished *A Brief and Tentative Analysis of Negro Leadership.*

BEN KEPPEL is currently an associate professor in the department of history at the University of Oklahoma. His areas of specialty include African American history; the mass media and social change in twentieth-century America; and twentieth-century cultural, intellectual, and political U.S. history. Keppel is the author of several publications, including *The Work of Democracy: Ralph Bunche, Kenneth B. Clark, Lorraine Hansberry and the Cultural Politics of Race.* He also served as a historical consultant on the PBS documentary *Ralph Bunche: An American Odyssey.*

BEVERLY LINDSAY is the first American to become a senior Fulbright specialist in South Korea and Zimbabwe where she engaged in peace and conflict resolution, initiated executive and faculty leadership development models, and fostered strategic planning and program evaluation processes. She is a former dean at Hampton University for international education and policy studies, at Penn State University for international programs, and is a professor and senior scientist at the latter university. She is a member of the Council on Foreign Relations. Recently, she was an executive fellow of multitrack diplomacy and international policy administration at the Institute for Multitrack Diplomacy in Washington, D.C., and was a president of the Comparative and International Education Society. After being an American Council on Education government fellow, Lindsay wrote over eighty-five articles, chapters, and essays and four books, including *The Quest for Equity in Higher Education* (with Manuel J. Justiz) and *African Migration and National Development.*

PRINCETON N. LYMAN is adjunct senior fellow and director of Africa policy studies at the Council on Foreign Relations, former Ralph Bunche Chair at the Council on Foreign Relations, and the former director of the Global Interdependence Initiative at the Aspen Institute. He is a former U.S. ambassador to Nigeria and to South Africa. Lyman was assistant secretary of state for international organizations and has published numerous articles on Africa, foreign policy, and development and the book *Partner to History,* which recounts U.S. policy in South Africa during the transition from apartheid to democracy.

EDWIN SMITH is the Leon Benwell Professor of Law and International Relations at the University of Southern California. Smith served as attorney for the National Oceanic and Atmospheric Administration. He also served as special counsel for foreign policy to U.S. senator Daniel Patrick Moynihan and was a presidential appointee as a science and policy advisor to the U.S. Arms Control and Disarmament Agency. Smith belongs to the Council on Foreign Relations and served as vice president of the American Society of International Law. He has lectured internationally on United Nations–NATO cooperation in peacekeeping and written several publications, including *The United Nations in a New World Order.* Special thanks to Jeanette Yazadjian, Shanaiara Udwadaia, and Fawn Wright for their invaluable assistance.

HANES WALTON JR. is a professor of political science at the University of Michigan. He specializes in American politics, race and politics, parties and elections, and state and local government. He has been a Guggenheim, Ford, and Rockefeller fellow during his career. Walton is the author of eleven books, including *The African Foreign Policy of Secretary of State Henry Kissinger: A Documentary Analysis.*

Index

The University of Illinois Press
is a founding member of the
Association of American University Presses.

Composed in 10.5/13 Adobe Minion Pro
by Jim Proefrock
at the University of Illinois Press
Manufactured by Thomson-Shore, Inc.

University of Illinois Press
1325 South Oak Street
Champaign, IL 61820-6903
www.press.uillinois.edu